1001
Cocktails

1001 Cocktails

p

This is a Parragon Publishing Book

First published in 2004

Parragon Publishing
Queen Street House
4 Queen Street
Bath BA1 1HE, UK

Copyright © Parragon 2004

Designed, produced, and packaged by Stonecastle Graphics Limited

Photography by Steve Moss, Chris Linton, Roddy Paine, Calvey Taylor-Haw, Pinpoint
Text complied by Alex Barker
Designed by Sue Pressley and Paul Turner

ISBN 1-40543-709-X

Printed in China

Warning
Recipes containing raw eggs are not suitable for children, convalescents, the elderly or pregnant women. Please consume alcohol responsibly.

Contents

A World of Cocktails

1001 Cocktails

The coolest drinks around at the moment are cocktails. They're an invitation to combine fun and creativity with an enduring aura of glamor from the racy 1920s and '30s. You can go into the newest bar in town, most likely to be an imitation of the famous Harry's Bar, to order the latest creation from New York. Or visit the classiest traditional bar around – you can't beat London's Savoy or Manhattan's Algonquin Hotel when it comes to class – and ask for the all-time classic cocktail – a dry Martini.

Sit and watch the bartender perform – the fast action and easy chat, the smooth sharp shake, the perfect balance of flavors created with effortless speed, the decorative finishing touches and flourishes that make you think he has invented it especially for you! Yet this is only a drink. Maybe you could do that too, in the comfort of your own home?

This is just what this book is all about – giving you the most comprehensive collection of cocktails you will ever need. Included here are 1001 classic and contemporary cocktails from around the world. They are described simply, and beautifully photographed, so you know exactly how to recreate them and how to present them. Naturally, you can dress or finish them as you prefer, flamboyant or not, according to your taste and mood. Making cocktails is great fun, both for you and for your appreciative guests.

Cocktails made easy

1001 Cocktails is divided into five simple sections – Bubbly, Long, Short, Fruity, and Quirky. The recipes in each section are grouped according to their most important base ingredient – gin, vodka, whiskey, rum, brandy, liqueur, tequila, vermouth. Non-alcoholic drinks in each section are identified with key symbol, and finally classic cocktails are also highlighted with a symbol (see page 9), so you can easily find your favorite gin or vodka classic cocktail, for instance.

Bubbly cocktails are based on champagne, sparkling wine, cider, beer, and many other drinks. This is the place to search for a glamorous or sexy champagne cocktail, or an unusual yet economical sparkling summer punch for the weekend barbecue.

Long cocktails are classified as an alcohol lengthened with a non-alcoholic drink such as one of the many mixers, fruit juices, or sparkling waters. Here you will find the ubiquitous Piña Colada, variations of a Tom Collins, or an Americano, as well as new cocktails, such as The Champion or Suffering Fool!

Short cocktails are generally a spirit, neat, on the rocks, or topped up with ice and very little fruit, or flavored with an additional spirit or liqueur. Look here for the majority of the famous classics – Dry Martini, Daiquiri, Between the Sheets, White Lady, Manhattan, Rusty Nail. The list is almost endless and includes many of the latest vodka favorites together with examples of the new trend toward flavored spirits.

Fruity cocktails have a fruit base, fresh fruit juice or sometimes puréed fruit, as in the case of smoothies. Some contain alcohol, but many do not, and these are therefore perfect for family occasions when youngsters wish to drink the same cocktails as the adults.

Quirky cocktails, as the word implies, are the more unusual drinks. Ones served for special occasions, such as after dinner treats, or to relieve hangovers, or even as health cures. Here you will also find drinks with cream, egg, or ice cream whisked in; drinks topped with a layer of cream or creamy liqueur; the exotic pousse-café which are simply layers of iced colorful spirits; or frappés, where the spirit is served over finely crushed ice. This quirky collection is fascinating and well worth exploring when you are looking for adventure.

Have fun making cocktails, the recipes are all easy to follow, but you may find it difficult to decide where to start!

The history of cocktails

Precisely where the word "cocktail" originated is uncertain, and many theories abound. One such theory is that the name was taken from the term "cock-tailed," which was an expression used in eighteenth- and nineteenth-century American racecourse slang to describe a non-Thoroughbred horse. The tails of such horses were always docked which made them look like a cockerel's tail. The name given to a horse of mixed blood seemed an appropriate one to bestow on a drink of similar diverse qualities.

But whatever the origins of the word, mixed drinks have existed since ancient times and the first recognizable cocktail dates from about the sixteenth century. Indeed, many classic recipes have been around for much longer than most people think. The bourbon-based Old Fashioned, for example, first appeared at the end of the eighteenth century. We know that the word cocktail was already in use in 1809 in the United States and, thirty-five years later, when Charles Dickens described one of his characters, Major Hawkins, as able to drink "more rum-toddy, mint-julep, gin-sling, and cock-tail, than any private gentleman of his acquaintance," it had reached Britain too. Popular among the

style-conscious and wealthy in the United States, cocktails were often served before dinner in the most exclusive houses and hotels until World War I made them unfashionable. They have gone in and out of vogue ever since.

Following the war, young people desperately seeking new experiences, pleasures, stimuli and styles, developed a taste for an innovative range of cocktails. Ironically the National Prohibition Act in the United States in the 1920s banned the manufacture, sales, transportation, import, or export of intoxicating liquors of any kind. Illegally-produced liquor soon became common-place and its consumption was driven underground into speakeasies and smoke-filled clubs. Bootlegging became widespread. Frequently, this illegal liquor tasted poisonous – and sometimes was – so its flavor needed to be disguised with fruit juices and mixers. No doubt, the thrill of drinking illicit alcoholic cocktails also added to their appeal to the "bright young things" of the time.

The cocktail craze quickly crossed the Atlantic and reached the best hotels in London, Paris, and Monte Carlo which soon boasted their own cocktail bars. The celebrated American Bar at London's exclusive Savoy Hotel and Harry's New York Bar were especially fashionable venues often frequented by the famous and glamorous. Not surprisingly some of the best Classic cocktails were created for, and named after, romantic icons and popular film stars or venues of the day.

World War II brought an end to such revelry and, although enjoyed occasionally, cocktails remained out of style for decades, until an exuberant renaissance in the 1970s. This resulted in a new generation of recipes, often featuring the contemporary and more fashionable white rum, vodka,

and tequila (which was just becoming known outside its native Mexico). Inevitably, the pendulum swung against cocktails again until recent times. Now, once more, the cocktail shaker is essential equipment in every fashionable city bar.

Creative cocktails

The world of cocktails is ever changing and you will no doubt create your own variations as you travel through this book to prove it. The choice of drinks and ingredients available today is more exciting and creative than ever before. The scope for the home barman is endless, with something for every mood.

There are short but strong Classics like the Martini in its many new guises – simply stirred over ice and shimmering with a frosty chill, or long subtle blends like the Collins – with gentle undertones of alcohol topped by familiar sparkling mixers. The revival of the shooter, the slammer, and the colorful pousse-café by the young and more adventurous has raised many an eyebrow as drink after drink is swallowed in one. Champagne cocktails have always been popular, but the have seen so many changes and additions that you can now create bubbly concoctions of almost every color and flavor! There are drinks for any occasion, from quirky creamy after-dinner mixes, to hangover and morning-after specials, from fizzy alcoholic ice cream sodas to festive and fruity punches and mulls. So why not start right now – you are bound to have drinks in your cupboard just waiting to be enjoyed in some exciting new way.

Key to symbols:

 Classic cocktails

 Alcohol-free cocktails

Techniques, Tricks, and Equipment

Anyone can make a good cocktail with little or no experience. But it helps to have the right equipment, an understanding of what you are aiming for, a keenness to experiment, and a good variety of ingredients and drinks with which to work. Reading these few pages first is a good start to increasing your knowledge and then you are ready to get shaking!

Measures

Measuring the quantities is one of the keys to making a good cocktail. The standard single measure is 1 1/2 oz, as used throughout this book, and you can buy stainless steel measures (jiggers) for 1, 2 and 1/3 quantities in many stores. However, like any experienced bartender, you can decide to use your own standard measure as long as you follow the proportions given in the recipes. An appropriately small tumbler, glass or even eggcup will serve as the basic measure.

Most short cocktails are a precise balance of flavors, whereas longer drinks which can be topped up with mixers to your liking are not so crucial. For instance, when making up the rather risqué-sounding combination known as Between the Sheets, equal measures of Cointreau, brandy, and white rum are always used – whether the measures are jiggers or jugs is up to you! With time, you can begin to vary your favorite cocktails and experiment with flavors and tastes.

Terms

Classic cocktails are either shaken, stirred, built, blended, or layered. The famous James Bond quote "shaken not stirred" speaks volumes about how particular cocktail drinkers can be. Shaking a cocktail is fun for you and flamboyant entertainment for your guests.

As a general rule of thumb, a cocktail shaker is used when heavier ingredients such as liqueurs, fruit juices, cream, and such like are to be blended. The idea behind the shaker is to mix and cool the drink as quickly as possible, keeping the ice constantly moving so it melts as little as possible. To make a shaken cocktail, put the cracked ice into the chilled cocktail shaker first and immediately pour over the other ingredients. Secure the lids and shake vigorously with a sharp movement for 10–20 seconds, until the outside of the shaker is lightly frosted and coated in condensation. Strain the liquid into a glass and serve at once. Any cocktail that you can make by shaking can also be made in a blender.

Stirred cocktails are quick, easy, stay perfectly clear, and retain the full strength of the spirits. Use a large glass or mixing jug filled with uncracked ice. Add the ingredients and stir well for a few seconds until the mixing glass is frosted, then strain the cocktail into iced glasses. Building a cocktail sounds strange, but it means quite simply adding all the ingredients in sequence to the chilled glass and stirring once or twice before serving.

Many drinks are blended, especially in this era of smoothies and juices. All the ingredients are blended together until smooth, generally with cracked or crushed ice. When producing small quantities it is a good idea to use a small blender or a handheld blender in a jug, as food processors are generally too large for one quantity.

Layering is the technique used for drinks known as pousse-café where you see several colored liqueurs layered one above the other. You need to ice all of the drinks and glasses very well first, follow the recipe, and have a steady hand! Using a teaspoon or barspoon resting on the surface of the base drink, carefully pour the next drink down the back of the spoon. When creating your own pousse-café, it is important to remember that the density of each liqueur used will affect its tendency to float and so the first into the glass must be the heaviest – you may find you need to experiment!

Some recipes suggest muddling ingredients in the bottom of the glass first – mint with sugar for instance – this means to mash or bruise the ingredients to release the flavor before adding ice and spirits. A dash is an expression used for approximately the tip of a tilted teaspoon. Neat or straight up is a drink served full strength and without ice. On the rocks is a drink served over ice.

Shooters and pousse-cafés are great fun – although often incredibly potent! The pousse-café originated in France as an after-dinner cocktail. Both the pousse-café and the shooter use hard spirit or liqueurs, served neat in small glasses known as shot glasses. A shooter, sometimes referred to as a shot, should be swallowed in one gulp, whereas the layers of a pousse-café are usually designed to complement each other, and so for this reason the latter is best sipped slowly.

Equipment

A shaker is the most essential piece of equipment. It consists of a container with an inner, perforated lid and an outer lid. Both lids are secured while the mixture is shaken and then the cocktail is strained through the perforated lid into a glass. However, a clear glass jug and shaker, sometimes known as the Boston shaker, is useful when you wish to see what you are mixing. The jug is also useful for preparing stirred cocktails.

A mixing glass or bar glass is a medium-sized jug in which stirred cocktails can be mixed. It is usually made of clear glass so you can see the mix and is generally large enough to prepare several drinks.

A long-handled bar spoon is necessary for stirring cocktails in long glasses. A typical bar spoon resembles an elongated flat teaspoon with a shaft that is long enough to reach the bottom of the mixing glass. Some long spoons have an end that doubles as a muddler (a flat disc), which is useful when crushing fresh mint or sugar cubes for certain cocktails.

A small strainer prevents unwanted ice cubes finding their way into the cocktail glass. The Hawthorne strainer (so called because of the company that makes it) is a metal strainer with a coil spring around it that clips on to a mixing glass. Although not strictly an essential item, the Hawthorne strainer does make the job of straining a "stirred" cocktail much easier.

Measuring cups (jiggers) and various sizes of spoons are essential for getting the proportions of ingredients right.

Other useful, but non-essential tools, include a citrus reamer, canelle or channeling cutter, an insulated ice bucket and tongs, a punch bowl, a glass serving

jug, and a zester or grater. If you have a juicer, this is useful for making large quantities of fresh juice for cocktails or smoothies and for preparing a hangover cure for the morning after!

A sharp knife and cutting board are essential for paring an elegant twist of lemon peel, or simply preparing a neat slice of fresh fruit.

A good corkscrew/ bottle opener is essential; even better, an all-in-one gadget known as the "bartender's friend" combining a corkscrew, foil-cutter, and bottle-opener, is widely available and it is an indispensable tool to have around.

Glasses

You can serve a cocktail in any glass you wish, but the right one makes all the difference and of course, it should be really well chilled. If possible, put sparkling clean glasses into the freezer the night before you need them.

When choosing the most suitable glass in which to present your freshly created cocktail, try to achieve a good balance between the contents and the glass. An elegant cocktail will look most attractive in a stylish glass with a long slender stem, whereas a short spirit-based cocktail served on the rocks would be best in a chunkier lowball tumbler, sometimes referred to as an old-fashioned glass.

Martini glass: With its conical-shaped bowl and tall stem, the Martini glass is often depicted as the classic cocktail glass and is most often used for Martinis and Margaritas.

Champagne flute: An elegant glass, the narrow flute is perfect for preserving the sparkling bubbles in champagne and other fizzy drinks.

Above:

1 juicer **2** blender **3** cocktail shakers
4 mixing jug with stirrer
5 jiggers (measuring cups) **6** grater/zester
7 wooden ice mallet **8** strainer
9 long-handled bar spoons
10 cocktail sticks **11** bartender's friend
12 measuring spoons **13** stirrers
14 zester/canelle knife

Left: A large cocktail shaker is a vital piece of equipment.

Brandy balloon: The traditional brandy glass has a short stem and a large well-rounded bowl that narrows at the rim. The design of the brandy balloon makes it easy to warm the glass and its contents using the palm of the hand; the narrow rim captures the compelling bouquet. In the United States, the brandy balloon is often referred to as a snifter.

Pousse-café: A tall narrow glass designed to show off the stunning, colorful layers of a pousse-café to full effect. Also referred to as an elgin.

Old-fashioned (lowball): A short chunky tumbler, often used for short drinks that are served "on the rocks."

Highball (Collins): A highball glass is a tall, straight-sided tumbler designed for long drinks and is sometimes also referred to as a Collins glass – although, strictly speaking, the Collins glass is usually slightly taller.

Shot glass: A small glass designed to take a single shot of spirit that is boldly swallowed in one gulp. Larger shot glasses are suitable for double measures and are used for shooters.

Ingredients

Although cocktails frequently use more than one alcohol the other ingredients – sugar, fruit, fruit juice and syrup, and various mixers each play crucial roles. A great deal of the fun and adventure in cocktail mixing – and of course drinking – is the variety of tastes and colors that can be used and created.

Alcoholic drinks: You can stock your bar over a period of time with the basics – it is not necessary to buy everything at once. A good, all-round selection of alcoholic drinks would include:
• A good mixture of spirits – brandy, fruit brandies, bourbon, Cointreau, Drambuie, gin, tequila, vodka, whiskey, and rum (light and dark). You could also include Pernod. Select your stock according to your tastes – for example, if you never drink whiskey, it would be extravagant to buy Scotch, Irish, Canadian, American blended, and bourbon.
• Dry and sweet vermouth (red and white)
• Cassis, crème de menthe, and blue Curaçao – the colorful liqueurs.
• Herbal and uniquely flavored liqueurs such as Amaretto, Chartreuse, Galliano, kümmel.
• Coffee, chocolate and nut liqueurs are occasionally used, such as Kahlua, Malibu and Tia Maria.
• Colorful but non-alcoholic syrups like grenadine – green or red.
• Beer, red and white wine, cider, and sparkling wine.
• Keep champagne cocktails for special occasions.
• Mixers – soda water, lemonade, ginger ale, ginger beer, and cola.

Angostura bitters: The most famous of all the aromatic bitters, Angostura bitters are based on a blend of gentian with vegetable spices and some coloring. They create the "pink" coloring in a Pink Gin.

Cream: Some cocktails and shooters require the addition of cream. Always use fresh, heavy dairy cream unless otherwise stated in the recipe.

Fruit: A good supply of fresh lemons, limes, and oranges is essential. Remember that you will frequently use the peel so you may prefer to buy organic or unwaxed fruits.

Fruit juices: Freshly squeezed lemon and lime juice are essential and if you can freshly squeeze other fruit juices, such as orange and grapefruit, then so much the better. Alternatively, shop-bought freshly squeezed juices will make a perfectly acceptable substitute, but it is best to

avoid those with added sugar or extra "padding." Commercial brands of grapefruit, orange, cranberry, tomato juice, and lime cordial are very useful.

Mixers: First check that you have the required mixers available. Those most frequently used are soda water, lemonade, ginger ale, fruit juices (including tomato juice), citrus juices, cola, and soda water or sparkling water.

Sugar syrup/syrup de gomme: Some cocktails require sugar syrup, known as "syrup de gomme." It is used by professional bartenders and can be bought commercially, but it is very easy to make at home. Simply take equal quantities of sugar and water and heat them gently in a really clean pan until the sugar has dissolved. Allow the syrup to cool, bottle and refrigerate until required, for up to two weeks.

Worcestershire sauce: Worcestershire sauce is created from a spicy, slightly fiery blend of vinegar, molasses, tamarind, and anchovies and is renowned for putting the zap into a Bloody Mary.

Ice: Ice is the second most important element to making a good cocktail, although many would say it is the first, as you can never make a good cocktail without it. So always make plenty, well in advance, and whenever possible use pure bottled water.

Cracking and crushing ice: Store ice in the freezer until just before use. Cracked ice is used in both shaken and stirred cocktails. To crack ice, put ice cubes into a strong

Top: Frosting the rim of a Martini glass.
Centre: Making sugar syrup.
Below: Crushing ice with a wooden mallet.

plastic bag and hit it against an outside wall, or put the ice between clean cloths on a sturdy surface and bash with a wooden mallet or rolling pin to crack into smaller pieces but not to crush. Crushed ice melts almost immediately and is used in cocktails made in a blender and in some shaken cocktails. To crush ice, crack it as before but break it into much smaller pieces, or whizz it in a food processor where there is plenty of room so it turns to a even mixture of not-too-fine crystals.

Special occasion ice cubes: Throughout this book you will find a variety of unusual ice cubes designed to suit specific cocktails. For instance, you can freeze small pieces of fruit in ice cubes – cranberries, raspberries or blackberries are ideal. Small slices of orange, lemon, and lime are great and chopped mint and other herbs work well too. For brightly colored cubes, mix a bright liqueur with water. As pure alcohol will not freeze, you will need to use $1/3$ liqueur and $2/3$ water. The best ingredients to use are grenadine, blue Curaçao, and green crème de menthe.

Decorations

Much of the glamor and sophistication of a cocktail is conjured up by its visual presentation, and fresh decorations can play a major part in this. The following are some suggestions for garnishes and these should be used appropriately to complement the ingredients of each cocktail in the book.

Celery: Best for tomato-based cocktails such as Bloody Mary or Virgin Mary.

Citrus fruits: Make citrus peel into twists, or spirals to float in the drink, or to decorate the rim of the glass.

Fruit slices or wedges: To garnish the edge of the glass.

Maraschino cherry: Provides an elegant touch of color.

Olives: A single green olive is the essential garnish for a classic Martini. A black olive is very elegant in a clear white sharp (non-sweet) mix.

Fresh mint: To add a touch of color and a zing of flavor.

Tropical fruit: The occasional, subtle use of tropical fruit as a decoration can further enhance the glamor of a cocktail. Take care not to go overboard and turn the drink into something resembling a miniature fruit salad!

Frosting glasses: Glasses can be frosted with sugar – or fine or coarse salt in the case of the Margarita or Salty Dog – to give added glamor and an extra flavor. Simply rub the rim of the glass with a wedge of lemon or lime, a drop of one of the liquids in the cocktail, or if you are making several you could use egg white, then dip the rim into a saucer of powdered sugar until evenly coated. Leave it to dry for several minutes if possible before serving the drink. Sugar may be flavored with citrus zest, cocoa powder and ground cinnamon, although various other ingredients are occasionally used.

Cocktail Tips

Cocktail shaker: If you do not yet have a cocktail shaker, use two very large sturdy tumblers which fit together, one over the other. For single cocktails, use one large glass with a suitable lid or cover for shaking. When choosing a shaker, make sure it is large enough to ensure a really good shake.

Ice: Remember that the more ice you can use in shaking and the faster and more firmly you can shake the liquid, the quicker the drink will cool and the less the ice will melt and dilute the cocktail. Never use the same ice for different drinks, as it will always retain the flavor and will not be cold enough to serve its purpose. Ice is crucial to the end result, so do be sure you have made sufficient before you start.

Chilled glasses: A well-chilled glass will make all the difference to a cocktail. Plan ahead and store cleaned and polished glasses overnight on a safe flat shelf in the freezer. If you have very little time, fill the glasses with cold water and ice cubes, and allow them to chill. Handle glasses as little as possible once chilled. Avoid freezing cut crystal or very delicate glasses to prevent breakages and accidents.

Be prepared: To enjoy the fun of making and drinking cocktails, it is worth planning ahead to ensure you have all the right elements to hand. A variety of glasses, suitable decorations, fruit, straws, cocktail sticks, ice, all the right equipment and, of course, the relevant drinks and mixers.

Favorites: If you intend to make cocktails often, it would be a good idea to make a note of the recipes you have tried and the favorites of your family and friends. If you change, add to, or make your own variations, you will then have a record for the future and a growing collection of your household's very own specialties.

Bubbly Cocktails

Le Crystal

Poire William liqueur schnapps is a great drink on its own, but it makes a really super champagne cocktail with a very serious kick.

Serves : 1

1/2 measure Poire William
1 dash orange Curaçao
1 slice firm pear
ice
champagne
peice of fesh pear

1 Shake all, except the champagne, over ice until really cold.

2 Pour into a flute and top up with the cold champagne.

3 Finish with a slice of pear.

The Acrobat

Cider is not often used in cocktails, which is a pity as it is a great way to add length with a little strength to a drink.

Serves : 1

2 measures whiskey
1 measure Cointreau
1 measure lime juice
ice
cider
piece of lime

1 Mix all the ingredients except cider over ice until frosted.

2 Strain into an ice-filled long glass.

3 Dress with a slice of lime or lemon.

Buck's Fizz

③

Invented at Buck's Club in London, the original was invariably made with Bollinger champagne and it is true that the better the quality of the champagne, the better the flavor.

Serves : 1

2 measures chilled fresh orange juice
2 measures champagne, chilled

1 Half fill a chilled flute with orange juice, then gently pour in the chilled champagne.

Amarettine

④

Inexpensive sparkling white wine is the base of this pretty cocktail. Use the sweeter bubblies if you like a sweet drink, otherwise go for dry. And be warned, it is not just a pretty drink!

Serves : 1

$^1/_3$ measure Amaretto
$^1/_3$ measure dry vermouth
sparkling white wine

1 Mix the Amaretto and vermouth in a chilled tall cocktail glass.
2 Top up with wine to taste.

Alfonso

⑤

This is a delicious way to turn a simple sparkling white wine into a sophisticated cocktail. Probably not the time to use expensive champagne.

Serves : 1

1 measure Dubonnet
2 dashes Angostura bitters
1 sugar lump
champagne, chilled
orange peel

1 Pour the Dubonnet into a chilled flute.
2 Add the sugar lump with the bitters splashed on to it.
3 When ready to serve, pour on the chilled bubbly and add a twist of orange peel.

6

Bombay Sherry Punch

An unusual mix for a party, ideal to dilute as much as you wish.

Serves : 16
1 bottle brandy, chilled
1 bottle sherry, chilled
1 measure maraschino
1 measure Curaçao
2 bottles champagne or sparkling
white wine, chilled
soda water, chilled
large ice cubes (set with fruit in them)
fruit to decorate

1 Mix the first four ingredients in a large punch bowl.
2 Add the wine and soda to taste and then add the fruit and ice cubes at the last minute.

7

Long Tall Sally

A seriously strong champagne cocktail with the perfume of herbs.

Serves : 1
$^1/_4$ measure brandy
$^1/_4$ measure dry vermouth
$^1/_4$ measure Galliano
$^1/_4$ measure mandarin liqueur
ice
champagne or sparkling wine

1 Stir the first four ingredients over ice and pour into a tall chilled glass.
2 Top up with champagne.

Serpentine

Living up to its name, this green bubbly concoction has hidden secrets. Don't forget to chill the champagne for at least 2 hours before mixing.

Serves : 1

½ measure green crème de menthe
cracked ice
curl or twist of lime peel
champagne, chilled
1 tsp lime zest

1 Pour the crème de menthe into the base of a flute with ice and the curl of lime peel.
2 Pour in the champagne and finish with a sprinkle of zest.

Chicago

Do use a dry champagne, or even a good sparkling wine, for cocktails where you add sweet ingredients and especially if you want to sugar the rim of the glass for extra sparkle.

Serves : 1

egg white or lemon juice
powdered sugar
1 measure brandy
1 dash Cointreau
1 dash Angostura bitters
ice
champagne

1 Prepare a frosted rim glass with the egg white and sugar.
2 Shake the rest of the ingredients together (except the champagne) with ice until frosted.
3 Strain into the prepared glass and top up with champagne.

Mimosa

So called because it resembles the color of a mimosa's attractive yellow bloom.

Serves : 1

juice of 1 passion fruit
½ measure orange Curaçao
crushed ice
champagne, chilled
slice of star fruit and twist of peel

1 Scoop out the passion fruit flesh into a jug or shaker and shake with the Curaçao and a little crushed ice until frosted.
2 Pour into the base of a champagne glass and top up with champagne.
3 Dress with fruit.

 11

Disco Dancer

Make it nice and long and you have the perfect disco drink.

Serves : 1
1 measure crème de banane
1 measure rum
few drops Angostura bitters
ice
sparkling white wine

1 Shake all the first three ingredients well over ice.
2 Pour into a high ball glass and top up with sparkling wine to taste.
3 Add plenty of ice to keep you cool and lengthen your drink.

 12

Campari Fizz

The bitter-sweet of Campari is a natural with orange juice and sparkling wine or champagne. You need very little to add the distinctive color and flavor.

Serves : 1
1 measure Campari
1 measure orange juice
crushed ice
champagne

1 Shake the first three ingredients together well until frosted and pour into a flute.
2 Top up with champagne.

 13

Kir Royale

A wicked improvement on the simple cassis and white wine drink.

Serves : 1
few drops cassis or to taste
1/2 measure brandy
champagne, chilled

1 Put the cassis and brandy into the base of a flute.
2 Top up with champagne to taste.

Daydreamer

You won't need more than one of these before you are daydreaming.

Serves : 1

¹/₃ measure brandy
1 tsp maraschino
1 tsp dark Curaçao
1 tsp Angostura bitters
ice
champagne or sparkling white wine
fresh cherry

1 Stir the first four ingredients over ice, strain into a cocktail glass and top up with champagne.
2 Dress with a cherry.

Raspberry Mist

The perfect celebration drink for a ruby wedding anniversary.

Serves : 24

6 measures Irish Mist honey liqueur
1lb raspberries
crushed ice
4 bottles sparkling dry white wine, well chilled
24 raspberries

1 Whiz the liqueur and raspberries in a blender with a cup of crushed ice.
2 When lightly frozen, divide between chilled champagne bowls and top up with the wine.
3 Top each with a raspberry.

Pink Sherbet Royale

This is perfect for very special occasions on hot days, or after dinner watching a warm sun setting slowly.

Serves : 2

1¹/₂ cups sparkling white wine, really cold
2 measures cassis
1 measure brandy
1 scoop crushed ice
blackberries

1 Whizz half the wine in a blender with the rest of the ingredients until really frothy and frosted (mind it doesn't bubble over).
2 Slowly whisk in a little more wine and pour into tall thin frosted glasses.
3 Top with a few blackberries.

 # Black Sparkler

Simply using sparkling water makes this a delicious summer party drink. If you wish to make it more celebratory, use sparkling white wine.

Serves : 1

1 3/4 measures cognac

1/4 measure Crème de Mure

1/4 measure lemon juice

1 tsp powdered sugar

ice

soda water or sparkling white wine

frozen blackcurrants or berries

1 Shake the first four ingredients over ice until frosted.

2 Strain into a tall chilled cocktail glass and top up with soda water or wine.

3 Dress with fruit.

Black Velvet

Don't ever say that it ruins good champagne, just enjoy a long heady draught of a timeless treasure.

Serves : 1

stout or Guinness, chilled
champagne, chilled

1 Pour both drinks in equal quantities carefully (may fizz up well) into a long beer or highball glass.

Velvet Mule

This mule has an interesting kick of anise and ginger – a surprisingly good mix, especially with unique flavors from the cola.

Serves : 1

1 measure cassis
1 measure black Sambuca
2 measures ginger wine
cola
soda or sparkling white wine

1 Stir the first three ingredients over ice until well frosted.
2 Strain into a frosted flute and top up with equal quantities of cola and soda.

Velvet Cooler

A very unusual long summer party drink, refreshing and yet surprisingly strong.

Serves : 1

2-3 tbsp pineapple juice
lager, iced
champagne or sparkling wine, iced

1 Pour the pineapple juice into the base of a chilled highball glass.
2 Slowly add equal quantities of lager and champagne.

Champagne Cocktail

The classic champagne cocktail can be too sweet for some. It is the brandy that gives the treat and the kick, so you could leave out the sugar!

Serves : 1
1 sugar cube
2 dashes Angostura bitters
1 measure brandy
champagne, chilled

1 Place the sugar cube with the drops of bitters in the base of a chilled flute.
2 Pour on the brandy and top up slowly with champagne.

Caribbean Champagne

Both rum and bananas are naturally associated with the Tropics, but wine does not spring so readily to mind when the Caribbean is mentioned. However, remember that France and many of the Caribbean islands, such as Martinique and Guadeloupe, share a long history.

Serves : 1
$1/2$ measure white rum
$1/2$ measure crème de banane
champagne, chilled
slice of banana, to decorate

1 Pour the rum and crème de banane into a chilled flute.
2 Top up with champagne.
3 Stir gently to mix and dress with a slice of banana.

James Bond

Surprisingly and very definitely not shaken on this occasion, or stirred!

Serves : 1
1 sugar cube
2 dashes Angostura bitters
1 measure vodka, chilled
champagne, chilled

1 Moisten the sugar with the Angostura and place in the base of a chilled flute.
2 Cover with the vodka and then top up with champagne.

 24

Dawn

Look for a good fruity sparkling wine to use in this cocktail or even a sparkling red.

Serves : 1

1 measure lime juice
1 measure medium to medium dry sherry
champagne, chilled

1 Stir the lime and sherry in a chilled flute.
2 Top with chilled champagne and stir briefly.

 25

Prince of Wales

A knockout version of a champagne cocktail, not to be drunk too quickly.

Serves : 1

1 measure brandy
1 measure Madeira wine or muscatel
3 drops Curaçao
2 drop Angostura bitters
ice
champagne, chilled
orange peel

1 Shake the first four ingredients together over ice and strain into a chilled flute.
2 Top up with champagne to taste and finish with a fine curl of orange peel.

 26

Royal Julep

As with all juleps, the mint needs crushing or muddling first to help release its flavor into the sugar and water. Simply chopping it won't produce enough flavor.

Serves : 1

1 sugar lump
3 sprigs fresh mint
1 measure Jack Daniels
champagne, chilled

1 In a small glass, crush the sugar and mint together with a little of the whiskey.
2 When the sugar has dissolved, strain it into a chilled flute with the rest of the whiskey and then top up with champagne.

Millennium Cocktail

Specially created to mark the beginning of the 21st century – and an even better way to continue it.

Serves : 1

1 measure raspberry vodka
1 measure fresh raspberry juice
1 measure orange juice
ice
champagne, chilled
raspberries, to decorate

1 Shake the vodka, raspberry juice and orange juice vigorously over ice until well frosted.
2 Strain into a chilled flute and top up with chilled champagne.
3 Stir gently to mix and dress with raspberries.

28. Leap Year: Shake 2 measures gin, $^1/_2$ measure Grand Marnier, $^1/_2$ measure sweet vermouth, and $^1/_2$ tsp lemon juice vigorously over ice until well frosted. Strain into a chilled cocktail glass.

29. Thanksgiving Special: Shake 2 measures gin, $1^1/_2$ measures apricot brandy, 1 measure dry vermouth, and $^1/_2$ measure lemon juice vigorously over ice until well frosted. Strain into a chilled cocktail glass. Dress with a cocktail cherry.

30. Cool Yule Martini: Shake 3 measures vodka, $^1/_2$ measure dry vermouth, and 1 tsp peppermint schnapps over ice until well frosted. Strain into a chilled cocktail glass. Dress with a peppermint candy cane.

Champagne Cobbler

(31)

The Cobbler was popular in Dickens'
time when it was a concoction of
sherry, sugar, lemon, and ice. This
version has much more kick and
lots more bubbles.

Serves : 1

1 glass champagne
¹/₄ measure Curaçao
1 tsp syrup de gomme
ice
raspberry and soft fruit slices

1 Mix the champagne, Curaçao and
syrup in a chilled mixing glass.
2 Pour into a tall glass filled with ice
and simply dress with pieces of fresh
soft fruit.

Pearl Cocktail

(32)

No pearls or oysters here, just a pearl of a drink to enjoy before or after dinner.

Serves : 1
¹/₂ measure cognac
¹/₂ measure coffee liqueur
crushed ice
champagne, chilled
black cherry or grape

1 Stir the first two ingredients together
over ice in a chilled champagne glass.
2 Top up with champagne and dress with a
cherry or grape.

Lady Luck

The pear and apple flavors give a deep fruitiness to the final cocktail so you could use a sparkling white wine as the base.

Serves : 1

1 measure Calvados
1 measure pear nectar or ¹/₂ measure pear liqueur
slice of firm ripe pear
champagne, chilled

1 Pour the Calvados and pear nectar into a chilled flute with a slice of pear.
2 Top up with chilled champagne.

(34)

Grape Expectations

Add the remaining grapes at the very last minute, then watch them liven up your drink as they jump around, making ever more bubbles.

Serves : 1

5-6 red or black grapes
ice
splash of mandarin liqueur
pink champagne or sparkling wine, chilled

1 Save 2 grapes for the glass.
2 Crush or muddle the others in a small bowl to let the juice flow.
3 Add ice and liqueur, stir well and strain into a chilled champagne glass.
4 Top up with champagne. Halve and pip the remaining grapes and add to the glass.

 # Kismet

A romantic era produced some delightful music and this elegant drink brings that mood bang up to date.

Serves : 1

1 measure gin
1 measure apricot brandy
1/2 tsp stem ginger syrup
champagne, chilled
slices of ripe fresh mango

1 Pour the gin and brandy into a chilled flute.
2 Trickle the ginger syrup slowly down the glass and then top up with champagne.
3 Add a piece of fruit to finish.

 # Orange Sparkler

Serve this exotic version of a classic champagne cocktail for any occasion or simple celebration.

Serves : 1

2/3 measure brandy
1/3 measure orange liqueur
1/3 measure lemon juice
ice
Asti Spumante dry, iced

1 Shake the first three ingredients well together over ice.
2 Strain into a chilled champagne glass and top up with Asti Spumante to taste.

 # Pear and Cinnamon Sling

If you can't find cinnamon syrup, you may have to make your own!

Serves : 1

2 measures vodka
2 measure pear purée
3/5 measure cinnamon syrup
4/5 measure cranberry and
blackcurrant juice
ice
champagne, chilled
slices of pear

1 Shake the first four ingredients together over ice until frosted.
2 Strain into a chilled flute and top up with champagne.
3 Dress with pear.

Death in the Afternoon

It is rumoured this was Ernest Hemingway's favorite drink when he lived in Paris. The anise gives it a mysterious cloudiness and it is certainly moreish!

Serves : 1
1 measure Pernod
dry champagne, chilled
ice

1 Put two ice cubes into a champagne glass.
2 Pour the Pernod over them and carefully pour in the champagne.
3 Drink quickly before the bubbles disperse!

 39

Pick-me-up

Champagne always gives you a lift and this one, with its added ingredients, is the perfect anytime booster.

Serves : 1
ice
3 dashes Fernet Branca
3 dashes Curaçao
1 measure brandy
champagne, chilled

1 Place the ice in a wine glass to chill.
2 Stir in the other ingredients gradually and top up with the champagne.
3 Dress with a twist of lemon peel.

Josiah's Bay Float

This is a wonderful cocktail for a special occasion in the summer. Designed for two to share, perhaps an engagement or a romantic al fresco dinner would be appropriate. For the more prosaic, serve in tall, chilled tumblers, rather than a pineapple shell.

Serves : 2

cracked ice cubes
2 measures golden rum
1 measure Galliano
2 measures pineapple juice
1 measure lime juice
4 tsp sugar syrup
champagne, to top up
slices of lime and lemon
cocktail cherries
scooped-out pineapple shell

1 Shake the rum, Galliano, pineapple juice, lime juice and sugar syrup vigorously over ice until well frosted.

2 Strain into the pineapple shell, top up with champagne and stir gently.

3 Decorate with lime and lemon slices and cocktail cherries and serve with two straws.

41. Royal Matador: Cut the top off a pineapple and reserve the lid. Scoop out the flesh, leaving the shell intact. Put the flesh in a blender and purée. Strain the juice from the purée and return it to the blender. Add 8-10 crushed ice cubes, 4 measures golden tequila, 1 1/2 measures crème de framboise, 2 measures lime juice and 1 tbsp Amaretto. Blend until slushy, then pour into the pineapple shell, adding more ice if required. Replace the lid and serve with straws. **Serves : 2**

Jade

You can tell good jade because it always feels cold to the touch – and that should apply to cocktails, too. No cocktail bar, nor home bar, can ever have too much ice.

Serves : 1

1/4 measure Midori
1/4 measure blue Curaçao
1/4 measure lime juice
dash Angostura bitters
champagne, chilled
cracked ice cubes
slice of lime, to decorate

1 Shake the Midori, Curaçao, lime juice and Angostura bitters vigorously over ice until well frosted.

2 Strain into a chilled flute. Top up with chilled champagne and dress with a slice of lime.

Mexican Fizz

The tart fruitiness of tequila is not often appreciated neat, but it is great with many of the sweetened and fuller flavored mixers.

Serves : 1

2 measures tequila
1/2 measure grenadine
5-6 measures dry ginger ale
crushed ice

1 Shake the tequila, grenadine and half the ginger over ice until slushy and frosted.
2 Pour into a chilled tall glass and top up with more ginger to taste.
3 Drink through a straw.

(44)

French 75

CLASSIC

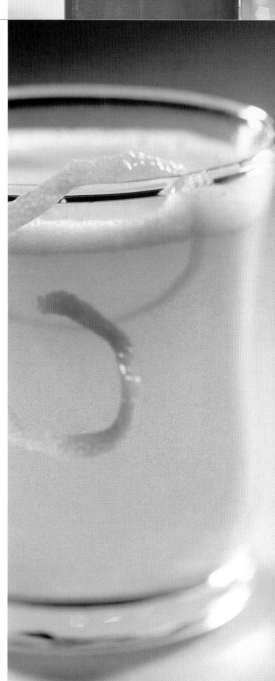

Described in a cocktail book of the early 20th century as a drink that "definitely hits the spot," there seems to be some confusion about the actual ingredients for this classic. All recipes include champagne, but disagree about the spirits included.

Serves : 1

2 measures brandy
1 measure lemon juice
1 tbsp sugar syrup
cracked ice cubes
champagne, chilled
twist of lemon peel

1 Shake the brandy, lemon juice and sugar syrup vigorously over ice until well frosted.
2 Strain into a chilled highball glass and top up with champagne.
3 Dress with lemon twist.

45. French 75 (second version): Shake 2 measures Plymouth gin and 1 measure lime juice vigorously over ice until well frosted. Strain into a chilled wine glass and top up with chilled champagne. Dress with a cocktail cherry. **Serves : 1**

46. French 75 (third version): Put 1 tsp powdered sugar into a tall, chilled tumbler. Add 1 measure lemon juice and stir until the sugar has dissolved. Fill the glass with cracked ice cubes. Pour 2 measures gin over the ice and top up with chilled champagne. Dress with slices of orange. **Serves : 1**

47. London French 75: Make the second version of a French 75, but substitute London gin for the Plymouth gin and lemon juice for the lime. **Serves : 1**

48. French Kiss: Shake 2 measures bourbon, 1 measure apricot liqueur, 2 tsp grenadine and 1 tsp lemon juice vigorously over ice until well frosted. Strain into a chilled cocktail glass. **Serves : 1**

 (49)

Ruby Fizz

This low-alcohol fizz is very refreshing and can be made with almost any rich sweet fruit syrup. It's especially good with home-made syrups such as redcurrant shrub.

Serves : 1

juice of ½ lemon
2 tsp powdered sugar
1 small egg white
2 dashes raspberry syrup or grenadine
2 measures sloe gin
ice
soda water

1 Shake all the ingredients except the soda water well over ice until frosted.
2 Strain into a chilled long glass and top up with soda water.

 (50)

Cranberry Whizz

The perfect long and refreshing bubble for non-drinkers at festive times or for anyone just resting before the next party!

Serves : 1

ice
juice ½ lime
cranberry juice
lemonade or elderflower pressé
strawberry

1 Sugar-frost the rim of a tall glass or flute.
2 Two-thirds fill with ice and pour in the lime juice and cranberry juice.
3 Top up with lemonade and stir gently.
4 Dress with a strawberry.

 (51)

Wild Silk

A wildly fruity cocktail topped with a riot of bubbles and really well-iced champagne.

Serves : 2

½ measure cream
½ measure raspberries
1 measure framboise or raspberry syrup
little crushed ice
champagne, chilled

1 Set aside 2-3 nice raspberries.
2 Whizz the first three ingredients with ice in a blender until frosted and slushy.
3 Pour into a flute and top up with champagne. Float a raspberry or two on the top.

52 Cherry Kiss

A refreshing and almost calorie-free cocktail perfect for dieting or simply one of those non-alcohol occasions.

Serves : 2

8 ice cubes, crushed
2 tbsp cherry syrup
2 cups sparkling water
2-3 splashes fresh lime juice
maraschino cherries on cocktail sticks

1 Divide the crushed ice between two glasses and pour over the syrup.
2 Add the lime juice and top up with sparkling water.
3 Decorate with the maraschino cherries on cocktail sticks and serve.

---

53 QM2

A new ship deserves a new cocktail and no doubt quite a few will be made and drunk on her many majestic voyages.

Serves : 8

juice of 1 lime
powdered sugar
$1/2$ measure sugar syrup
2 measures Drambuie
$1^1/2$ cups sparkling water
1 bottle sparkling red or rosé wine
maraschino cherries

1 Rub the rim of the flutes with lime juice, then dip in sugar and set aside to chill.
2 Stir the rest of the juice over ice with the sugar syrup, Drambuie and sparkling water.
3 Divide evenly between the glasses, top up with the sparkling wine and add a few cherries to each flute.
4 Serve with a decorative straw.

 54

San Joaquin Punch

A fabulous bubbly punch enriched with brandy-soaked Californian dried fruits.

Serves : 4
1 tbsp raisins or chopped prunes
6 tsp brandy
1 cup sparkling white wine or champagne
1 cup white cranberry and
grape juice
ice

1 Mix the dried fruit and brandy in a small bowl and leave to soak for 1-2 hours.
2 In a jug mix the sparkling wine, juice and brandy-soaked fruit.
3 Pour into ice-filled glasses.

 55

The Footman

If you are preparing several glasses, make the gin base in advance and keep it well chilled until you are ready.

Serves : 1
¹/₂ measure gin
1 measure orange juice
1 slice peach
1 ice cube
champagne, chilled
1 slice of peach to finish

1 Whizz all except the champagne in a blender until smooth, about 10 seconds.
2 Pour into a flute and top up with champagne when ready.
3 Finish with a slice of peach.

 56

San Remo

Next time you cut up a citrus fruit, put any left-over slices in the freezer, as they make great flavored ice cubes.

Serves : 1
¹/₂ measure grapefruit juice
¹/₄ measure Triple Sec
¹/₄ measure mandarin liqueur
ice
champagne
slices of citrus fruit, frozen

1 Mix the first three ingredients with ice in a tall glass.
2 Top up with champagne and dress with fruit.

CLASSIC

Christmas Cocktail

This bright and cheerful cocktail is easy to prepare for lots of guests and you certainly don't need to wait for Christmas to enjoy it.

Serves : 1
1 cube sugar
splash brandy
generous splash cranberry juice, chilled
champagne, chilled
few raspberries to float

1 Place a sugar cube in the base of a chilled champagne glass.
2 Add the brandy and allow to soak in, then splash on the cranberry juice.
3 At the last moment, top up with champagne and float one or two raspberries on the top.

Sparkling Gold

For a very special occasion like a golden wedding anniversary, you could float tiny pieces of edible gold leaf on the top of each glass.

Serves : 1
1 measure golden rum
1/2 measure Cointreau
champagne, chilled

1 Pour the rum and liqueur into a chilled flute and top up with chilled champagne.

Shangri-la

This an excellent mix to liven up a not-so-exciting bottle of bubbly! Also an unusual mix for several people for a party.

Serves : 1

1/2 measure gin
1/4 measure apricot brandy
1/2 measure orange juice
few drops grenadine
ice
Asti Spumante dry sparkling wine
slices of orange and lemon

1 Stir the first four ingredients with ice in a chilled highball or large wine glass.
2 Top up with sparkling wine and dress with fruit.

Valencia Cocktail

Valencia is the home of some of the best oranges, so what better way to enjoy the local produce. A forerunner to Buck's Fizz no doubt.

Serves : 1

4 dashes orange bitters
1 tsp apricot cordial
1/3 measure orange juice
1/3 measure apricot brandy
ice
champagne, chilled

1 Shake the first four ingredients well over ice until frosted.
2 Strain into a tall chilled flute and top up with champagne to taste.

Tequila Slammer

Slammers are also known as shooters. The idea is that you pour the ingredients directly into the glass, without stirring. Cover the glass with one hand to prevent spillage, slam it on to a table to mix and drink the cocktail down in one! Do ensure you use a strong glass!

Serves : 1

1 measure white tequila, chilled
1 measure lemon juice
sparkling wine, chilled

1 Put the tequila and lemon juice into a chilled glass.

2 Top up with sparkling wine.

3 Cover the glass with your hand and slam.

62. Alabama Slammer: Pour 1 measure Southern Comfort, 1 measure Amaretto and $^1/_2$ measure sloe gin over cracked ice in a mixing glass and stir. Strain into a shot glass and add $^1/_2$ tsp lemon juice. Cover and slam. **Serves : 1**

63. B52: Pour 1 measure chilled dark crème de cacao into a shot glass. With a steady hand, gently pour in 1 measure chilled Baileys Irish Cream to make a second layer, then gently pour in 1 measure chilled Grand Marnier. Cover and slam. **Serves : 1**

64. B52: (second version): Pour 1 measure chilled Kahlua into a shot glass. With a steady hand, gently pour in 1 measure chilled Baileys Irish Cream to make a second layer, then gently pour in 1 measure chilled Grand Marnier. Cover and slam. **Serves : 1**

65. Banana Slip: Pour 1 measure chilled crème de banane into a shot glass. With a steady hand, gently pour in 1 measure chilled Baileys Irish Cream to make a second layer. Cover and slam. **Serves : 1**

Sabrina

Perfect for lovers of sweet and fruity cocktails and the base is easy to prepare in advance.

Serves : 1

$^1/_2$ measure gin
$^1/_8$ measure apricot brandy
$^1/_2$ measure fresh orange juice
1 tsp grenadine
$^1/_4$ measure Cinzano
ice
sweet sparkling wine
orange and lemon slices

1 Shake the first five ingredients together over ice.

2 Pour into a tall glass and top up with sparkling wine.

3 Finish with slices of orange and lemon.

The Trade Winds

Whether it blows hot or cold, champagne cocktails are a treat for any occasion and this one is as refreshing as it is colorful.

Serves : 1

1 measure gin
$^1/_2$ measure cherry brandy
$^1/_2$ measure lemon juice
1-2 dashes syrup de gomme
$^1/_2$ scoop crushed ice
champagne, chilled
cherries

1 Shake together all but the champagne over ice until frosted and strain into the base of a champagne glass.
2 Top up with chilled champagne and decorate with fresh cherries.

68

Peardrops

Pear is one fruit that adds an alcoholic type of flavor, whether it is in alcohol form or not. When you cook pears, they become more aromatic and in this cocktail they certainly give off a wonderfully rich and heady aroma.

Serves : 1

1 measure pear schnapps
perry, chilled
slice of pear or a cherry

1 Pour the schnapps into the base of a chilled champagne glass and slowly add the perry.
2 Dress with a cherry.

The Bentley

Champagne cocktails tend to get better and better the more you drink.

Serves : 1

¹/₂ measure cognac or brandy

¹/₂ measure peach liqueur, peach brandy or schnapps

juice of 1 passion fruit, sieved

1 ice cube

champagne

1 Mix the first three ingredients gently together in a chilled glass.

2 Add one ice cube and slowly pour in champagne to taste.

Sparkling Julep

Sparkling wine is good to enjoy any time and this is a particularly refreshing way to drink it.

Serves : 1
1 lump sugar
2 sprigs mint
sparkling white wine, chilled

1 Place the sugar in the base of a chilled flute with one bruised sprig of mint.
2 Add the bubbly and the other sprig of mint and any fruit in season you wish.

71. Diamond Head: Shake 4 measures gin, 2 measures lemon juice, 1 measure apricot brandy, 1 tsp sugar and 1 egg white syrup vigorously over ice until well frosted. Strain into two chilled cocktail glasses. **Serves : 2**

72. Diamond Fizz: Shake 2 measures gin, $^1/_2$ measure lemon juice and 1 tsp sugar syrup over the ice until well frosted. Strain into a chilled flute. Top up with chilled champagne. **Serves : 1**

73. Sapphire Martini: Put 4-6 cracked ice cubes into a mixing glass. Pour 2 measures gin and $^1/_2$ measure blue Curaçao over the ice. Stir well to mix then strain into a chilled cocktail glass. Dress with a blue cocktail cherry. **Serves : 1**

74. Topaz Martini: Put 4-6 cracked ice cubes into a mixing glass. Pour 2 measures gin and $^1/_2$ measure orange Curaçao over the ice. Stir well to mix then strain into a chilled cocktail glass. Dress with a slice of lemon. **Serves : 1**

Sparkler

The simplest and cleverest of all non-alcoholic drinks. It can look like a gin and tonic or a spritzer, and it tastes great too!

Serves : 1
few drops Angostura bitters
ice
your favorite sparkling water
cherry or slice of lemon
lemon or orange juice, optional

1 Splash the bitters into an ice-filled highball glass.
2 Fill up with the water and dress with a cherry or a slice.
3 Add a few drops lemon or orange juice too, if you wish.

Monte Carlo

The motor racing world always drinks champagne, especially in Monte Carlo, so this well-laced cocktail will be very popular.

Serves : 1
$^1/_2$ measure gin
$^1/_4$ measure lemon juice
ice
champagne or sparkling white wine
$^1/_4$ measure crème de menthe
mint leaf

1 Stir the first two ingredients well over ice until well chilled.
2 Strain into chilled flutes and top up with champagne.
3 Finally drizzle the crème de menthe over the top and dress with a mint leaf.

Jersey Lily

This clear, golden refresher is named for the Edwardian beauty, actress Lillie Langtry (1852-1929). Whether the most famous of her lovers, the Prince of Wales (later King Edward VII), enjoyed it too, history does not record.

Serves : 1
1 glass fizzy apple juice
sugar to taste
1 dash Angostura bitters
ice cubes
maraschino cherry and apple slice

1 Mix a little sugar into the apple juice, add the bitters and ice cubes and stir until well frosted.
2 Strain into a chilled glass. Spear a thin slice of apple and a cherry on a cocktail stick to garnish or simply drop the cherry into the bottom of the glass.

(78) Apple Fizz

Cider makes a great punch base as it can be blended with many alcoholic drinks. This mix can't be made in advance, but it's easy to prepare for several people and then add more cider at the last minute to create extra fizz.

Serves : 1

1/2 cup sparkling cider or
apple juice
1 measure Calvados
juice 1/2 lemon
1 tbsp egg white
generous pinch sugar
ice
slices of lemon and apple

1 Shake the first five ingredients together over ice and pour immediately into a highball glass (it may fizz up well).
2 Finish with a slice of lemon or apple or both. For more fizz at the last moment top up with more cider.

(79) Hedgerow Apple Tipple

If you ever make your own cider or blackberry gin this is the ideal drink in which to combine them.

Serves : 1

ice cubes
1 tsp blackberry purée, syrup or liqueur
1 measure apple juice
sparkling cider to taste
a few blackberries

1 Place one ice cube in the base of a tall thin glass.
2 Spoon over the purée, then the apple juice and gently pour on the cider.
3 Dress with a few blackberries.

Cider Punch

This may sound seriously strong but it isn't, and you can add more soda or ice to taste once the base is made.

Serves : 10

2 cups dry sparkling cider

$^1/_2$ cup cognac or brandy

$^1/_2$ cup Cointreau

ice

apple slices

2 cups soda water or dry ginger

1 Mix the first three ingredients together and chill in the refrigerator until required.

2 Pour into a large punch bowl with ice, apple slices and the soda water or dry ginger.

3 Serve in small cups or glasses.

Antoinette

For a light sparkling drink on any occasion, this is a lovely mix. Add more Calvados to taste and freshen it up with extra lemon or lime juice.

Serves : 1

$1^1/_2$ measures Calvados

$^1/_2$ measure fresh lemon juice

$^1/_2$ measure syrup de gomme

ice

sparkling cider

twist of apple peel

1 Shake the first three ingredients over ice until frosted.

2 Strain into a highball or tall cocktail glass and top up with sparkling cider to taste.

3 Finish with a curl or twist of apple peel.

Long
Cocktails

 82

Alice Springs

This fruity cocktail with a generous kick of gin can be well diluted to taste.

Serves : 1

3 measures gin

$^1/_2$ tsp grenadine

1 measure orange juice

1 measure lemon juice

ice

soda water

3 drops Angostura bitters

1 Shake the first four ingredients together over ice until frosted.

2 Strain into a chilled tall glass and top up with soda water.

3 Sprinkle in the bitters and drink with a straw.

Gin Fizz

This could be the forerunner to gin and tonic, as it makes a great drink – long, economical and refreshing.

Serves : 1
1 ¹/2 measures gin
1 tsp sugar
few long shreds lemon peel
crushed ice
soda water

1 Mix the gin, sugar and peel together until sugar has dissolved.
2 Pour into a long glass full of crushed ice and top up with chilled soda water.

Gin Sling

Many say the original gin sling was hot, but there are numerous cool variations to enjoy too!

Serves : 1
1 cube sugar
1 measure dry gin
freshly grated nutmeg
slice of lemon

1 Dissolve the sugar in ¹/2 cup hot water in an old-fashioned glass.
2 Stir in the gin, sprinkle with nutmeg and serve with a slice of lemon.

85. Gin Sling Cocktail: Into a tumbler put a large chunk of ice, juice of ³/4 lemon, ¹/2 tbsp powdered sugar and 1 measure gin. Top up with water and float a slice of lemon on top with a dash of Angostura bitters. **Serves : 1**

86. Orange Gin Sling: Pour 2 measures gin into a cocktail glass then carefully splash on 4 dashes orange bitters. **Serves : 1**

Leap-Frog

Gin and tonic fans will enjoy this variation with its gutsy flavor of lemon and gin.

Serves : 1

1 cube ice

juice of $1/2$ lemon

2 measures gin

ginger ale

1 Chill a long tumbler and then add in the ice, lemon and gin. Stir just once.

2 Top up with ginger to taste and add a stirrer.

Mother-in-law's Gin

Made up in advance so no-one need know how much gin you put in!

Serves : 6

5 measures gin

7 measures orange juice

7 measures lemon juice

2 measures syrup de gomme

1 small egg white

ice

tonic water

lemon peel

1 Blend the first four ingredients together and chill until required.

2 When ready to serve, whizz with the egg white and ice in a blender until frothy.

3 Pour into long chilled glasses and top up with tonic.

4 Dress with a little lemon zest or peel.

Bulldog

A refreshing variation on the classic gin and orange.

Serves : 1

2 measure gin
1 measure fresh orange juice
ice
ginger ale
slither of orange peel

1 Stir the gin and orange over ice in a medium tumbler.
2 Top up with ginger and add a twist of orange peel.

Bee's Knees

Use a well-flavored honey for this drink – acacia, orange blossom or heather, for instance. It makes all the difference to the final cocktail.

Serves : 1

1 measure gin
1/3 measure fresh lemon juice
2/3 measure clear honey
bitter lemon to taste
ice
lemon zest

1 Shake the first three ingredients over ice until well frosted.
2 Strain into a tall ice-filled glass and top up with bitter lemon.
3 Dress with a few shreds of lemon zest

91

Tom Collins

This cooling long drink is a celebrated cocktail and was the inspiration of several generations of the Collins drinks family scattered across the globe.

Serves : 1

3 measures gin
2 measures lemon juice
1/2 measure sugar syrup
5-6 cracked ice cubes
soda water
slice of lemon

1 Shake the gin, lemon juice and sugar syrup vigorously over ice until well frosted.
2 Strain into a tall, chilled tumbler and top up with soda water.
3 Dress with a slice of lemon.

92. Belle Collins: Crush 2 fresh mint sprigs and place in a tall chilled tumbler. Add 4-6 crushed ice cubes and pour in 2 measures gin, 1 measure lemon juice and 1 tsp sugar syrup. Top up with sparkling water, stir gently and decorate with a fresh mint sprig. **Serves : 1**

93. Juan Collins: Half fill a chilled tumbler with cracked ice and pour in 2 measures white tequila, 1 measure lemon juice and 1 tsp sugar syrup. Top up with sparkling mineral water and stir gently. Dress with a cocktail cherry. **Serves : 1**

94. Country Cousin Collins: Blend 2 measures apple brandy, 1 measure lemon juice and 1/2 tsp sugar syrup with crushed ice and a dash of orange bitters at medium speed for 10 seconds. Pour into a chilled tumbler and top up with sparkling water. Stir gently and dress with a slice of lemon. **Serves : 1**

95

Royal Grand Fizz

A very grand name for quite a low-key cocktail, but you could add more gin to taste.

Serves : 1

2 measures gin
juice 1/2 lemon
juice 1/2 orange
3 dashes syrup de gomme
1/2 measure maraschino
1/2 measure cream
crushed ice

soda water
orange slice

1 Shake the first six ingredients together over ice and pour into an ice-filled glass.
2 Top up with soda water and finish with a slice of orange.

96

Cat's Eye

A cat's eye is many things (apart from what a cat sees with!) including a semi-precious stone and a stripy marble. Now, it's a highly potent cocktail, as pretty as a gemstone and certainly more fun than playing marbles.

Serves : 1
2 measures gin
1¹/₂ measures dry vermouth
¹/₂ measure kirsch
¹/₂ measure Triple Sec
¹/₂ measure lemon juice
cracked ice
¹/₂ measure water

1 Shake the gin, vermouth, kirsch, Triple Sec and lemon juice over the ice until well frosted.
2 Strain into a chilled goblet, adding a touch of iced water to serve.

97. Cheshire Cat: Pour 1 measure brandy, 1 measure sweet vermouth, and 1 measure orange juice over cracked ice in a mixing glass. Stir well, then strain into a chilled flute and top up with chilled champagne. Squeeze over a twist of orange peel and decorate with an orange peel spiral. **Serves : 1**

98. Tiger by the Tail: Blend 2 measures Pernod, 4 measures orange juice, and ¹/₄ tsp Triple Sec with crushed ice until smooth. Pour into a chilled wine glass and dress with a wedge of lime. **Serves : 1**

99. Tiger's Milk: Blend 2 measures golden rum, 1¹/₂ measures brandy, 1 tsp sugar syrup, and ¹/₂ cup milk with crushed ice until combined. Pour into a chilled wine glass. Sprinkle with ground cinnamon. **Serves : 1**

100. White Lion: Shake 4-6 cracked ice cubes in a cocktail shaker with a dash of Angostura bitters and grenadine, 2 measures white rum, 1 measure lemon juice and 1 tsp sugar syrup until a frost forms. Strain into a chilled cocktail glass. **Serves : 1**

 # Oasis

This bright blue shining pool is as refreshing as it looks, thanks to lots of ice and refreshing soda water.

Serves : 1

ice

1 measure blue Curaçao

2 measures gin

soda water

slice of lemon

sprig of mint

1 Fill a highball glass with ice cubes, pour in the Curaçao and gin and stir once.

2 Add the soda water and stir.

3 Dress with a slice of lemon and sprig of mint.

 # Paradise Fizz

This lovely long drink is also great made with white rum and should be poured over lots of ice to enjoy it really cold.

Serves : 1

1 measure gin

juice 1/2 lime

1 tsp powdered sugar

1/2 measure melon liqueur

1/2 egg white

ice

soda water

shreds of lime peel

1 Shake the first five ingredients over ice until well frosted.

2 Strain into an ice-filled long glass and top up with soda water to taste.

3 Sprinkle with shreds of lime peel and add a straw.

 # Bleu Bleu Bleu

It may well be blurr blurr after this heady combination, so don't rush for the second one.

Serves : 1

1 measure gin

1 measure vodka

1 measure tequila

1 measure blue Curaçao

1 measure fresh lemon juice

2 dashes egg white

crushed ice

soda water

1 Shake all ingredients except the soda water together over ice until frosted.

2 Pour into a tall glass filled with ice and top up with soda water to taste.

Gin Rickey

The classic version of this cocktail is based on gin, but other spirits are also used, mixed with lime or lemon juice and soda water, with no sweetening.

Serves : 1

2 measures gin
1 measure lime juice
cracked ice cubes
soda water
slice of lemon

1 Build this cocktail straight into a chilled highball glass or goblet.
2 Pour the gin and lime juice over the ice.
3 Top up with soda water.
4 Stir gently to mix and dress with the lemon slice.

105. Whiskey Rickey: Substitute American blended whiskey for the gin and dress with a slice of lime. **Serves : 1**

106. Sloe Gin Rickey: Substitute sloe gin for the dry gin. Dress with a slice of lime. **Serves : 1**

107. Apple Rum Rickey: Shake 1 measure apple brandy, $\frac{1}{2}$ measure white rum and $\frac{1}{2}$ measure lime juice vigorously over ice until well frosted. Half fill a chilled tumbler with cracked ice cubes and strain the cocktail over them. Top up with sparkling water and dress with lime. **Serves : 1**

108. Kirsch Rickey: Pour 2 measures kirsch and 1 tbsp lime juice in a chilled tumbler half-filled with crushed ice cubes. Top up with sparkling water and stir gently. Decorate with stoned fresh cherries. **Serves : 1**

Blue Blooded

A rather sinister looking drink until it has settled down – but don't let that put you off as it tastes great and is very light and fruity.

Serves : 1
1 measure gin
1 measure passion fruit nectar
4 cubes melon or mango
scoop crushed ice
1-2 tsp blue Curaçao

1 Whizz all the ingredients except the Curaçao in a blender until smooth and frosted.
2 Pour into a chilled tall glass filled with more ice and finally top with the Curaçao so it trickles through like blue blood!

Gimlet

The fresh aromatic scent of lime is so much nicer with gin than the traditional lemon and this one is seriously tangy.

Serves : 1
1 measure gin or vodka
1/2 measure fresh lime juice
soda water or tonic
slice of lime

1 Pour the gin and lime over ice in a chilled old-fashioned glass.
2 Top up with tonic and add a slice of lime.

111 Leave It To Me

Pretty but with a sting to its tail, this is a good party cocktail, as you can easily make several at once.

Serves : 1

$^1/_2$ measure gin
$^1/_4$ measure dry vermouth
$^1/_4$ apricot brandy
1 dash lemon juice
1 dash grenadine
crushed ice

1 Shake first four ingredients well over ice and strain into a cocktail glass.
2 Swirl in the grenadine at the last minute with the piece of lemon peel.

112 Daisy

A Daisy is a long cocktail with a high proportion of alcohol and sweetened with fruit syrup. Perhaps it gets its name from the now old-fashioned slang when the word "daisy" referred to something exceptional and special.

Serves : 1

3 measures gin
1 measure lemon juice
1 tbsp grenadine
1 tsp sugar syrup
cracked ice cubes
soda water
slice of orange, to decorate

1 Pour the gin, lemon juice, grenadine and sugar syrup over cracked ice and shake vigorously until well frosted.
2 Strain into a chilled highball glass and top up with soda water.
3 Stir gently, then decorate with an orange slice.

113. Star Daisy: Pour 2 measures gin, 1$^1/_2$ measures apple brandy, 1$^1/_2$ measures lemon juice, 1 tsp sugar syrup and $^1/_2$ tsp Triple Sec over ice and shake vigorously until well frosted. Strain into a chilled tumbler and top up with soda water.
Serves : 1

114. Rum Daisy: Pour 2 measures golden rum, 1 measure lemon juice, 1 tsp sugar syrup, $^1/_2$ tsp grenadine over ice and shake until well frosted. Half fill a small, chilled tumbler with cracked ice and strain the cocktail over it.
Dress with a slice of orange. **Serves : 1**

115 St Clement's Gin

This can be seriously strong or very refreshing so add soda water to your taste.

Serves : 1

juice of 1/2 orange
juice of 1/2 lemon
1 tsp powdered sugar
2 measures gin
ice
soda water
twists of orange and lemon peel

1 Mix the juices, sugar and gin together and pour over ice in a highball glass.
2 Top up with soda water and finish with twists of orange and lemon peel.

116 Pimm's No. I

Pimm's No. 1 is a long, deliciously dry but fruity concoction, with a gin base flavored with herbs. It was devised by James Pimm, a London restaurateur in the late 19th century and was quite probably the original gin sling.

Serves : 1

ice
1 measure Pimm's No. 1
lemonade
strips of cucumber peel, sprigs of mint or borage
slices of orange and lemon

1 Fill a chilled large glass two-thirds full with ice and pour in the Pimm's.
2 Top up with lemonade and stir gently.
3 Dress with a twist of cucumber peel, a sprig of fresh mint and a slice of orange and lemon.

117 Cherry Fizz

A fizz used to be a morning drink, perhaps as a refresher. Add plenty of soda water to make this one as long as you wish.

Serves : 1

3/4 measure gin
1/4 measure cherry brandy
3 dashes kirsch
juice of 1/2 lime
1 tsp syrup de gomme
ice
soda water

1 Shake all the ingredients except the soda water over ice until frosted.
2 Strain into an ice-filled highball glass and top up with soda water to taste.

Singapore Sling

In the days of the British Empire, the privileged would gather at their exclusive clubs in the relative cool of the evening to gossip about the day's events. Times may change, but a Singapore Sling is still the ideal thirst-quencher on a hot summer evening.

Serves : 1

2 measures gin

1 measure cherry brandy

1 measure lemon juice

1 tsp grenadine

cracked ice cubes

soda water

lime peel and cocktail cherries

1 Shake the gin, cherry brandy, lemon juice and grenadine vigorously over ice until well frosted.

2 Half fill a chilled highball glass with cracked ice cubes and strain in the cocktail.

3 Top up with soda water and dress with lime peel and cocktail cherries.

119. Sweet Singapore Sling: Shake 1 measure gin and 2 measures cherry brandy with a dash of lemon juice vigorously over ice until well frosted. Half fill a chilled tumbler with cracked ice cubes and strain in the cocktail. Top up with soda water and decorate with cocktail cherries. **Serves : 1**

120. Gin Slinger: Stir 1 tsp sugar with 1 measure lemon juice and 1 tsp water until the sugar has dissolved. Pour in 2 measures gin and stir. Half fill a small, chilled tumbler with ice and strain the cocktail over it. Decorate with an orange twist. **Serves : 1**

121. Whiskey Sling: In a mixing glass stir 1 tsp sugar with 1 measure lemon juice and 1 tsp water until the sugar has dissolved. Pour in 2 measures American blended whiskey and stir to mix. Half fill a small chilled tumbler with ice and strain the cocktail over it. Dress with an orange twist. **Serves : 1**

122. Raffles Knockout: Shake 1 measure Triple Sec and 1 measure kirsch with a dash of lemon juice vigorously until well frosted. Strain into a chilled cocktail glass. **Serves : 1**

Suffering Fool

You will have to make up your own mind whether this cocktail is a cure for someone already suffering or whether it is the cause of suffering still to come!

Serves : 1

1 tbsp Angostura bitters
cracked ice cubes
2 measures gin
1¹/₂ measures brandy
¹/₂ measure lime juice
1 tsp sugar syrup
ginger beer
slice cucumber and lime
sprig of fresh mint

1 Pour the Angostura bitters into a chilled Collins glass and swirl around until the inside of the glass is coated.

2 Pour out the excess and discard. Half fill the glass with cracked ice cubes.

3 Pour the gin, brandy, lime juice and sugar syrup over the ice.

4 Stir well to mix.

5 Top up with ginger beer and stir gently.

6 Dress with the cucumber, lime and mint.

124. Ankle Breaker: Shake 2 measures dark rum, 1 measure cherry brandy, 1 measure lime juice, and 1 tsp sugar syrup over ice until well frosted. Strain into a chilled tumbler. **Serves : 1**

125. Third Degree: Put cracked ice cubes into a mixing glass. Dash Pernod over the ice and pour in 2 measures gin and 1 measure dry vermouth. Stir well to mix then strain into a chilled cocktail glass. **Serves : 1**

126. Self-destruct: Shake 3 measures vodka, ¹/₂ tsp lime juice and ¹/₂ tsp Triple Sec over ice until well frosted. Strain into a chilled cocktail glass and dress with a wedge of lime. **Serves : 1**

127. Barbed Wire: Shake 3 measures vodka, 1 tsp sweet vermouth, ¹/₂ tsp Pernod, and ¹/₂ measure dry sherry over ice until well frosted. Strain into a chilled cocktail glass and dress with a twist of lemon peel. **Serves : 1**

128   Londoner

The soft fruitiness of berries and the herbal aroma of vermouth make this gin mix a lovely long cocktail.

Serves : 1

2 measures London dry gin
1/2 measure fraise, rosehip or any fruit syrup
2 measures lemon juice
1/2 measure dry vermouth
ice
soda water
slice of lemon peel

1 Mix the first four ingredients over ice in a highball glass or large tumbler.
2 Top up with soda water and dress with a twist of peel.

129   New Orleans Gin Fizz

The cocktail is part of New Orleans' society and it is always flamboyantly presented, so go to town on this one!

Serves : 1

juice 1/2 lemon
2 tsp powdered sugar or to taste
1 small egg white
2 measures gin
2 dashes orange flower water
1 tbsp half and half cream
ice
soda water
orange peel and a flower to finish

1 Shake the first six ingredients over ice until well frosted.
2 Strain into a chilled tall tumbler and top up with soda water to taste.
3 Dress with a flower or a shred of orange peel.

130   Mediterranean

Whatever the weather, this eye-catching drink should transport your imagination to the blue skies and seas of the Mediterranean. The exotic color needs no decoration to set it off.

Serves : 1

ice cubes
2 measures gin
1 measure blue Curaçao
lemonade

1 Put ice cubes in a glass and pour the gin and Curaçao over them.
2 Top up with lemonade.

Gordon Bennett

Don't be too surprised that this is no simple gin – it has more than a little kick and lots of limey zing.

Serves : 1

1 measure gin, iced
1 measure Cointreau, iced
cracked ice
slices of lime
soda water

1 Place the gin, Cointreau and ice in a chilled highball glass and stir until well frosted.
2 Squeeze the lime slice and add to the glass. Add soda water to taste.

(132)

A Sloe Kiss

Sloe gin has a rich fruity flavor that mixes well and is a great base for long drinks.

Serves : 1

¹/₂ measure sloe gin
¹/₂ measure Southern Comfort
1 measure vodka
1 tsp Amaretto
ice
splash of Galliano
orange juice
twists of orange peel

1 Shake the first four ingredients over ice until well frosted.
2 Strain into a chilled long glass filled with ice.
3 Splash on the Galliano and top up with a little orange juice.
4 Dress with peel and a stirrer.

133 Angelic

It may look angelic, but, unless you are very liberal with the fruit juice, this is certainly not a mild cocktail.

Serves : 1
1/2 measure Galliano
1/2 measure Southern Comfort
1 measure vodka
dash egg white
ice
orange or pineapple juice to taste
slice of pineapple

1 Shake the first four ingredients over ice until well frosted.
2 Strain into an ice-filled tall glass and top up with orange or pineapple juice to taste.
3 Dress with a slice of fresh pineapple.

134 Long Island Iced Tea CLASSIC

Dating back to the days of the American Prohibition when it was drunk out of cups in an attempt to fool the FBI that it was harmless, this cocktail has evolved from the original simple combination of vodka with a dash of cola!

Serves : 1
2 measures vodka
1 measure gin
1 measure white tequila
1 measure white rum
1/2 measure white crème de menthe
2 measures lemon juice
1 tsp sugar syrup
cracked ice cubes
cola
wedge of lime or lemon

1 Shake the vodka, gin, tequila, rum, crème de menthe, lemon juice and sugar syrup vigorously over ice until well frosted.
2 Strain into an ice-filled highball glass and top up with cola.
3 Dress with lime or lemon wedges.

135. Artillery Punch: Pour 1 1/3 bottles bourbon, 1 1/3 bottles red wine, 8 cups strong, black tea, 2 cups dark rum, 1 cup gin, 1 cup apricot brandy, 4 measures lemon juice, 4 measures lime juice and 4 tbsp sugar syrup in a large bowl. Refrigerate for 2 hours. To serve, place a large block of ice in a punch bowl. Pour the punch over the ice and decorate with thinly sliced lemon and lime. **Serves : 30**

Bay Breeze

The new white cranberry juices are perfect for mixing a refreshing cocktail combination. Not as sharp as red cranberry, but deliciously fruity.

Serves : 1
2 measures white cranberry and apple juice
2 measures pineapple juice
2 measures vodka
ice
tonic water
slices of lime or pineapple

1 Shake the first three ingredients well over ice until frosted.
2 Strain into a tall glass and top up with tonic to taste.
3 Dress with slices of lime or pineapple.

Dry Smile

If you like really dry mixes, go easy on the pineapple juice until you have tasted it.

Serves : 1
1 measure Cinzano extra dry
1 measure mandarin vodka
1/2 measure orange Curaçao
juice 1/2 lemon
1 tbsp strawberry syrup
ice
pineapple juice
strawberry to finish

1 Shake the first five ingredients well over ice.
2 Pour into a long glass and top up with pineapple juice to taste.
3 Finish with a slice of strawberry.

Kamikaze

No turning back on this one. It's so delicious – you won't be able to put it down.

Serves : 1
1 measure vodka
1 measure Triple Sec
$^{1}/_{2}$ measure fresh lime juice
$^{1}/_{2}$ measure fresh lemon juice
ice
dry white wine, chilled
piece of lime and cucumber

1 Shake the first four ingredients together over ice until well frosted.
2 Strain into a chilled glass and top up with wine.
3 Dress with lime and cucumber.

Twister

Fresh lime juice and lime slices swirled through help to make this a seriously sharp, but long and refreshing mix.

Serves : 1
2 measures vodka
juice of $^{1}/_{2}$ fresh lime
$^{1}/_{2}$ fresh lime, sliced
ice
lemonade

1 Stir the vodka and lime juice over ice in a large tumbler with slices of fresh lime.
2 Top up with lemonade to taste.

Salty Dog

When this cocktail first appeared, gin-based mixes were by far the most popular, but nowadays, a Salty Dog is more frequently made with vodka. Choose which you prefer, but the cocktails will have different flavors.

Serves : 1
1 tbsp granulated sugar
1 tbsp coarse salt
lime wedge
6-8 cracked ice cubes
2 measures vodka
grapefruit juice

1 Mix the sugar and salt in a saucer. Rub the rim of a chilled Collins glass with the lime wedge, then dip it in the sugar and salt mixture to frost.
2 Fill the glass with cracked ice cubes and pour the vodka over them.
3 Top up with grapefruit juice and stir to mix. Drink with a straw.

141. Bride's Mother: Shake 1¹/₂ measures sloe gin, 1 measure gin, 2 ¹/₂ measures grapefruit juice and ¹/₂ measure sugar syrup vigorously over ice until well frosted. Strain into a chilled cocktail glass. **Serves : 1**

142. A.J: Shake 1¹/₂ measures applejack or apple brandy and 1 measure grapefruit juice vigorously over ice until well frosted. Strain into a chilled cocktail glass. **Serves : 1**

143. Blinker: Shake 2 measures rye whiskey, 2¹/₂ measures grapefruit juice and 1 tsp grenadine vigorously over ice until well frosted. Strain into a chilled cocktail glass. **Serves : 1**

Screwdriver

Always use freshly squeezed orange juice to make this refreshing cocktail – it is just not the same with bottled juice. This simple, classic cocktail has given rise to numerous and increasingly elaborate variations.

Serves : 1

cracked ice cubes
2 measures vodka
orange juice
slice of orange

1 Fill a chilled glass with cracked ice cubes.
2 Pour the vodka over the ice and top up with orange juice.
3 Stir well to mix and dress with a slice of orange.

145. Slow Screw: Substitute sloe gin for the vodka. **Serves : 1**

146. Cordless Screwdriver: Pour 2 measures chilled vodka into a shot glass. Dip a wedge of orange into powdered sugar. Down the vodka in one go and suck the orange. **Serves : 1**

147. Creamy Screwdriver: Blend 2 measures vodka, several crushed ice cubes, 6 measures orange juice, 1 egg yolk, and $1/2$ tsp sugar syrup until smooth. Half fill a tall chilled tumbler with cracked ice cubes and pour the cocktail over them without straining. **Serves : 1**

(148)

Moscow Mule

 CLASSIC

This cocktail came into existence through a happy coincidence during the 1930s. An American bar owner had overstocked ginger beer and a representative of a soft drinks company invented the Moscow Mule to help him out.

Serves : 1

2 measures vodka
1 measure lime juice
cracked ice cubes
ginger beer
slice of lime

1 Shake the vodka and lime juice vigorously over ice until well frosted.
2 Half fill a chilled highball glass with cracked ice cubes and strain the cocktail over them.
3 Top up with ginger beer. Dress with a slice of lime.

149. Delft Donkey: Make a Moscow Mule but substitute gin for the vodka. **Serves : 1**

150. Mississippi Mule: Shake 2 measures gin, $^1/_2$ measure crème de cassis and $^1/_2$ measure lemon juice vigorously over ice until well frosted. Strain into a small chilled tumbler. **Serves : 1**

151. Mule's Hind Leg: Shake $^1/_2$ measure apricot brandy, $^1/_2$ measure apple brandy, $^1/_2$ measure Benedictine, $^1/_2$ measure gin, and $^1/_2$ measure maple syrup vigorously over ice until well frosted. Strain into a chilled cocktail glass. **Serves : 1**

152. Jamaica Mule: Shake 2 measures white rum, 1 measure dark rum, 1 measure golden rum, 1 measure Falernum (wine-based ginger syrup), and 1 measure lime juice vigorously over ice until well frosted. Strain the mixture into a tall chilled tumbler. Top up with ginger beer and dress with pineapple wedges and crystallised ginger. **Serves : 1**

(153)

Rainy Days

A good cocktail should cheer up any rainy day, especially when it is as exciting to look at as this one – add more cassis to taste or on request.

Serves : 1

2 measures vodka
$^1/_2$ measure lime juice
ice
orange juice
cassis

1 Stir the vodka and lime with ice in a small tumbler.
2 Strain into a highball glass filled with ice.
3 Top up with orange juice and add a dash of cassis at the last minute.

1001 Cocktails

Blue Lagoon

Let your imagination carry you away while you sink into this luxuriously blue lagoon cocktail. It has a refreshing lemon zing and sparkle too.

Serves : 1

1 measure blue Curaçao
1 measure vodka
dash fresh lemon juice
lemonade

1 Pour the blue Curaçao into a highball or cocktail glass, followed by the vodka.
2 Add the lemon juice and top up with lemonade to taste.

Lumberjack

When you put your back into a day's hard work, you deserve something with a bit of a kick in it to refresh you at the end.

Serves : 1

2 measures vodka
2 measure applejack (apple brandy)
1 measure lemon juice
$^1\!/_2$ measure syrup de gomme
6 stoned cherries
scoop crushed ice
soda water
cherry to finish

1 Whizz all the ingredients except the soda water together in a small blender until slushy.
2 Pour into a tall chilled glass.
3 Top up with soda water and finish with a cherry on the top.

Midnight Sunset

Punt e Mes is an unusual aperitif – as bitter as Campari but more like a sweet sherry. It is the perfect mixer in a cocktail such as this.

Serves : 1

1 measure Cinzano rosso
1/2 measure lime juice
1/2 measure Punt e Mes
ice
pineapple juice
slice of pineapple

1 Shake the first three ingredients well over ice.
2 Strain into a chilled highball glass with more ice and top up with pineapple juice.
3 Dress with the piece of pineapple on the edge of the glass.

Ice Maiden

If you keep frozen orange juice in the freezer, it will instantly provide the source for many cocktails.

Serves : 1

2 tbsp frozen orange juice
2 tbsp crushed ice
1 measure dry vermouth
lemonade
2 measures Marsala
slice of lime or lemon

1 Whizz the orange juice, ice and vermouth to a slush in a small blender.
2 Pour into an iced wine glass or large cocktail glass and top up with lemonade.
3 Pour on the Marsala and add a slice of fruit to finish.

Merry Widow Fizz

Dubonnet, a French vermouth-type aperitif made by adding quinine and other flavors to sweet heavy wine, makes a versatile cocktail ingredient.

Serves : 1

3 measures Dubonnet
1 measure fresh lemon juice
1 measure fresh orange juice
egg white
cracked ice
soda water

1 Shake the first four ingredients together over ice until well frosted.
2 Pour into a chilled glass and top up with soda water.

(159)

CLASSIC

Addington

Vermouth is a fortified wine flavored with various herbs, spices and flowers so it makes a refreshing and aromatic drink.

Serves : 1

1 measure red vermouth

1 measure dry vermouth

ice

soda water

slice of orange

1 Stir the two vermouths briefly with ice in a glass.

2 Top up with soda water to taste and dress with a slice of orange.

(160)

Country Club

Vermouths vary from extra dry to dry or sweet and, of course, red, so you can vary this drink to suit your taste.

Serves : 1

2 measures dry vermouth

1 tsp grenadine

ice

soda water

1 Stir the vermouth and grenadine over ice in a chilled tumbler.

2 Top up with soda water to taste.

Walk Tall

(161)

Looks and smells like orange juice but don't be deceived, there is lots going on here!

Serves : 1

¹/₂ measure sweet white vermouth
¹/₄ measure gin
¹/₄ measure Campari
¹/₄ measure orange liqueur
sweet orange juice
ice
soda water
orange peel

1 Mix the first five ingredients well and pour into a tall glass or large tumbler full of ice.
2 Top up with a splash of soda water if you wish and a twist of orange peel.

Americano

(162)

CLASSIC

A light refreshing cocktail for lovers of the bitter-sweet Campari, easy anytime drinking to make as strong or weak as you like.

Serves : 1

1 measure Campari
1 measure sweet vermouth
ice
soda water
twist of orange or lemon peel

1 Pour the Campari and vermouth into a highball glass filled with ice.
2 Stir well and then top up with soda water.
3 Dress with a twist of orange or lemon peel.

Mars Explosion

(163)

We may never know what happens on Mars but we can let the imagination wander.

Serves : 1

2 measures orange juice, chilled
1 measure vodka, frozen
¹/₄ measure white rum, frozen
1 dash grenadine, chilled
cherry and spiral of orange peel

1 Stir the orange juice and vodka over ice until well frosted.
2 Strain into a chilled goblet or wine glass.
3 Stir the rum and grenadine together and pour slowly into the middle of the juice so the red color gently spreads outwards.
4 Finish with a cherry and a spiral of orange peel.

Blackcurrant Cocktail

If you have young children who like to drink the same as you, this one is easy to copy, using blackcurrant cordial and soda water.

Serves : 1

2 measures dry vermouth

1 measure cassis

ice

soda water

few blackcurrants, blackberries or blueberries

1 Shake the two liquors over ice until well frosted.

2 Strain into a medium-size glass and top up with soda water to taste.

3 Add a few berries at the last minute.

(165)

Bloody Mary

This classic cocktail was invented in 1921 at the legendary Harry's Bar in Paris. There are numerous versions – some much hotter and spicier. Ingredients may include horseradish sauce in addition to or instead of Tabasco sauce.

Serves : 1

dash Worcestershire sauce
dash Tabasco sauce
cracked ice cubes
2 measures vodka
splash dry sherry
6 measures tomato juice
juice 1/2 lemon
pinch celery salt
pinch cayenne pepper
celery stick with leaves
slice of lemon

1 Dash the Worcestershire sauce and Tabasco sauce over ice in shaker and add the vodka, splash of dry sherry, tomato juice and lemon juice.
2 Shake vigorously until frosted.
3 Strain into a tall chilled glass, add a pinch of celery salt and a pinch of cayenne and decorate with a celery stick and a slice of lemon.

(166) # Special Clam Cocktail

The flavor of clam and tomato juice is unusual, but goes well with dry fruity sherry.

Serves : 1

1 measure schnapps
1 measure dry sherry
1/2 measure clam and tomato juice
3-4 dashes lemon juice
2 dashes Worcestershire sauce
ice
cayenne, celery salt and black pepper
lemon zest

1 Stir all the ingredients together over ice and strain into an ice-filled old-fashioned glass or tumbler.
2 Top with a sprinkling of pepper and grated lemon.

Illusions

Start adding the orange juice to this blue-green combination and you will be having illusions as it changes its color once again.

Serves : 1

1 measure vodka

1 measure Malibu

1/2 measure Midori

1/2 measure blue Curaçao

ice

fresh orange juice

melon

1 Stir the first four ingredients over ice until frosted.

2 Strain into a chilled highball glass or large cocktail or wine glass, and top up with more ice and orange juice to taste.

3 Dress with slices of melon.

Indian Summer

The coffee liqueur is the key ingredient in this delicious long mix – it would be good with crème de noyeau or crème de cacao too.

Serves : 1

1 measure vodka

2 measures Kahlua

1 measure gin

2 measures pineapple

ice

tonic water

1 Shake the first four ingredients well over ice until frosted.

2 Strain into a medium cocktail glass or wine glass and top up with tonic water to taste.

19th Green

Whiskey with a kick, perfect for cold wet days and ideal to carry undiluted in a hip flask to help you keep your head down!

Serves : 1

1^1/$_2$ measures Irish whiskey

1 measure green Curaçao

ice

dry ginger

1 Stir the whiskey and Curaçao in a tumbler with the ice.

2 Top up with ginger.

Mint Cooler

Whiskey and mint is a great after dinner combination, but as a long drink with soda water it is delicious almost any time of the day.

Serves : 1

2 measures whiskey

3 dashes crème de menthe

ice

soda water

1 Pour the whiskey over ice in a chilled tumbler and stir in the crème de menthe.

2 Top up with soda water to taste.

 171

Green Dimples

Originating from the days of Haig Dimple whiskey and flavored with another old favorite – the herb-based green Chartreuse.

Serves : 1
$^1/_2$ measure whiskey
$^1/_2$ measure apple juice
good dash of green Chartreuse
soda water
sprig of mint

1 Stir the first three ingredients over ice and strain into an ice-filled highball glass.
2 Top up with soda water and a sprig of mint.

Mint Julep

A julep is simply a mixed drink sweetened with syrup. The Mint Julep was probably first made in the United States, and is the traditional drink of the Kentucky Derby.

Serves : 1

leaves from 1 fresh mint sprig
1 tbsp sugar syrup
crushed ice cubes
3 measures bourbon whiskey
fresh mint sprig, to dress

1 Put the mint leaves and sugar syrup into a small chilled glass and mash with a teaspoon.
2 Add crushed ice to fill the tumbler, then add the bourbon.
3 Decorate with the mint sprig.

173. Frozen Mint Julep: Put crushed ice cubes into a blender or food processor. Add 2 measures bourbon whiskey, 1 measure lemon juice, 1 measure sugar syrup, and 6 fresh mint leaves. Blend at low speed until slushy. Pour into a small chilled tumbler and dress with a fresh mint sprig. **Serves : 1**

174. Jocose Julep: Put 4-6 crushed ice cubes into a blender or food processor. Pour 3 measures bourbon whiskey, 1 measure green crème de menthe, 1 $1/2$ measures lime juice, and 1 tsp sugar syrup over the ice. Add 5 fresh mint leaves. Process until smooth. Fill a chilled tumbler with cracked ice cubes and pour in the cocktail. Top up with sparkling water and stir gently to mix. Dress with a fresh mint sprig. **Serves : 1**

175. Brandy Julep: Fill a chilled tumbler with cracked ice. Add 2 measures brandy, 1 tsp sugar syrup and 4 fresh mint leaves. Stir well to mix, dress with a fresh mint sprig, a slice of lemon and a straw. **Serves : 1**

Bruno

Whiskey and vermouth are a popular mix, but the addition of the banana liqueur adds a very unusual and exciting touch.

Serves : 1

1 measure whiskey
1/2 measure red vermouth
1/2 measure crème de banane
ice
ginger ale
banana slices

1 Stir the first three ingredients together and pour into a tumbler full of ice.
2 Top up with ginger and dress with a few slices of banana.

On the Fence

It's the Angostura bitters that are sitting on the fence here – on the top waiting for that final mix when you take the first sip.

Serves : 1

1 measure whiskey
ice
cider
2 dashes Angostura bitters

1 Stir the whiskey with ice in a tall glass.
2 Top up with cider to taste and finish with a few dashes of Angostura bitters.

Blood and Sand

Cherry brandy is quite a full-flavored liqueur. You could use brandy instead, but do not expect as punchy a cocktail.

Serves : 1

1 measure Scotch whiskey
1 measure cherry brandy
1 measure red vermouth
ice
orange juice

1 Shake the first three ingredients over ice until frosted.
2 Strain into a medium-size glass and top up with orange juice.

Highland Cooler

Whiskey packed with other tastes – ginger, lemon and bitters – is a great long drink.

Serves : 1

1 tsp powdered sugar
juice of $^1/_2$ lemon
2 dashes Angostura bitters
2 measures Scotch whiskey
ice
ginger ale

1 Stir the first four ingredients together over ice in a chilled tumbler.
2 Top up with ginger to taste.

Highland Raider

This is a unique blend of three great Scottish drinks. Finish them off with a few fresh Scottish raspberries and you have a really great mix.

Serves : 1

1 measure Drambuie
1 measure whiskey
1 measure Glayva liqueur
ice
soda water
few raspberries

1 Stir the first three ingredients over ice until well chilled.
2 Strain into a tall glass or tumbler with more ice and top up with soda water to taste.
3 Dress with a few raspberries.

 (181)

Out of the Glen

Raspberries have quite a dominant fresh tang and mix well with stronger spirits.

Serves : 1

$^1/_2$ measure Scotch whiskey

$^1/_3$ measure brandy

juice $^1/_2$ lemon

2 dashes syrup de gomme

4 dashes raspberry syrup

$^1/_2$ egg white

ice

soda water

1 Shake all the ingredients except the soda water together over ice until well frosted.

2 Strain into a highball glass filled with ice and top up with soda water.

Oh! Henry!

Whiskey lovers enjoy this variation when they want something a little sweeter and deeper.

Serves : 1
1 measure Benedictine
1 measure whiskey
2 cubes ice
ginger ale

1 Stir the Benedictine and whiskey gently in a medium tumbler with ice.
2 Top up with ginger ale to taste.

183

Samba

You could make this one short and strong if you prefer a good kick of whiskey.

Serves : 1
¹/₂ measure Scotch whiskey
¹/₄ measure golden rum
¹/₄ measure sweet red vermouth
¹/₈ measure apricot brandy
soda water
1 maraschino cherry

1 Mix the first four ingredients in a large tumbler and top up with soda water to taste.
2 Finish with a cherry.

Isobella

Quite a cocktail of spirits in one glass, so add soda water to mellow the flavors.

Serves : 1

¹/₂ measure Canadian Club whiskey
¹/₄ measure brandy
¹/₄ measure red vermouth
¹/₈ measure Galliano
¹/₈ measure mandarin liqueur
ice cubes
juice of 1 orange and few shreds of peel
chilled soda water

1 Mix the first six ingredients together over ice in a mixing glass.
2 Strain into a chilled medium-sized tumbler with a few ice cubes and a stirrer.
3 Dress with the orange shreds and top with soda water to taste.

Mammy

The peel of any citrus fruit has the most pungent and aromatic flavor, but do use a zester or fine peeler so you leave the bitter white pith on the fruit.

Serves : 1

juice and zest of 1 lime
2 measures whiskey
ice
ginger ale

1 Remove some long shreds of lime peel first.
2 Then stir the lime juice and whiskey over ice in a highball glass and top up with ginger ale.
3 Dress with lime peel.

Perry Highball

Pear drinks are much softer and mellower in flavor than apple and even the bubbly perries are quite unlike cider, but great in this mix.

Serves : 1

2 measures whiskey

1 large lump ice

perry or cider

1 Pour the whiskey over ice in a highball glass and top up with perry or cider.

Black Watch

An unusual version of whiskey and soda which makes a great drink for any time of day or evening.

Serves : 1

$^2/_3$ measure Scotch whiskey

$^1/_3$ measure Kahlua or coffee liqueur

ice

soda water

1 Mix the whiskey and liqueur with a few lumps of ice in a large tumbler.

2 Top up with soda water to taste.

1001 Cocktails

The Champion

Four great drinks blended in one has to produce a champion cocktail – try it for yourself and see!

Serves : 1

1/2 measure dry vermouth
1/2 measure Scotch whiskey
1/4 measure Benedictine
1/4 measure white Curaçao
ice
soda water

1 Shake the first four ingredients over ice until well frosted.
2 Strain into a small tumbler filled with ice and top up with a little soda water.

Thai Cocktail Sling

A Thai-style version of a classic cocktail – a long drink with a strong kick of whiskey.

Serves : 1

2 tbsp whiskey
1 tbsp cherry brandy
1 tbsp orange-flavored liqueur
1 tbsp lime juice
1 tsp jaggery
dash of Angostura bitters
2 ice cubes
1/2 cup pineapple juice
1 small pineapple wedge

1 Shake first six ingredients well over ice until frosted.
2 Place the ice cubes in a large glass.
3 Pour the cocktail over and top off with the pineapple juice.
4 Finish with a pineapple wedge on the edge of the glass.

Barbados Sunset

There is certainly a warm evening glow to this cocktail and you can make it even more pink with the addition of more strawberry syrup.

Serves : 1

1 1/2 measures golden rum
1 measure coconut rum
2 measures orange juice
2 measures pineapple juice
dash strawberry syrup
ice

cherries
orange and lime slices

1 Shake the first five ingredients well over ice and pour into a chilled glass.
2 Add more ice to taste, a cherry and slices of fruit to finish.

Jamaican Cooler

 191

A long, refreshing and very simple cocktail – perfect for rum lovers.

Serves : 1

1¹/₂ measures Jamaican rum
crushed iced
soda water
squeeze of lemon or lime peel

1 Pour the rum into an ice-filled highball glass.
2 Top up with soda water to taste and dress with a piece of lemon peel.

192

Jamaican Mule

Jamaican rum is dark and strong, perfect to dilute and makes a great long drink with numerous mixers.

Serves : 1

2 measures Jamaican rum
ice
ginger beer
segment of lime and squeeze of juice

1 Pour the rum into a highball glass filled with ice.
2 Top up with ginger beer to taste and finish with a squeeze of lime.

Fat Man Running

Blue Curaçao can make beautiful cocktails of strange colors – you may find you prefer to use a clear Curaçao in this cocktail!

Serves : 1
2 measures dark rum
1/2 measure blue Curaçao
1/2 measure lime juice
ice cubes
ginger ale

1 Whizz all the ingredients except the ginger ale in a blender on fast speed for about 10 seconds.
2 Pour into a tall glass filled with crushed ice and top up with ginger.
3 Serve with a stirrer.

Bajan Sun

There is certainly a feeling of warm tropical sunshine in this cocktail.

Serves : 1
1 measure white rum
1 measure mandarin brandy
1 measure fresh orange juice
1 measure pineapple juice
splash of grenadine
ice
fresh pineapple slice
cherry

1 Shake all the ingredients well over ice.
2 Pour into a tall glass and finish with a slice of pineapple and a cherry.

Tamara's Tipple

The dark secrets at the bottom of this glass add rich sweetness, so you shouldn't need to add too much cola.

Serves : 1

2 measures dark rum

1 measure crème de cacao

ice

cola

slice of lime, lemon or orange

1 Mix the first two ingredients in a tall glass filled with ice.

2 Top up with a little cola and finish with a slice of fruit.

(196)

Space Odyssey

Remember those colored cherries? Well, here is one reason to keep some in the cupboard – they are great fun in cocktails!

Serves : 1

1 measure golden rum

2 dashes Angostura bitters

colored cherries

ginger beer

1 Mix the rum and bitters in a highball glass filled with ice and colored cherries.

2 Top up with ginger beer to taste.

Ocean Breeze

(197)

It's a breeze to make and as colorful as the whipped-up ocean on an early morning. Just don't dilute too much.

Serves : 1

1 measure white rum
1 measure Amaretto
1/2 measure blue Curaçao
1/2 measure pineapple juice
crushed ice
soda water

1 Shake the first four ingredients together over ice.
2 Pour into a tall glass and top up with soda water to taste.

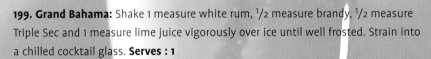

198. Miami Beach: Shake 2 measures Scotch whiskey, 1 1/2 measures dry vermouth and 2 measures grapefruit juice over the ice. Shake vigorously until well frosted, then strain into a chilled cocktail glass. **Serves : 1**

199. Grand Bahama: Shake 1 measure white rum, 1/2 measure brandy, 1/2 measure Triple Sec and 1 measure lime juice vigorously over ice until well frosted. Strain into a chilled cocktail glass. **Serves : 1**

200. Costa del Sol: Shake 2 measures gin, 1 measure apricot brandy and 1 measure Triple Sec vigorously over ice until well frosted. Strain into a chilled glass. **Serves : 1**

201. Palm Beach Sour: Shake 1/3 measure gin, 1/3 measure grapefruit juice, 1/6 measure dry vermouth, 2-3 drops Angostura bitters, 1 tsp powdered sugar, and 1 egg white with ice. Strain into a chilled cocktail glass. **Serves : 1**

Palm Beach

(202)

If it's been a long time since your last holiday, conjure up the blue skies of Florida and the rolling surf with this sunny cocktail.

Serves : 1

1 measure white rum
1 measure gin
1 measure pineapple juice
cracked ice cubes

1 Shake the rum, gin and pineapple juice vigorously over ice until well frosted.
2 Strain into a chilled highball glass.

Cuba Libra

The 1960s and 1970s saw a meteoric rise in popularity of this simple long drink.

Serves : 1
cracked ice cubes
2 measures white rum
cola
wedge of lime, to decorate

1 Half fill a highball glass with cracked ice cubes.
2 Pour the rum over the ice and top up with cola.
3 Stir gently to mix and dress with a wedge of lime.

204. Brandy Cuban: Pour
1^1/$_2$ measures brandy and ^{1}/$_2$ measure lime juice into a tumbler half-filled with ice. Top up with cola and stir gently. Dress with lime. **Serves : 1**

205. Cuban: Pour 2 measures brandy, 1 measure apricot brandy, 1 measure lime juice, and 1 tsp white rum over ice and shake vigorously until well frosted. Strain into a chilled cocktail glass. **Serves : 1**

206. Cuban Special: Pour 2 measures rum, 1 measure lime juice, 1 tbsp pineapple juice, and 1 tsp Triple Sec over ice and shake until well frosted. Strain into a chilled cocktail glass and dress with a pineapple wedge. **Serves : 1**

Old Soak

Sit back and relax with a seriously warming mix of flavors from the Deep South.

Serves : 1

2 measures golden rum

1 measure Southern Comfort

1 measure ginger syrup

cracked ice

soda water

1 Stir the first three ingredients over ice in a chilled tumbler or large wine glass.

2 Top up with soda water to taste.

Railroadster

Decorate the rim carefully well in advance for a really good effect.

Serves : 1

1 tsp fine zest of lime

1 tsp powdered sugar

$1\frac{1}{2}$ measures white rum

$\frac{1}{2}$ measure Galliano

1 measure lime juice

crushed ice

dry ginger

1 Mix the zest and sugar together.

2 Rub the rim of a glass with a little rum then dip it into the sugar to coat thoroughly.

3 Set aside to dry.

4 Shake all the remaining ingredients except dry ginger together with the crushed ice until well chilled.

5 Pour into the glass and top up with a little dry ginger to taste.

(209)

Club Mojito

Dark rum is rich in flavor and redolent of sunshine holiday memories.

Serves : 1

1 tsp syrup de gomme
few mint leaves
juice ¹/₂ lime
ice
2 measures Jamaican rum
soda water
dash Angostura bitters
mint to finish

1 Put the syrup, mint leaves and lime juice in a highball glass and crush or muddle the mint leaves.
2 Add ice and rum, then top up with soda water to taste.
3 Finish with a dash of Angostura bitters and a mint leaf.

(210)

Santa Cruz Daisy

Traditionally Daisies were made with raspberry syrup, but any good sugar or fruit syrup will produce a delicate sweetness.

Serves : 1

3 dashes syrup de gomme
1 tsp Curaçao
juice ¹/₂ small lemon
2 measures rum
crushed ice
soda water

1 Shake the first four ingredients well over ice and strain into a tumbler or highball glass.
2 Top up with soda water.

Dark and Stormy

Golden rum has a mellow, slightly milder taste, but you could use dark rum here for a really stormy mix.

Serves : 1

2 measures Mount Gay rum

1 measure lime juice

1/2 measure sugar syrup

ice

ginger beer

twist of lime peel

1 Shake the first three ingredients over ice until well frosted.

2 Strain into a chilled highball glass and top up with ginger beer to taste.

3 Dress with lime zest.

212

Dragon Lady

The rich fruit flavors of orange, pomegranate (provided by the grenadine) and lemon, blended with light rum make a really lovely long summer drink.

Serves : 1
1 measure golden rum
1 measure orange juice
dash white Curaçao
dash grenadine
ice
bitter lemon, chilled
slice of orange and twist of peel

1 Stir the first four ingredients well over ice, strain into an ice-filled highball glass and top up with bitter lemon.
2 Add the fruit and top with peel.

213

Nirvana

It may not be possible to obtain a perfect state of harmony and bliss through a cocktail, but this has to be the next best thing.

Serves : 1
2 measures dark rum
1/2 measure grenadine
1/2 measure tamarind syrup
1 tsp sugar syrup
cracked ice cubes
grapefruit juice

1 Shake the rum, grenadine, tamarind syrup and sugar syrup vigorously over ice until well frosted.
2 Half fill a chilled Collins glass with cracked ice cubes and strain the cocktail over them.
3 Top up with grapefruit juice.

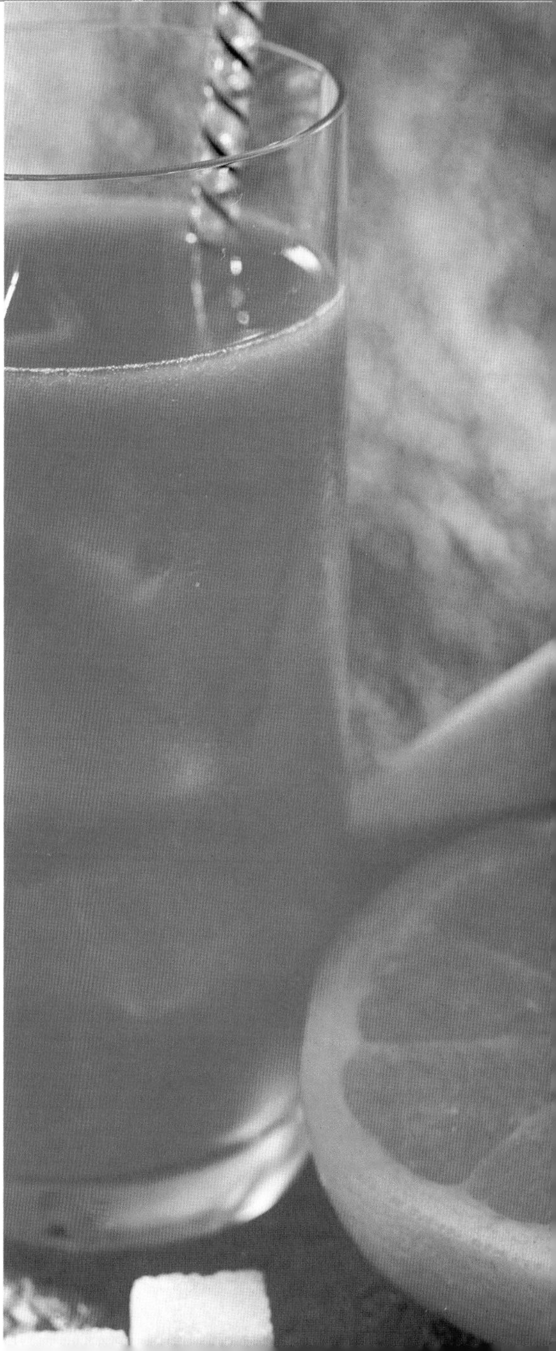

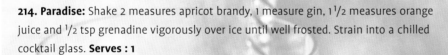

214. Paradise: Shake 2 measures apricot brandy, 1 measure gin, 1 1/2 measures orange juice and 1/2 tsp grenadine vigorously over ice until well frosted. Strain into a chilled cocktail glass. **Serves : 1**

215. Seventh Heaven: Shake 2 measures gin, 1/2 measure maraschino and 1/2 measure grapefruit juice vigorously over ice until well frosted. Strain into a chilled cocktail glass. Dress with fresh mint. **Serves : 1**

216. Heavenly: Put cracked ice cubes into a mixing glass. Pour 1 1/2 measures brandy, 1/2 measure cherry brandy and 1/2 measure plum brandy over the ice and stir well to mix. Strain into a chilled cocktail glass. **Serves : 1**

217. Ambrosia: Shake 1 1/2 measures brandy, 1 1/2 measures apple brandy and 1/2 tsp raspberry syrup vigorously over ice until well frosted. Strain into a chilled wine glass. Top up with chilled champagne and dress with a raspberry. **Serves : 1**

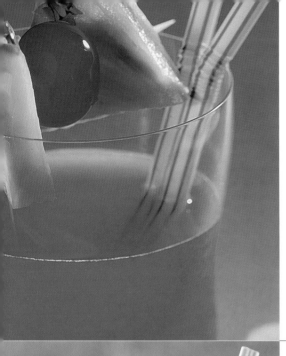

Mai Tai

Created in 1944 by restaurateur "Trader Vic" it was described as "Mai Tai – Roe Ae" meaning "out of this world." It is always flamboyantly dressed.

Serves : 1

2 measures white rum
2 measures dark rum
1 measure orange Curaçao
1 measure lime juice
1 tbsp orgeat
1 tbsp grenadine
cracked ice cubes

slices of pineapple and pieces of fruit peel
cocktail cherries and straws

1 Shake the white and dark rums, Curaçao, lime juice, orgeat and grenadine vigorously over ice until well frosted.
2 Strain into a chilled Collins glass and decorate as you wish.

Piña Colada

One of the younger generation of classics, this became popular during the cocktail revival of the 1980s and has remained so ever since.

Serves : 1

4-6 crushed ice cubes
2 measures white rum
1 measure dark rum
3 measures pineapple juice
2 measures coconut cream
pineapple wedges, to decorate

1 Whizz the crushed ice in a blender with the white rum, dark rum, pineapple juice and coconut cream until smooth.
2 Pour, without straining, into a tall, chilled glass and dress with pineapple wedges.

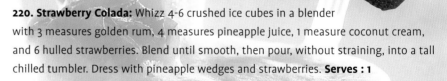

220. Strawberry Colada: Whizz 4-6 crushed ice cubes in a blender with 3 measures golden rum, 4 measures pineapple juice, 1 measure coconut cream, and 6 hulled strawberries. Blend until smooth, then pour, without straining, into a tall chilled tumbler. Dress with pineapple wedges and strawberries. **Serves : 1**

221. Banana Colada: Whizz 4-6 crushed ice cubes in a blender with 2 measures white rum, 4 measures pineapple juice, 1 measure Malibu, and 1 peeled and sliced banana. Blend until smooth, then pour, without straining, into a tall chilled tumbler and serve with a straw. **Serves : 1**

222. Amigos Piña Colada: Whizz 10-12 crushed ice cubes in a blender with 1/2 cup rum, 1 cup pineapple juice, 5 measures coconut cream, 2 measures dark rum, and 2 measures half and half cream. Blend until smooth. Pour, without straining, into tall chilled tumblers and decorate with pineapple wedges. **Serves : 4**

Rum'n'Currant

This old-fashioned drink is making a comeback, drunk either short or long.

Serves : 1

1 measure dark rum
$^1/_2$ measure blackcurrant cordial
ice
lemonade

1 Mix the rum and blackcurrant over ice in a tumbler. Top up with lemonade to taste.

Black Widow

Not as wicked as its title suggests, but if you are feeling adventurous you could take it straight, on the rocks!

Serves : 1

$^2/_3$ measure dark rum
$^1/_3$ measure Southern Comfort
juice $^1/_2$ lime
dash Curaçao
ice
soda water
lime peel

1 Shake the first four ingredients together well over ice and strain into a chilled tumbler.
2 Top up with soda water to taste and finish with a twist of lime.

Caribbean Blues

(225)

The cool crystal blue cocktail invites you to think of Caribbean sea and sand, and enjoy this tropical mix.

Serves : 1

1 measure white rum
1/2 measure blue Curaçao
good squeeze lime juice
1/4 measure syrup de gomme
ice
soda water
3 frozen slices of lime

1 Mix the first four ingredients in a large cocktail glass with a few ice cubes.
2 Top up with soda water to taste and dress with the frozen slices of lime.

(226)

Island Blues

This taste of the deep blue ocean comes from those romantic rum-producing Islands.

Serves : 1

lemon juice
powdered sugar
3/4 measure peach schnapps
1/2 measure blue Curaçao
1 small egg white
dash fresh lemon juice
ice
lemonade

1 Frost the rim of a glass using the lemon juice and sugar. Set aside to dry.
2 Place the first four ingredients into a cocktail shaker half full of ice.
3 Shake well and strain into a highball glass.
4 Top up with lemonade.

Planter's Punch

 CLASSIC

Derived from a Hindi word meaning five, punch is so called because, traditionally, it contained five ingredients. These should also include four basic flavors – strong, weak, sour and sweet.

Serves : 1

2 measures white rum
2 measures dark rum
1 measure lemon juice
1 measure lime juice
1 tsp sugar syrup
$^1/_4$ tsp Triple Sec
dash of grenadine
ice
sparkling water
slice of lemon, lime and pineapple
cocktail cherry

1 Shake the white rum, dark rum, lemon juice, lime juice, sugar syrup, Triple Sec and a dash of grenadine vigorously over ice until well frosted.

2 Half fill a tall chilled tumbler or Collins glass with cracked ice cubes and strain the cocktail over them.

3 Top up with sparkling water and stir gently.

4 Dress with the fruit.

228. Orange Planter's Punch: Mix 1 measure rum and 1 of orange Curaçao, 2 dashes Angostura bitters, 1 tsp grenadine and juice 1$^1/_2$ limes. **Serves : 1**

229. Plantation Punch: Shake 2 measures dark rum, 1 measure Southern Comfort and 1 measure lemon juice vigorously over ice with 1 tsp brown sugar until well frosted. Strain into a tall, chilled glass and top up, almost to the rim, with sparkling water. Float 1 tsp of ruby port on top by pouring it gently over the back of a teaspoon and garnish with a lemon and orange slice. **Serves : 1**

230. Planter's Cocktail: Mix 1 measure rum with juice $^1/_2$ lime, 1 tsp sugar syrup and dash Angostura bitters. **Serves : 1**

231. Pineapple Planter's Punch: Mix 1 measure white rum and 1 measure pineapple juice with juice $^1/_2$ lime, $^1/_2$ measure Curaçao and dash maraschino. Serve in a highball glass with ice and rum-soaked cherries. **Serves : 1**

232. Planter's Punch Refresher: Use equal quantities of rum and lime juice, 1-2 tsp grenadine, dash Angostura bitters and top up with soda.

233. Planter's Tea: Mix 2 measures strong black tea with 2 measures dark rum, 1 cup orange juice and $^1/_2$ cup fresh lemon juice. Heat, sweeten to taste and serve with orange slices. **Serves : 1**

(234)

Calypso Sting

There is definitely a sting in the tale of this one, so enjoy with caution.

Serves : 1

1 measure dark rum

1 measure Malibu

$^1/_2$ measure orange Curaçao

$^1/_2$ measure orange juice

dash fresh lime juice

ice

tonic water

Angostura bitters

cherry and lime twist

1 Shake the first five ingredients well over ice.

2 Pour into a highball glass and top up with tonic.

3 Finish with a drop or two of bitters, a cherry and a twist of lime.

(235)

San Paulo

Golden rum brings out the sweetness of the tomatoes giving this cocktail a warm fruitiness quite different to its lookalike, the Bloody Mary.

Serves : 1

1 measure golden rum

good squeeze lime juice

2 measures tomato juice

dash Tabasco sauce

celery salt and pepper

ice

1 Stir all the ingredients together well over ice and strain into an ice-filled highball glass.

Sailor's Rum Punch

Sail in the West Indies and you will come back with this classic recipe in your pocket.

Serves : 1

1 part sour – lemon or lime juice

2 parts sweet – honey or sugar syrup

3 parts strong rum (90% proof if possible!)

few shakes of Angostura bitters

4 parts weak, chilled fruit juice: orange,
pineapple, grapefruit

lots of ice

freshly grated nutmeg and fruit pieces

1 Mix the first four ingredients together in advance, chill and leave the flavors to develop for a while.

2 To serve, mix in the fruit juice, pour into a highball glass with a little more ice and sprinkle with nutmeg.

3 Serve with fruit and a straw.

Zander

A liquorice-flavored liqueur, Sambuca is traditionally drunk straight, but its intense flavor is great with fruit drinks, and makes a change for a long drink.

Serves : 1

1 measure Sambuca

1 measure orange juice

dash lemon juice

ice

bitter lemon

1 Shake the first three ingredients over ice well and strain into a highball glass filled with ice.

2 Top up with bitter lemon.

Cactus Café

An exciting variation on iced coffee that will be enjoyed on any hot day and can be made in advance, ready for a crowd.

Serves : 1

1 measure Bols coffee liqueur

½ measure tequila

ice

lemonade

1 Pour the coffee liqueur and tequila over ice in a tall glass and top up with lemonade to taste.

Muddy Waters

Coffee soda with a difference – not quite non-alcoholic but it could be. There again you could top up with a drop more liqueur if you have added just a little too much cola!

Serves : 1

1 measure coffee liqueur

crushed ice

cola

1 Stir the liqueur over ice in a tall glass and top up with cola to taste.

2 Drink through a straw.

 # Like Lightning

This unusual liqueur made from caraway seeds makes a great long drink with most mixers and other flavors.

Serves : 1

1 measure vodka
1 measure kümmel
ice
tonic water
red fruit to finish

1 Stir the vodka and kümmel together with ice in a tall glass.

2 Top up with tonic to taste and dress with a piece of fruit or berries.

Lime Swizzle

Lime juice and zest are both sharp and very aromatic, so don't let them overpower the soft sweetness of Drambuie.

Serves : 1

1 ¹/₂ measures Drambuie
¹/₄ tsp finely grated zest of lime
1 tsp powdered sugar
few drops lime juice
ice
soda water

1 Rub the rim of a large cocktail glass or wine glass with Drambuie.

2 Mix the lime zest and sugar and dip the glass rim in this.

3 Stir all the ingredients, including the remaining sugar and zest, in the glass filled with ice.

4 Top up with soda water to taste.

Tequila Sunrise

This is one cocktail you shouldn't rush when making, otherwise you will spoil the attractive sunrise effect as the grenadine slowly spreads through the orange juice.

Serves : 1

2 parts silver tequila
cracked ice cubes
orange juice
1 measure grenadine

1 Pour the tequila over cracked ice in a chilled highball glass and top up with the orange juice. Stir well to mix.
2 Slowly pour in the grenadine and serve with a straw.

243. Blinding Sunrise: Shake 1 measure white tequila, 1 measure vodka, 3 measures orange juice, and 1 tsp Triple Sec vigorously over ice until well frosted. Half fill a tumbler with cracked ice cubes and strain the cocktail over. Slowly pour in 1 measure grenadine. **Serves : 1**

244. Pacific Sunrise: Shake 1 measure white tequila, 1 measure blue Curaçao, 1 measure lime juice, and a dash of bitters vigorously over ice until well frosted. Strain into a chilled cocktail glass. **Serves : 1**

245. Mint Sunrise: Pour 1 1/2 measures Scotch whiskey, 1/2 measure brandy, and 1/2 measure white Curaçao over cracked ice in a chilled tumbler and stir gently. Decorate with a fresh mint sprig. **Serves : 1**

Tequila Mockingbird

In spite of the horrible literary pun in the name, this popular cocktail is fast becoming a modern classic.

Serves : 1
2 measures white tequila
1 measure white crème de menthe
1 measure fresh lime juice
cracked ice cubes

1 Shake the tequila, crème de menthe and lime juice vigorously over ice until well frosted.
2 Strain into a chilled highball glass.

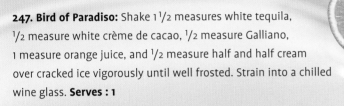

247. Bird of Paradiso: Shake 1$^1/_2$ measures white tequila, $^1/_2$ measure white crème de cacao, $^1/_2$ measure Galliano, 1 measure orange juice, and $^1/_2$ measure half and half cream over cracked ice vigorously until well frosted. Strain into a chilled wine glass. **Serves : 1**

248. Bird of Paradise Cooler: Shake 2 measures gin, 1 measure lemon juice, 1 tsp grenadine, 1 tsp sugar syrup, and 1 egg white over cracked ice vigorously until well frosted. Half fill a chilled tumbler with cracked ice cubes and pour the cocktail over them. Top up with sparkling water. **Serves : 1**

249. Blue Bird: Shake 3 measures gin, 1 measure blue Curaçao and a dash of Angostura bitters over cracked ice vigorously until well frosted. Strain into a chilled cocktail glass. **Serves : 1**

The Blues

This long bright cocktail would be quite sweet if it weren't for the lemon juice, so be careful with the balance of the ingredients the first time you make it.

Serves : 1
1$^1/_2$ measures tequila
$^1/_2$ measure maraschino
$^1/_2$ measure blue Curaçao
$^1/_2$ measure lemon juice
ice cubes
bitter lemon

1 Shake the first four ingredients well over ice until frosted.
2 Strain into a highball glass and top up with bitter lemon.

Wild Night Out

Tequila has a reputation for being an extraordinarily potent spirit, but most commercially exported brands are the same standard strength as other spirits, such as gin or whiskey. "Home-grown" tequila or its close relative, mescal, may be another matter.

Serves : 1

3 measures white tequila
2 measures cranberry juice
1 measure lime juice
cracked ice cubes
soda water

1 Shake the tequila, cranberry juice and lime juice vigorously over ice until well frosted.
2 Half fill a chilled highball glass with cracked ice cubes and strain the cocktail over them.
3 Add soda water to taste.

252. Buttafuoco: Shake 2 measures white tequila, ¹/₂ measure Galliano, ¹/₂ measure cherry brandy and ¹/₂ measure lemon juice vigorously over ice until well frosted. Half fill a tumbler with cracked ice and strain the cocktail over it. Top up with soda water and dress with a cherry. **Serves : 1**

253. Magna Carta: Rub the rim of a wine glass with a wedge of lime, then dip in powdered sugar to frost. Stir 2 measures white tequila and 1 measure Triple Sec over ice in a mixing glass. Strain into the prepared glass and top up with chilled sparkling wine. **Serves : 1**

254. Tequila Fizz: Shake 3 measures white tequila, 1 measure grenadine, 1 measure lime juice and 1 egg white vigorously over ice until well frosted. Half fill a chilled tumbler with cracked ice cubes and strain the cocktail over them. Top up with ginger ale. **Serves : 1**

255. Changuirongo: Half fill a tall chilled tumbler with cracked ice cubes. Pour in 2 measures white tequila and top up with ginger ale. Stir gently and dress with a slice of lime. **Serves : 1**

Huatusco Whammer

To be authentic, this cocktail should be topped up with Coca-Cola, but you can use other brands of cola if you prefer. Make sure that the cola is well chilled before adding it.

Serves : 1

1 measure white tequila

1/2 measure white rum

1/2 measure vodka

1/2 measure gin

1/2 measure Triple Sec

1 measure lemon juice

1/2 tsp sugar syrup

cracked ice cubes

cola

1 Shake the tequila, rum, vodka, gin, Triple Sec, lemon juice and sugar syrup vigorously over ice until well frosted.

2 Fill a chilled Collins glass with cracked ice cubes and strain the cocktail over them.

3 Top up with cola, stir gently and serve with straws.

257. Mexicola: Half fill a tall chilled tumbler with cracked ice cubes. Pour 2 measures tequila and 1 measure lime juice over the ice and top up with cola. Stir gently and decorate with a slice of lime. **Serves : 1**

258. Cherrycola: Half fill a tall chilled tumbler with cracked ice cubes. Pour 2 measures cherry brandy and 1 measure lemon juice over the ice. Top up with cola, stir gently and decorate with a slice of lemon. **Serves : 1**

259. Lounge Lizard: Half fill a tall chilled tumbler with cracked ice cubes. Pour 2 measures dark rum and 1 measure Amaretto over the ice. Top up with cola and stir gently. **Serves : 1**

CLASSIC

Kiss-Me-Quick

This cloudy looking combination is for serious anise lovers and the last few drops of bitters add a nice sharp finish.

Serves : 1

2 measures Pernod
1 tsp Cointreau
2 dashes Angostura bitters
ice
soda water

1 Pour the first three ingredients over the ice in a tumbler or tall glass.
2 Top up with soda water to taste and a few drops more Angostura bitters.

Suissesse

CLASSIC

This looks almost like a cool refreshing glass of milk, but I don't think you will be able to fool your friends for very long!

Serves : 1

1¹/₂ measures Pernod
1 measure lemon juice
¹/₄ measure orange flower water
1 egg white
ice
soda water

1 Shake all ingrecients except soda water over ice until well frosted.
2 Strain into a tumbler and top up with a little soda water to taste.

262

Iceberg

If you are an anise fan, you may only want to top up with very little lemonade – it's up to you.

Serves : 1

2 measures Pernod or pastis
good squeeze of lime
cracked ice
lemonade or ginger beer to taste
twist of lime peel

1 Stir the Pernod and lime over ice.
2 Strain into a chilled highball glass with extra ice and top up with lemonade to taste.
3 Dress with a twist of lime peel.

263

Misty Morning

If the weather really looked like this in the morning, you'd need another one of these quickly!

Serves : 1

1 1/2 measures Pernod or Ricard
1 measure crème de menthe
ice
slices of cucumber
soda water

1 Stir the first two ingredients well over ice in a highball glass.
2 Add the cucumber, top up with soda water.

Knuckleduster

Just sip quietly and your blues will soon drift away...

Serves : 1

1 measure coconut liqueur
1 measure blue Curaçao
1/2 measure white rum
1/4 measure pineapple juice
crushed ice
toasted shredded coconut

1 Whizz the first five ingredients together in a blender until frothy and partly frozen.
2 Pour into a tall iced glass, top up with more ice and finish with a little toasted shredded coconut.

265

Paddlesteamer

For a party, prepare lots of ice cubes with pieces of fruit in to add a little glamor and rim the glasses too if you wish.

Serves : 10

6 measures Southern Comfort
6 measures gin
6 measures Curaçao
6 measures orange juice or more
ice cubes
ginger ale
straws or stirrers

1 Mix the first four ingredients together well and chill until required.
2 When ready to serve pour measures into chilled tumblers or glasses with ice cubes and top up with ginger.
3 Serve with straws or a stirrer.

Orange Demons

Don't despair if at first mixing you think this is going to look grim. Pour it over plenty of ice, top up with tonic and it begins to look so different!

Serves : 1

1/2 measure green crème de menthe

1 measure Dubonnet

1/3 measure orange juice

ice

soda water

slice of orange

1 Stir the first three ingredients with ice in a tumbler or old-fashioned glass.

2 Top up with tonic and dress with a slice of orange.

Luisita

If you are not feeling in a blue mood remember you can buy orange Curaçao and change the whole mood without changing the taste!

Serves : 1

1 measure blue Curaçao

lemon barley water

few dashes lemon juice

ice

tonic water

lemon or lime slices

1 Stir the Curaçao, barley water and lemon over ice in a chilled long tumbler.

2 Add tonic water to taste and dress with a few slices of lemon.

Le Triomphe

This is fruity and very refreshing, and you can make it longer still by adding soda water or crushed ice.

Serves : 1

1 measure cognac
3/4 measure Grand Marnier
3/4 measure pineapple
1/2 measure grapefruit juice
good splash grenadine
ice
fresh cherries

1 Shake the first five ingredients together over ice.
2 When well chilled and mixed, strain into a long glass, top up with ice and finish with a cherry.

(269)

Napoleon

These two rich fruity liqueurs mix well and make a great long cocktail.

Serves : 1

1 measure Mandarine Napoleon
1 measure cherry brandy
ice
lemonade

1 Pour the liqueurs into a highball glass filled with ice.
2 Stir gently and then gradually top up with lemonade.

Wake up Call

Very refreshing and revitalising any time of the day and not just for hangovers!

Serves : 1

$^1/_2$ measure fresh orange juice

$^1/_2$ measure Fernet Branca

ice

soda water

1 Stir the first two ingredients over ice in a medium-size glass and top up with soda water to taste.

Lime 'n' Lemon Hour

This advocaat cocktail may look like a milkshake, but when mixed with citrus and given a kick of vodka, it certainly doesn't taste like one!

Serves : 1

1 measure advocaat

$^1/_2$ measure vodka

$^1/_2$ measure lime cordial

ice

lemonade

twist of lime peel

1 Shake the first three ingredients well over ice until frosted.

2 Pour into a chilled highball glass and top up with lemonade.

3 Finish with a twist of lime peel and drink through a straw.

 272

Star-Bangled Spanner

Although only half measures of each spirit are used, there are seven of them, so it is a potent cocktail. It is probably fortunate that after getting your tongue around a couple, your hand will become too unsteady to pour more. The drinks must all be iced.

Serves : 1

1/2 measure chilled green Chartreuse
1/2 measure chilled Triple Sec
1/2 measure chilled cherry brandy
1/2 measure chilled crème violette
1/2 measure chilled yellow Chartreuse
1/2 measure chilled blue Curaçao
1/2 measure chilled brandy

1 Pour the green Chartreuse into a chilled flute, then, with a steady hand, gently pour in the Triple Sec to make a second layer.
2 Gently add the cherry brandy to make a third layer, the crème violette to make a fourth, the yellow Chartreuse to make a fifth and the Curaçao to make a sixth.
3 Finally, float the brandy on top.

273. Stars and Stripes: Pour 3/4 measure chilled cherry brandy into a chilled shot glass, pousse café glass or flute. With a steady hand, gently pour in 1 1/2 measures chilled half and half cream to make a second layer and, finally, gently pour in 3/4 measure chilled blue Curaçao. **Serves : 1**

274. Union Jack: Pour 1 measure chilled maraschino into a chilled shot glass. With a steady hand, gently pour in 1 measure chilled blue Curaçao to make a second layer and, finally, gently pour in 1 measure chilled grenadine. **Serves : 1**

275. Tricolor: Pour 1 measure chilled crème de menthe into a chilled shot glass. With a steady hand, gently pour in 1 measure chilled Baileys Irish Cream to make a second layer and, for the final layer, gently pour in 1 measure chilled red maraschino. **Serves : 1**

 276

Belladora

If you love the kick of mint in your cocktails, add more to this one, varying it to taste for each drinker.

Serves : 1

3/4 measure cognac
3/4 measure Cointreau
3/4 measure grapefruit juice
ice
tonic water
2 tsp crème de menthe

1 Shake the first three ingredients together over ice until well frosted.
2 Strain into a chilled tall glass and top up with tonic water.
3 Pour in the crème de menthe at the end and serve with a stirrer.

Frivolous Dubonnet

A sweet and fruity favorite with the girls.

Serves : 1

1 measure Dubonnet
1 measure cherry brandy
1/2 measure lemon juice
1/2 egg white
ice
soda water
slice of lemon

1 Shake the Dubonnet, brandy and lemon juice over ice with the egg white until frothy.
2 Strain into long glasses and top up with soda water.
3 Serve with a slice of lemon.

Azure

The blue Curaçao added at the end of mixing this cocktail certainly produces a stunning effect, but it also adds to the delicious mix of orange and lemon flavors.

Serves : 1

1 1/4 measures cognac
3/4 measure Cointreau
3/4 measure lemon juice
ice
3 measures bitter lemon or to taste
1 tbsp blue Curaçao

1 Shake the first three ingredients over ice until frosted.
2 Strain into a chilled wine glass or large cocktail glass and mix in the bitter lemon.
3 Carefully pour the Curaçao down the side of the glass and leave 1-2 minutes whilst it settles to the base.
4 Dress with fruit and drink through a straw.

The Apple Teaser

The flavor of apple comes through gently, giving a soft fruitiness to these liqueurs.

Serves : 1

$^1/_3$ measure whiskey

$^1/_3$ measure Amaretto

$^1/_3$ measure Calvados

dash grenadine

1 measure apple juice

ice

soda water

apple slice

1 Shake the first five ingredients together over ice until well frosted.

2 Strain into a highball glass filled with ice and top up with a little soda water.

3 Dress with a slice of apple.

Massimo

Marsala is a delicious sweet fortified wine heated to give an added mellow burnt flavor. In cocktails, this characteristic gives a rich depth.

Serves : 1

2 measures Marsala

1 measure gin

ice

sprig of mint

slice of orange, lemon and lime

lemonade

dash Angostura bitters

1 Pour the Marsala and gin over ice in an old-fashioned glass.

2 Add the mint, sliced fruit and lemonade to taste, then finish with a dash of Angostura bitters.

Snowball Classic

The familiar golden egg yellow of advocaat is preferred by many when it is lengthened with soda or tonic and given an added tang of lemon.

Serves : 1

1 measure advocaat

good dash fresh lemon juice

ice

lemonade

slices of orange and lemon

1 Stir the advocaat and lemon over ice in a mixing glass.

2 Strain into a highball glass filled with ice and top up with lemonade to taste.

3 Dress with slices of orange and lemon.

(282)

Widow's Kiss

With a name like that it has to be daring – and it is – until you add the soda water!

Serves : 1

$^1/_2$ measure Benedictine

$^1/_2$ measure Chartreuse

1 measure Calvados

ice

dash Angostura bitters

soda water

1 Pour the liqueurs into a highball glass filled with ice.

2 Stir once and top up with soda water and Angostura bitters to taste.

Trixie Dixie

As there is lots of fruit and fruit juice in this cocktail, you may not want to add much soda water, just ice well and offer soda water to taste.

Serves : 4

3 measures gin

6 measures Southern Comfort

3 measures lime juice

4 slices fresh pineapple

ice

soda water

sliced pineapple

1 Whizz the first four ingredients in the blender on slow until creamed and frothy.
2 Pour into ice-filled glasses and top up with the soda water to taste just before serving.
3 Dress with slices of pineapple.

Ruffled

This strange combination could ruffle anyone's feathers if you have too many!

Serves : 1

1 measure Dubonnet
1/2 measure coffee liqueur
1/2 measure Calvados
ice
stout
apple peel

1 Mix together the first three ingredients and pour over ice into a long glass.
2 Top up with stout and finish with a twist of apple peel.

(285) # Ace of Spades

This mild looking drink is long, cold and refreshing, great for warm summer evenings, but it is not quite as mild as it looks!

Serves : 1

1/2 measure coffee liqueur
1/2 measure Cointreau
1 measure Dubonnet
ice cubes
1/2 bottle stout or Guinness

1 Mix the first three ingredients together over ice in a large glass.
2 Slowly pour in the stout so it doesn't bubble over.
3 Serve with a stirrer.

 286

Sparkling Rose

The ever popular Dubonnet mixes with so many flavors. This combination may be new to you, so give it a try – you won't be disappointed.

Serves : 1

2 measures Dubonnet

3 measures cider

5 measures lemonade

ice

slice of apple

1 Stir the ingredients over ice in a chilled highball glass and dress with a slice of apple.

287

American Rose

"A rose by any other name…" this pretty cocktail is truly a thing of beauty and a joy forever.

Serves : 1

1 1/2 measures brandy

1 tsp grenadine

1/2 tsp Pernod

1/2 fresh peach, peeled and mashed

cracked ice cubes

sparkling wine

slice of fresh peach

1 Shake the brandy, grenadine, Pernod and peach vigorously over ice until frosted.

2 Strain into a chilled wine goblet and top up with sparkling wine.

3 Stir gently, then dress with the slice of peach.

Sherwood

Enjoy this rich fruit and cream cocktail after lunch or dinner, or even in place of dessert, as it is quite sweet.

Serves : 1

1/2 measure Cointreau, chilled
1/2 measure Glayva, chilled
3/4 measure fraise de bois
ice
3/4 measure cream

1 Stir the Cointreau, Glayva and fraise in a mixing glass with a little ice.
2 Strain into an iced cocktail glass and float a layer of cream gently on the top.

Cherry Kitch

This is a velvety smooth cocktail, fruity but with a rich brandy undertone. A touch of maraschino liqueur added at the end would be good, too.

Serves : 1

1 measure cherry brandy
2 measures pineapple juice
1/2 measure kirsch
1 egg white
1 scoop crushed ice
frozen maraschino cherry

1 Shake all the ingredients well over ice until frosted.
2 Pour into a chilled tall thin glass and top with a frozen maraschino cherry.

Scotchman in Philadelphia

Applejack is the US name for apple brandy but don't waste your best Calvados in this long mix.

Serves : 1

2 measures applejack or apple brandy
2 measures port
juice of 1 orange
ice
ginger ale

1 Stir the first three ingredients in a chilled highball glass until frosted.
2 Fill up with ginger and ice and serve with a a stirrer.

(291) # Bermudan Beauty

The glorious rose color of this cocktail is partly the result of the grenadine. Made from pomegranates, it also adds a delightful perfume and fresh fruity taste.

Serves : 1

2 ready-to-eat dried apricots

1 measure apricot brandy

1 measure gin

1/4 measure grenadine

ice

soda water or apricot-flavored water

1 Soak the apricots in half the brandy for 15 minutes.

2 Shake the gin, remaining brandy, and grenadine over ice until well frosted.

3 Strain into a tall cocktail glass and top up with a little soda water.

4 Add the apricots, chopped or halved, and the last few drops of brandy to finish.

(292) Sleepy Afternoon

For lazy Sunday afternoons in the sun, try this long and very fruity drink.

Serves : 1

1 measure cognac
1/2 measure Benedictine
1/2 measure pineapple juice
1/4 measure lemon juice
ice
ginger ale
lemon peel

1 Shake the first four ingredients well over ice.
2 Strain into a long glass and top up with ginger ale.
3 Finish with a piece of lemon peel.

(293) Pinadora

Try this lovely pineapple and melon blend when you want to get back into that holiday mood.

Serves : 1

1 measure brandy
1/3 measure Midori
1/3 measure white rum
1/5 measure crème de menthe
ice
pineapple juice, chilled
soda water, chilled
piece of melon to finish

1 Shake the first four ingredients together well over ice.
2 Strain into a highball glass, add the pineapple and top up with soda water to taste.
3 Finish with a piece of melon.

(294) Apple Classic

Apple lovers and cider makers will put this top of their list, but it is definitely better made with sweet rather than dry cider.

Serves : 1

1/2 measure gin
1/2 measure brandy
1/2 measure Calvados
ice
sweet cider
slice of apple

1 Shake the first three ingredients over ice until frosted.
2 Strain into a medium or tall glass and top up with cider to taste.
3 Dress with a slice of apple.

1001 Cocktails

Horse's Neck

This refreshing drink can also be made with gin or with bourbon, adding a couple of dashes of Angostura bitters. The same name is also used for a brandy and champagne pick-me-up.

Serves : 1

lemon peel spiral
ice cubes
1 measure brandy
dry ginger ale

1 Drop the lemon peel spiral into a tall glass, and anchor it with ice cubes.
2 Pour in the brandy, and top up with ginger ale.

Sleepy Head

As its name implies, this is a lovely bedtime soother, so there is no need to ice it.

Serves : 1

2 measures brandy
piece of orange peel
3-4 mint leaves
ginger ale

1 Stir the brandy, peel and mint together in a medium tumbler.
2 Top up with ginger to taste.

(297) Italian Summer Punch

With a kick of Italian brandy and a few sprigs of basil, you will soon be transported to the Tuscan hills.

Serves : 2

$1^1/_3$ cups dry white wine

3 measures Tuaca or Italian brandy

squeeze of lemon, lime, and orange juice

ice

slices of citrus fruits

few sprigs of basil

soda water

1 Shake the first three ingredients well over ice.

2 Pour into a jug with the fruit and basil sprigs.

3 Serve each glassful topped up with soda water.

---

(298) Kir

CLASSIC

As with the best mustard, crème de cassis production is centred on the French city of Dijon. This cocktail is named in memory of a partisan and mayor of the city, Félix Kir.

Serves : 1

cracked ice cubes

2 measures crème de cassis

white wine

twist of lemon peel

1 Put the crushed ice cubes into a chilled wine glass.

2 Pour the crème de cassis over the ice.

3 Top up with chilled white wine and stir well.

4 Dress with the lemon twist.

---

299. Osborne (named after Queen Victoria's Isle of Wight residence and apparently a favorite tipple of Her Majesty): Pour 3 measures claret and 1 measure Scotch whiskey into a goblet and stir. **Serves : 1**

300. Bellinitini: Shake 2 measures vodka, 1 measure peach schnapps and 1 measure peach juice vigorously until well frosted. Strain into a chilled goblet. Top up with chilled champagne. **Serves : 1**

301. Rikki-Tikki-Tavi: Put a sugar cube into a chilled flute and dash Angostura bitters over it until red but still intact. Pour in 1 tsp brandy and 1 tsp white Curaçao and top up with chilled champagne. **Serves : 1**

302. Champagne Pick-me-up: Shake 2 measures brandy, 1 measure orange juice, 1 measure lemon juice and a dash of grenadine vigorously over ice until well frosted. Strain the mixture into a wine glass and then top up with chilled champagne. **Serves : 1**

Sangria

  CLASSIC

A perfect long cold drink for a crowd of friends at a summer barbie!

Serves 6
juice of 1 orange
juice of 1 lemon
2 tbsp powdered sugar
ice
1 orange, thinly sliced
1 lemon, thinly sliced
1 bottle red wine, chilled
lemonade

1 Stir orange and lemon juice with sugar in a large bowl or jug.
2 When sugar has dissolved, add few cubes ice, sliced fruit and wine.
3 Marinate for 1 hour if possible, and then add lemonade to taste and more ice.

(304)

Blonde Sangria

Like its red wine-based cousin, this is an excellent party drink to prepare for a crowd any time of year.

Serves : 10
4 measures clear acacia or almond blossom honey
2 lemons
2 oranges
8-12 cups white wine
ice
soda water

1 Warm the honey a little for easy mixing.
2 Pour into a large jug or mixing container.
3 Cut 2-3 good slices off the fruit then squeeze the rest of the juice into the honey and mix well.
4 Slowly add the wine and mix.
5 Pour over ice into tall glasses and top up with soda water.
6 Add a slice of fruit and a straw.

The Gunner

A good alternative to a pint in the pub, as no-one will know what it is but they will all want to try it.

Serves : 1

few ice cubes

1 measure lime juice

2-3 dashes Angostura bitters or to taste

³/4 cup ginger beer

³/4 cup lemonade

1 In a long glass mix all the ingredients adding equal quantities of ginger beer and lemonade.

2 Taste and add more Angostura bitters if you wish.

Wine with Tea Punch

This is a light and fruity punch perfect for a party in the garden, really well iced. Serve in a flower-filled ice bowl if you have got the time to make one.

Serves : 20

8oz powdered sugar

5 bottles Rhine wine

6 cups soda water

2 measures brandy

2 measures maraschino

2 tbsp tea, in bags or leaves tied in muslin

sliced fruits

1 Surround a large punch bowl with cracked ice.

2 Add in all the ingredients and leave for about 10 minutes to marinate.

3 Remove the tea and add lots of sliced fruits in season.

Long Jump

An unusual mix of creamy and bubbly. Make sure the bubbly is really cold, but the liqueur not so cold, or it might separate.

Serves : 1

1 measure Amarula liqueur

champagne or sparkling white wine, chilled

1 Pour the Amarula into a chilled long glass and top up slowly with champagne.

2 Drink immediately.

(308)

Bellini

This delicious concoction was created by Giuseppe Cipriani at Harry's Bar in Venice, around 1943.

Serves : 1

1 measure fresh peach juice made from lightly sweetened liquidised peaches
powdered sugar
3 measures champagne, chilled

1 Dip the rim of a flute into some peach juice and then into the sugar to create a sugar-frosted effect. Set aside to dry.
2 Pour the peach juice into the chilled flute.
3 Carefully top up with champagne and stir gently.

(309)

Ginger Fizz

This is a cool, refreshing cocktail for a hot day, easiest made in a blender.

Serves : 1

ginger ale
sprigs of fresh mint
cracked ice
raspberries
sprig of mint

1 Put the ginger ale and several mint leaves into a blender and whizz together.
2 Strain into a chilled highball glass two-thirds filled with ice.
3 Dress with a few raspberries and a sprig of fresh mint.

Prost

This German cocktail is best made with one of the slightly sweeter and fruitier German Rhine wines.

Serves : 1
1/2 measure cherry brandy
4 measures white wine
1 scoop crushed ice
soda water
2 maraschino cherries

1 Shake the brandy and wine together over ice until well frosted.
2 Pour into a tall glass or wine goblet, top up with soda water and dress with a maraschino cherry.

311

Long Boat

A long and pleasant cocktail, with a gentle hint of ginger.

Serves : 1
ice
1 measure lime cordial
ginger beer
fresh lime and a sprig of mint

1 Fill a chilled highball or tall glass two-thirds full with ice and pour in the lime cordial.
2 Top up with ginger beer and stir gently.
3 Dress with a wedge of fresh lime and a sprig of mint.

Shirley Temple

Shirley Temple Black became a respected diplomat, but this classic cocktail – one of the most famous non-alcoholic drinks, dates from her earlier days when she was an immensely popular child film star of the 1930s.

Serves : 1

2 measures lemon juice
1/2 measure grenadine
1/2 measure sugar syrup
cracked ice cubes
ginger ale
orange slice
cocktail cherry

1 Shake the lemon juice, grenadine and sugar syrup vigorously over ice until well frosted.

2 Strain into a small, chilled glass half filled with cracked ice cubes.

3 Top up with ginger ale.

4 Dress with an orange slice and a cocktail cherry.

313. St Clements: Put cracked ice cubes into a chilled tumbler. Pour in 2 measures orange juice and 2 measures bitter lemon. Stir gently and dress with a slice of orange and a slice of lemon. **Serves : 1**

314. Black and Tan: Pour 1/2 cup chilled ginger ale into a chilled tumbler. Add 1/2 cup chilled ginger beer. Do not stir. Dress with lime. **Serves : 1**

315. Heavenly Days: Shake 2 measures hazelnut syrup, 2 measures lemon juice and 1 tsp grenadine vigorously over ice until well frosted. Half fill a tumbler with cracked ice cubes and strain the cocktail over them. Top up with sparkling water. Stir gently and dress with orange. **Serves : 1**

Italian Soda

Italian syrup comes in a wide variety of flavors, including a range of fruit and nuts, and is available from most Italian delicatessens and supermarkets. French syrups are similar. You can substitute your favorite and vary the quantity to taste.

Serves : 1

cracked ice cubes
1 1/2 measures hazelnut syrup
sparkling water, to top up
slice of lime

1 Fill a chilled Collins glass with cracked ice cubes.

2 Pour the hazelnut syrup over and top up with sparkling water.

3 Stir gently and dress with lime.

(317) Island in the Sun

Anise is a flavor that blends well with fruit and gives only a subtle background taste in this cocktail.

Serves : 1

1 thick-skinned orange

1 measure ouzo or other anise spirit

3 dashes grenadine

few ice cubes

soda water

slice of orange

maraschino cherry

1 Cut one good slice of orange and grate ¹/₂ tsp zest and set aside.

2 Stir 1 measure of orange juice over ice with the orange zest, ouzo and grenadine.

3 Mix until well frosted. Pour into a tall glass or large wine glass with more ice, top up with soda water and dress with a slice of orange and a cherry.

Non-alcoholic Pimm's

For occasions when you are drinking the real thing, drivers and the younger members of the family can also join in.

Serves : 6

2 1/2 cups lemonade, chilled
2 cups cola, chilled
2 cups dry ginger, chilled
juice of 1 orange
juice of 1 lemon
few drops Angostura bitters
sliced fruit and sprigs of mint
ice

1 Mix the first six ingredients together in a large jug or punch bowl.
2 Float in the fruit and mint, keep in a cold place and add the ice cubes at the last minute.

Pom Pom

Lemonade is transformed into an extravaganza that's pretty in pink, with a frothy topping to match its frivolous name.

Serves : 1

juice of half a lemon
1 egg white
1 dash grenadine
crushed ice
lemonade
slice of lemon

1 Shake the lemon juice, egg white and grenadine together and strain over crushed ice in a tall glass.
2 Top up with lemonade and dress with a lemon slice on the rim of the glass.

Slush Puppy

Pink, pretty and refreshing – it looks serious, but you won't need to book a cab home.

Serves : 1

juice 1 lemon or 1/2 pink grapefruit

1/2 measure grenadine

ice

few strips lemon peel

2-3 tsp raspberry syrup

soda water

maraschino cherry

1 Pour the lemon juice and grenadine into a chilled tall glass with ice.

2 Add lemon peel, syrup and soda water to taste. Finish off with a cherry.

Thai Fruit Cocktail

When choosing your favorite combination of juices do use some of the delicate oriental flavors.

Serves : 1

1 measure pineapple juice

1 measure orange juice

1/2 measure lime juice

1 measure passion fruit juice

2 measures guava juice

crushed ice

flower to finish

1 Shake all the juices together with the crushed ice.

2 Pour into a chilled long glass and finish with a flower.

Sober Sunday

An interesting variation for those not drinking and any who are driving.

Serves : 1

1 measure grenadine

1 measure fresh lemon or lime juice

ice

lemonade

slices of lemon and lime

1 Pour the grenadine and fruit juice into an ice-filled highball glass.

2 Top up with lemonade and finish with slices of lemon and lime.

Clam Digger

A good cocktail for a Sunday brunch, when alcoholic drinks can be too soporific and you end up wasting the rest of the day, but you still want something to wake up the taste buds and set them tingling.

Serves : 1

cracked ice

Tabasco sauce

Worcestershire sauce

4 measures tomato juice

4 measures clam juice

1/4 tsp horseradish sauce

ice

celery salt

freshly ground black pepper

celery stick

wedge of lime

1 In a cocktail shaker, put the ice, dash of Tabasco sauce and Worcestershire sauce, the tomato juice and clam juice and then the horseradish sauce.

2 Shake vigorously until well frosted.

3 Fill a chilled Collins glass with more cracked ice and strain in the cocktail.

4 Season to taste with celery salt and pepper and dress with a celery stick and lime wedge.

324. New England Party: Into a blender put a little crushed ice, dash of Tabasco sauce, Worcestershire sauce and lemon juice, add 1 medium chopped carrot, 2 chopped celery sticks, 1 cup tomato juice and 1/2 cup clam juice. Blend until smooth. Transfer to a jug, cover with film and chill for about 1 hour. Pour into 2 chilled tumblers, season with salt and freshly ground black pepper and dress with olives on a cocktail stick. **Serves : 2**

Cocobelle

If you have a steady hand, this drink can be served with pretty swirls of color up the sides. Youngsters will no doubt be keen to help you with this one!

Serves : 1

3 measures cold milk

1 measure coconut cream

2 scoops vanilla ice cream

3-4 ice cubes

dash grenadine

long-shred coconut, toasted

1 Whizz the first four ingredients in a blender until slushy.

2 Chill a tall glass and gently dribble a few splashes of grenadine down the insides.

3 Pour in the slush slowly so not all the color is dissolved immediately and sprinkle with toasted coconut or flakes of fresh coconut.

(326) Coconut Islander

This can be very rich, so enjoy in small quantities or dilute a little with soda water.

Serves : 4

1 pineapple
4 measures pineapple juice
4 tbsp creamed coconut
4 measures milk
2 tbsp crushed pineapple
3 tbsp flaked coconut
ice
cherries

1 Cut the top off the pineapple and remove the flesh. Set aside for a salad or dessert.
2 Save some flesh to add to the cocktail.
3 Whizz all the ingredients except the cherries in a blender with a little crushed ice for 30-40 seconds.
4 When smooth and frothy, pour into the shell, dress with cherries or the pineapple leaves and drink with straws.

(327) Virgin Mary

This is simply a Bloody Mary without the vodka, but it is still a great pick-me-up with a good splash of Worcestershire sauce and Tabasco added.

Serves : 1

3 measures tomato juice
1 measure lemon juice
2 dashes Worcestershire sauce
1 dash Tabasco sauce
cracked ice
pinch celery salt
black pepper
lemon wedge and celery stick

1 Shake the first four ingredients vigorously over ice and season with celery salt and black pepper.
2 Strain into an iced old-fashioned glass.
3 Dress with a wedge of lemon and a stick of celery.

328. Ferdinand the Bull: Shake 4 measures tomato juice, 4 measures chilled beef stock and 1 measure lime juice with a dash Worcestershire sauce and Tabasco sauce over ice until well frosted. Half fill a tall chilled tumbler with cracked ice cubes and strain the cocktail over. Season to taste with salt and freshly ground black pepper and decorate with a slice of lime. **Serves : 1**

329. Texas Virgin: Shake over ice 1 measure lime juice and 1 measure barbecue sauce with a dash Worcestershire sauce and Tabasco sauce until well frosted. Pour into a chilled tumbler, top up with tomato juice and stir. Dress with a slice of lime and a pickled jalapeño chilli. **Serves : 1**

Soft Sangria

This is a version of the well-known Spanish wine cup that has caught out many an unwary tourist. A Soft Sangria poses no such danger of unexpected inebriation, but is just as refreshing and flavorsome. Chill everything thoroughly first.

Serves : 4

6 cups red grape juice
1 cup orange juice
3 measures cranberry juice
2 measures lemon juice
2 measures lime juice
4 measures sugar syrup
ice
slices of lemon, orange and lime

1 Pour all the juices and the sugar syrup into a chilled punch bowl and stir well.
2 Add the ice and the fruit slices.
3 Serve in chilled glasses.

331. Sangria Seca: Pour 2 cups tomato juice, 1 cup orange juice, 3 measures lime juice, ¹/₂ measure Tabasco sauce and 2 tsp Worcestershire sauce into a jug. Add 1 deseeded and finely chopped jalapeño chilli. Season to taste with celery salt and freshly ground white pepper and stir well. Cover with film and chill in the refrigerator for at least 1 hour. To serve, half fill chilled tumblers with cracked ice cubes and strain the cocktail over them. **Serves : 6**

Citrus Fizz

This is a clever and refreshing variation on the classic Buck's Fizz, which is perfect for all ages in the family.

Serves : 1

2 measures fresh orange juice, chilled
powdered sugar
few drops Angostura bitters
squeeze lime juice
2-3 measures sparkling water, chilled

1 Rub the rim of a flute with orange or lime juice and dip into powdered sugar.
2 Stir the rest of the juices together with the bitters and then pour into the glass.
3 Top up with water to taste.

Lassi

Originally Lassi was simply a flavored yogurt drink, slightly soured, often savory or spiced. There are many delicious drinks you can make from it.

Serves : 2

scant 1/2 cup plain yogurt
1 cup milk
1 tbsp rose water
3 tbsp honey
1 ripe mango, peeled and diced
6 ice cubes
rose petals (optional)

1 Pour the yogurt and milk into a processor and process gently until combined.
2 Add the rose water and honey and process until thoroughly blended, then add the mango and ice cubes and continue blending until smooth.
3 Pour into chilled glasses and dress with edible petals.

(334)

Mocha Slush

Definitely for people with a sweet tooth, this is a chocoholic's dream and is popular with adults, as well as children.

Serves : 1

crushed ice cubes

2 measures coffee syrup

1 measure chocolate syrup

4 measures milk

grated chocolate

1 Whizz the crushed ice in a small blender with the coffee and chocolate syrup and milk until slushy.

2 Pour into a chilled goblet and sprinkle with grated chocolate.

(335)

California Smoothie

The secret of success to a smoothie – alcoholic and non-alcoholic – is to blend it on medium speed until just smooth.

Serves : 1

1 banana, peeled and thinly sliced

$^1/_2$ cup strawberries

$^3/_4$ cup stoned dates

$4^1/_2$ tsp clear honey

1 cup orange juice

4-6 crushed ice cubes

1 Put the banana, strawberries, dates and honey into a blender and whizz until smooth.

2 Add the orange juice and crushed ice cubes and blend again until smooth.

3 Pour into a chilled Collins glass.

(336)

Mocha Cream

Although it sounds like lots of cream, it is quite a light and delicate result.

Serves : 2

$^3/_4$ cupl milk

$^1/_4$ cup half and half cream

1 tbsp brown sugar

2 tbsp cocoa powder

1 tbsp coffee syrup

6 ice cubes

a little whipped cream

grated chocolate

1 Put the milk, cream and sugar into a food processor and process until combined.

2 Add the cocoa powder and coffee syrup and process well.

3 Then add the ice cubes and process until smooth.

4 Pour the mixture into chilled glasses, top with whipped cream and a little grated chocolate.

 (337)

Eggmania

No need to wait until Easter to serve this delicious mint chocolate treat. Why not serve with small chocolate eggs for added luxury?

Serves : 1

1 measure chocolate mint liqueur

1 measure advocaat

$^1/_2$ measure whiskey

$^1/_2$ scoop vanilla ice cream

1 Whizz all the ingredients, except the eggs, together in a small blender on slow for about 10 seconds.

2 Pour into a chilled cocktail glass and serve with a straw.

Short
Cocktails

Gin Fix

338

A fix should contain spirit, sugar, fruit and often a lot of fizz. It works so well with gin but with other spirits are great too, so try some variations.

Serves : 1
2¹/₂ measures gin
1 measure lemon juice
1 tsp syrup de gomme
crushed ice
slice of lemon

1 Pour the gin, lemon, and syrup into a tumbler filled with crushed ice and stir once.
2 Finish with a slice of lemon.

339

CLASSIC

Pink Gin

Originally devised as a remedy for stomach complaints, the Pink Gin was subsequently adopted by the British Navy as part of its medicine chest.

Serves : 1
1 measure Plymouth gin
few drops Angostura bitters
1 measure iced water
maraschino cherry

1 Pour the first three ingredients into a mixing glass and stir.
2 Strain into a cocktail glass and garnish with a maraschino cherry.

Breakfast

It is difficult to believe that anyone would actually have the stomach to cope with cocktails first thing in the morning – but then, for those who party all night and sleep all day, cocktail time coincides with breakfast.

Serves : 1
2 measures gin
1 measure grenadine
cracked ice cubes
1 egg yolk

1 Pour the gin and grenadine over ice in a shaker and add the egg yolk.
2 Shake vigorously until frosted. Strain into a chilled glass.

341

Road Runner

Whether it is named after the real bird or after Wile E Coyote's nemesis, this is a cocktail for slowing down after a fast-moving day, not for speeding things up.

Serves : 1
2 measures gin
$^1/_2$ measure dry vermouth
$^1/_2$ measure Pernod
1 tsp grenadine
cracked ice cubes

1 Shake the gin, vermouth, Pernod and grenadine vigorously over ice until well frosted.
2 Strain into a chilled wine glass.

342. Road Runner (second version): Shake 1 measure vodka, $^1/_2$ measure Malibu, and $^1/_2$ measure Amaretto vigorously over ice until well frosted. Strain into a chilled cocktail glass. **Serves : 1**

343. End of the Road: Stir 3 measures gin, 1 measure crème de menthe, and 1 measure pastis over ice. Strain into a tall glass filled with ice and dress with a sprig of mint. Top up with soda water for a longer drink. **Serves : 1**

344. Elk's Own: Shake 2 measures rye whiskey, 1 measure ruby port, $^1/_2$ measure lemon juice, 1 tsp sugar syrup, and 1 egg white vigorously over ice until well frosted. Strain into a chilled cocktail glass and dress with a pineapple wedge. **Serves : 1**

345. Rattlesnake: Pour 1 measure chilled Baileys Irish Cream into a shot glass. With a steady hand, gently pour in 1 measure chilled dark crème de cacao to make a second layer, then gently pour in 1 measure chilled Kahlua to make a third layer. Do not stir. **Serves : 1**

 # Gloom Chaser

This bright and cheery drink is tempting enough to chase away any gloomy moods.

Serves : 1

1 measure dry vermouth

1 1/2 measures gin

1/2 tsp grenadine

2 dashes Pernod

ice

1 Shake ingredients together over ice and strain into a cocktail glass.

Red Cobbler

Although traditionally a short drink, for a cobbler to be extra refreshing, it is often drunk long over crushed ice, especially if it's very strong.

Serves : 1

piece or slice of orange and lemon
1 measure port
1 measure gin
few drops fraise
ice

1 Place the fruit in the shaker and crush or muddle them with a wooden spoon or small pestle.
2 Add the liquids and ice and shake well until frosted.
3 Strain into a frosted martini glass and add the squeezed fruit slices.

Moonlight

This light wine-based cocktail is ideal to make for several people.

Serves : 4

3 measures grapefruit juice
4 measures gin
1 measure kirsch
4 measures white wine
1/2 tsp lemon zest
ice

1 Shake all ingredients well over ice and strain into chilled cocktail glasses.

(349)

Fallen Angel

Mint and lemon make an unusual addition to gin, but do make sure it is a green mint liqueur or it will not have the same visual impact.

Serves : 1

1 dash Angostura bitters
juice of 1 lemon or lime
2 measures gin
ice
2 dashes green crème de menthe

1 Shake the first three ingredients well over ice and strain into a cocktail glass.
2 Top with two dashes of crème de menthe at the last minute.

(350)

Alaska

Yellow Chartreuse is slightly sweeter than the green Chartreuse, so it does benefit from being really well chilled.

Serves : 1

$^1/_2$ measure gin
$^1/_2$ measure yellow Chartreuse
ice

1 Shake the ingredients over ice until well frosted.
2 Strain into a chilled cocktail glass.

1001 Cocktails

 351

Charleston

 CLASSIC

This little number combines several tastes and flavors to produce a very lively drink.
Don't drink it when you are thirsty, you might want too many!

Serves : 1
$^{1}/_{4}$ measure gin
$^{1}/_{4}$ measure dry vermouth
$^{1}/_{4}$ measure sweet vermouth
$^{1}/_{4}$ measure Cointreau
$^{1}/_{4}$ measure kirsch
$^{1}/_{4}$ measure maraschino
ice and a twist of lemon

1 Shake all the ingredients except the lemon together well over ice and strain into a small chilled cocktail glass.
2 Dress with a twist of lemon.

Maiden's Blush

(352)

The name of this cocktail aptly describes its pretty color. It could also be a warning, however, that too much of this concoction could be the cause of the maiden's blush.

Serves : 1

cracked ice cubes
2 measures gin
1/2 tsp Triple Sec
1/2 tsp grenadine
1/2 tsp lemon juice

1 Put the cracked ice cubes into a cocktail shaker.
2 Shake the gin, Triple Sec, grenadine and lemon juice vigorously over the ice until well frosted.
3 Strain into a chilled cocktail glass or small highball glass.

353. Maidenly Blush: Stir 2 measures gin and 1 measure Pernod over ice to mix, then strain into a chilled cocktail glass. **Serves : 1**

354. Maiden's Prayer: Shake 1 measure gin, 1 measure Triple Sec, 1 tsp orange juice, and 1 tsp lemon juice vigorously over ice until well frosted. Strain into a chilled cocktail glass. **Serves : 1**

355. Virgin's Prayer: Shake 1 measure white rum, 1 measure dark rum, 1 measure Kahlua, 1 tsp lemon juice, and 2 tsp orange juice vigorously over ice until well frosted. Strain into a small, chilled tumbler. Dress with slices of lime. **Serves : 1**

356. Wedding Belle: Shake 2 measures gin, 2 measures Dubonnet, 1 measure cherry brandy, and 1 measure orange juice over ice until well frosted. Strain into a cocktail glass. **Serves : 1**

357. Widow's Wish: Shake 2 measures Benedictine with 1 egg vigorously over ice until well frosted. Strain into a chilled tumbler. Top up with half and half cream. **Serves : 1**

Absinthe Friend

(358)

The original absinthe was a popular cocktail ingredient and digestif. It was later banned by law in 1915 for many years as it was then flavored with wormwood and was said to react with alcohol and cause brain damage. Any pastis, like Pernod and Ricard, will do instead.

Serves : 1

1 measure gin
1 measure Pernod
dash Angostura bitters
dash sugar syrup
4-6 cracked ice cubes

1 Shake the ingredients vigorously over ice until well frosted.
2 Strain into a chilled medium-size glass or tumbler.

Orange Bloom

359

Some orange juices are made from the whole fruit and have a very bitter back taste. Avoid these in cocktails as they will over-power the spirits.

Serves : 1

1 measure gin
1/2 measure fresh orange juice
1/2 measure Cointreau
1/4 measure dry vermouth
cracked ice

1 Shake all the ingredients together over ice until really well frosted.
2 Strain into a chilled cocktail glass.

Blue Star Shaker

360

Stunningly pretty cocktail for blues fans who love the rich flavors of Lillet, a French aperitif made from red or white wine fortified with Armagnac, herbs and fruit.

Serves : 2

2/3 measure blue Curaçao
2/3 measure gin
1 measure Lillet
crushed ice
lime slices

1 Place the three liquids into a cocktail shaker with ice.
2 Shake until frosted, then pour into shallow cocktail glasses and finish with a slice of lime.

Bronx

361

Like Manhattan, the New York borough of the Bronx – and also the river of the same name – has been immortalised in cocktail bars throughout the world.

Serves : 1

2 measures gin
1 measure orange juice
1/2 measure dry vermouth
1/2 measure sweet vermouth
cracked ice cubes

1 Pour the gin, orange juice, dry, and sweet vermouth over ice in a mixing glass.
2 Stir to mix. Strain into a chilled cocktail glass.

 CLASSIC

Orange Blossom

During the Prohibition years in the USA gin was often quite literally made in the bathtub and flavored with fresh orange juice to conceal its filthy flavor. Made with good-quality gin, which needs no such concealment, this drink is delightfully refreshing.

Serves : 1

2 measures gin
2 measures orange juice
cracked ice cubes
slice of orange, to decorate

1 Shake the gin and orange juice vigorously over ice until well frosted.
2 Strain into a chilled cocktail glass and decorate with the orange slice.

363. Hawaiian Orange Blossom: Shake 2 measures gin, 1 measure Triple Sec, 2 measures orange juice, and 1 measure pineapple juice vigorously over ice until well frosted. Strain into a chilled wine glass. **Serves : 1**

364. Kentucky Orange Blossom: Shake 2 measures bourbon, 1 measure orange juice, and ¹/₂ measure Triple Sec vigorously over ice until well frosted. Strain into a chilled cocktail glass and dress with a slice of orange. **Serves : 1**

365. Magnolia Blossom: Shake 2 measures gin, 1 measure lemon juice, and 1 measure half and half cream vigorously over ice until well frosted. Strain into a chilled cocktail glass. **Serves : 1**

366. Apple Blossom: Pour 2 measures brandy, 1¹/₂ measures apple juice, and ¹/₂ tsp lemon juice over ice in a mixing glass and stir well. Half fill a small chilled tumbler with ice and strain the cocktail over it. Dress with a slice of lemon. **Serves : 1**

Depth Charge

Anise is a particularly unusual drink in that it turns cloudy when mixed with water but not when mixed with other alcoholic drinks, until the ice starts melting. So drink it slowly, with care, and watch it change.

Serves : 1

1 measure gin
1 measure Lillet
2 dashes Pernod
ice

1 Shake all the ingredients over ice until well frosted.
2 Strain into a chilled small cocktail glass.

Good Night Ladies

Sweetly scented with apricot and pomegranate, this is a great night cap for all cocktail lovers.

Serves : 1

$1/2$ measure gin
$1/6$ measure apricot brandy
$1/6$ measure grenadine
$1/6$ measure lemon juice
ice
slice of apricot or peach

1 Shake all the ingredients except the fruit well over ice and strain into a cocktail glass.
2 Finish with a slice of fresh apricot or peach on a cocktail stick.

Golden Dawn

Like the golden sun rising, the bright red of the grenadine peeps through the brandy and orange.

Serves : 1

¹/₂ measure gin
¹/₂ measure Calvados
¹/₂ measure apricot brandy
¹/₂ measure mango juice
ice
dash grenadine

1 Mix the first four ingredients together over ice.
2 Strain into a cocktail glass and gradually add a dash of grenadine so the color ripples through.

High Flyer

These two unusual liqueurs give a very aromatic and fruity cocktail.

Serves : 1

²/₃ measure gin
¹/₂ measure Strega
¹/₂ measure Van der Hum or Triple Sec
ice
orange or lemon peel

1 Stir the ingredients well over ice and strain into a cocktail glass.
2 Finish with a twist of peel.

(371) Pink Lady

Pretty in pink – they say! But this really is a truly great-tasting easy-drinking cocktail.

Serves : 1

1 measure gin
1 measure Cointreau
1/2 measure lemon juice
dash grenadine
ice
mandarin peel

1 Shake all the ingredients except the peel well over ice until frosted and strain into a chilled tall cocktail glass with a cube of ice.
2 Dress with a piece of mandarin peel.

(372) Jupiter One

Beautifully perfumed by the Parfait Amour – yet without the distinguishable purple color.

Serves : 1

2 tsp Parfait Amour
2 tsp orange juice
1 measure dry vermouth
1 measure gin
ice
lemon zest

1 Shake all the ingredients except the zest well over ice and strain into a cocktail glass.
2 Dress with pieces of lemon zest.

CLASSIC

Club

Groucho Marx is well known for claiming that he wouldn't want to belong to any club that was prepared to accept him as a member. This Club and its many associates are unlikely ever to have any shortage of willing members.

Serves : 1

dash yellow Chartreuse
cracked ice cubes
2 measures gin
1 measure sweet vermouth

1 Dash the Chartreuse over cracked ice in a mixing glass and pour in the gin and vermouth.
2 Stir well to mix and strain into a chilled cocktail glass.

374. Clover Club: Pour 2 measures gin, 1 measure lime juice, and 1 measure grenadine over ice with 1 egg white. Shake vigorously until well frosted. Strain into a chilled cocktail glass. **Serves : 1**

375. Grand Royal Clover Club: Make a Clover Club and substitute lemon juice for the lime juice. **Serves : 1**

376. Racket Club: Dash orange bitters over ice in a mixing glass and pour in 1 measure gin and 1 measure dry vermouth. Stir well to mix, then strain into a chilled cocktail glass. **Serves : 1**

378. Fifty Fifty: This is the original version of the Martini using equal measures of gin and vermouth. **Serves : 1**

379. Gibson: Decorate with 2-3 cocktail onions, instead of an olive. **Serves : 1**

380. Tequini: Pour 3 measures white tequila and ¹/₂ measure dry vermouth over cracked ice in a mixing glass. Add a dash Angostura bitters and stir well. Strain into a chilled cocktail glass and dress with a twist of lemon. **Serves : 1**

381. Dirty Martini: Shake 3 measures gin, 1 measure dry vermouth, and ¹/₂ measure brine from a jar of cocktail olives vigorously over ice until well frosted. Strain into a chilled cocktail glass and dress with a cocktail olive. **Serves : 1**

382. Saketini: Shake 3 measures gin and ¹/₂ measure sake. Shake vigorously over ice until well frosted. Strain into a chilled cocktail glass and dress with a twist of lemon peel. **Serves : 1**

383. Bellini Martini: Shake 1 measure gin with ¹/₂ measure brandy, ¹/₂ measure peach purée, and splash of sweet vermouth over ice until well frosted. Strain into an iced martini glass and dress with a slice of peach. **Serves : 1**

384. Chocolate Martini: Shake 2 measures vodka with ¹/₄ measure crème de cacao and 2 dashes orange flower water over ice until really well frosted. Strain into a martini glass rimmed with cocoa powder. **Serves : 1**

385. Montgomery: To 3 measures gin or vodka add 1 tsp vermouth, stir with ice, strain and add olive or lemon zest. **Serves : 1**

(377)

Martini

CLASSIC

For many, this is the ultimate cocktail. It is named after its inventor, Martini de Anna de Toggia, not the famous brand of vermouth! It can vary hugely, from the Original (see below) to the Ultra Dry, when the glass is merely rinsed out with vermouth.

Serves : 1
3 measures gin
1 tsp dry vermouth, or to taste
cracked ice cubes
green pitted olive

1 Pour the gin and vermouth over cracked ice in a mixing glass and stir well to mix.
2 Strain into a chilled cocktail glass and dress with a cocktail olive.

Dry Martini

Unlike the Martini, this drink has almost no vermouth in. Traditionalists will tell you simply to wave the bottle over the glass!

Serves : 1

1 measure London Dry gin

dash dry vermouth

a single olive or a twist of lemon

1 Stir the gin and vermouth over a handful of ice in a stirring glass.

2 Stir well and strain into a cocktail glass.

3 Dress simply with a single olive or a twist of lemon.

387. The Ultimate Classic Martini: This has almost no vermouth in at all! Simply put a dash of iced vermouth in an iced martini glass, swirl it round and discard, before pouring in the vodka or gin. **Serves : 1**

388. The Legend Martini: Shake together 2 measures iced vodka, 1 measure crème de mure, 1 measure fresh lime juice and a dash sugar syrup until really well frosted. Strain into an iced martini glass. **Serves : 1**

389. The Modern Martini: Now more popularly based on vodka and often flavored with fresh fruits. For instance, Pomegranate Martini – spoon the flesh of one very ripe pomegranate into a shaker and lightly crush or muddle. Add ice, 2 measures vodka or gin, a dash sugar syrup, and shake well. Strain into an iced martini glass. Other good fruits to try are kiwi, cranberry, pear and watermelon. **Serves : 1**

Martinez

The original recipe may go back to 1849 and was made with an American gin called Old Tom which was slightly sweetened.

Serves : 1
2 measures iced gin
1 measure Italian vermouth
dash Angostura bitters
dash maraschino
ice cubes
twist or slice of lemon

1 Shake all the ingredients except the lemon over ice until frosted.
2 Strain into an iced martini glass and add the lemon.

The Journalist

Practice makes perfect with this one, as the balance of sweet to dry is important to the final drink.

Serves : 1
1 1/2 measures gin
dash sweet vermouth
dash dry vermouth
1-2 dashes fresh lemon juice
2 dashes Triple Sec
2 dashes Angostura bitters
ice
cocktail cherry

1 Shake all the ingredients over ice until really well frosted.
2 Strain into an iced martini glass and dress with a cocktail cherry.

Karina

(392)

The mandarin liqueur comes through nicely to give this cocktail a good citrus tang.

Serves : 1
1 measure gin
1/2 measure Dubonnet
1/2 measure mandarin liqueur
juice 1/2 lemon
ice

1 Mix all the ingredients together in a large tumbler filled with ice and stir until the glass is frosted.

Dubarry

(393)

 CLASSIC

The Comtesse du Barry, the mistress of King Louis XV of France, was renowned for her extraordinary beauty. The guillotine brought an abrupt ending to her life – be careful not to lose your head over this delicious concoction.

Serves : 1
dash Pernod
dash Angostura bitters
2 measures gin
1 measure dry vermouth
ice
lemon peel twist

1 Stir the Pernod, Angostura bitters, gin and vermouth in a mixing glass with ice.
2 Strain into a chilled cocktail or wine glass and decorate with a twist of lemon.

394. Nell Gwynn: Pour 1 measure Triple Sec, 1 measure peach schnapps, and 1 measure white crème de menthe over ice in a mixing glass and stir well. Strain into a chilled cocktail glass and decorate with an orange peel twist. **Serves : 1**

395. Wallis Simpson: Pour 1 measure Southern Comfort into a chilled champagne flute, add 1 tsp powdered sugar and stir well until dissolved. Add a dash Angostura bitters and top up with chilled champagne. Dress with a slice of orange. **Serves : 1**

396. Not Tonight Josephine: Pour 1 measure Mandarine Napoleon, 1 measure Campari, and 1 measure brandy over ice and stir well. Strain into a chilled champagne flute and top up with chilled champagne. **Serves : 1**

397. Mrs Fitzherbert: Pour 1 measure white port and 1 measure cherry brandy over ice in a mixing glass. Stir to mix. Strain into a chilled cocktail glass. **Serves : 1**

Bartender

There is certainly an art to mixing and blending several different alcohols to give the best result. This classic has been much enjoyed by many generations.

Serves : 1

¹/₄ measure dry vermouth

¹/₄ measure Dubonnet

¹/₄ measure sherry

¹/₄ measure gin

dash Grand Marnier

ice

slice of mango or pineapple

1 Shake all five drinks together in a cocktail shaker with plenty of ice.

2 Strain into a cocktail glass and top with a slice of fruit.

(399)

Inca

The legendary lost gold of the Incas – the "sweat of the sun" to those sun-worshippers – inspired the name of this golden cocktail.

Serves : 1
1 measure gin
1 measure sweet vermouth
1 measure dry sherry
dash orgeat syrup (a non-alcoholic almond-flavored syrup)
dash orange bitters

1 Pour all the ingredients into a glass and stir. This is one that does not need to be chilled.

(400)

Pink Phantom

The classic combination of gin and Noilly Prat is sweetened with grenadine and a serious kick of absinthe.

Serves : 1
$1/2$ measure dry gin
$1/2$ measure Noilly Prat
2 dashes grenadine
2 dashes absinthe
ice
lemon juice

1 Stir ingredients over ice, strain into a cocktail glass and squeeze lemon juice over the top.

Salome

Dark, mysterious and very risqué – just like an Arabian dancer!

Serves : 1

$^1/_3$ measure gin
$^1/_3$ measure Dubonnet
$^1/_3$ measure dry vermouth
cherry or pecan nut to finish

1 Stir the ingredients together and pour into a chilled cocktail glass.
2 Finish with a cherry or floating nut.

Negroni

Count Negroni at the Bar Giacosa in Florence created this aristocratic cocktail, although, since then, the proportions of gin to Campari have altered.

Serves : 1

6 cracked ice cubes
1 measure gin
1 measure Campari
$^1/_2$ measure sweet vermouth
twist of orange peel

1 Put the cracked ice cubes into a mixing glass.
2 Pour the gin, Campari and vermouth over the ice and stir well to mix.
3 Strain into a chilled glass and dress with the orange twist.

403. Italian Stallion: Put 4–6 ice cubes into a mixing glass. Add a dash Angostura bitters over the ice and pour in 2 measures bourbon, 1 measure Campari, and $^1/_2$ measure sweet vermouth. Stir well to mix, then strain into a chilled cocktail glass and dress with a twist of lemon peel. **Serves : 1**

404. Genoa Vodka: Shake 2 measures vodka, 1 measure Campari, and 3 measures orange juice vigorously over ice until well frosted. Strain into a small chilled tumbler. Dress with a slice of orange. **Serves : 1**

405. Rosita: Put 4–6 ice cubes into a mixing glass. Pour 2 measures Campari, 2 measures white tequila, $^1/_2$ measure dry vermouth, and $^1/_2$ measure sweet vermouth over the ice. Stir well to mix, then strain into a small chilled tumbler and dress with a twist of lemon peel. **Serves : 1**

Mah-Jong

No Chinese games here, but you may not be walking in perfect straight lines if you drink too many!

Serves : 1
1 measure gin
1/4 measure Cointreau
1/4 measure white rum
ice
strip of orange peel

1 Stir all the ingredients over ice in a mixing glass and strain into a chilled small cocktail glass.
2 Dress with a piece of orange peel.

407

The Blue Bird

Orange and bittersweet, but not too strong.

Serves : 1
1 measure gin
3-4 dashes Angostura bitters
1-2 tsp orange Curaçao
maraschino cherry

1 Shake the ingredients together over ice and strain into a small cocktail glass.
2 Serve with a cherry on its stalk.

Jockey Club Special

A short cocktail with a good kick in its tail, but you can mellow it by serving on the rocks if you prefer!

Serves : 1

1 measure gin

$^1/_2$ measure crème de noyeau

good splash lemon juice

2 dashes orange bitters

2 dashes Angostura bitters

ice

1 Stir all the ingredients well over ice and strain into a cocktail glass.

409

Stressed Out

This well-iced cocktail will soon relax you and take away all the stresses of the day.

Serves : 1

1 measure gin, iced
$^1/_2$ measure green Chartreuse, iced
$^1/_2$ measure lime juice, chilled
dash absinthe, iced
syrup de gomme to taste
ice
twist of lime

1 Stir all the ingredients together over ice until well frosted.

2 Strain into a small cocktail glass filled with crushed ice and add a twist of lime.

410

Spring in the Air

It certainly looks like spring is on the way and has such a zing, it should make you feel like it too.

Serves : 1

1 measure gin
1 measure lime cordial
$^1/_2$ measure green Chartreuse
lime zest

1 Stir the ingredients over ice in a mixing glass and strain into a chilled cocktail glass.

2 Add one lump of fresh ice and sprinkle with lime zest.

411

Firefly

A light and frothy mixture that looks delicate and innocent – but watch out, there are three alcohols in this brew!

Serves : 1

1 measure gin
$^1/_2$ measure tequila
$^1/_2$ measure dry orange Curaçao
$^1/_2$ measure lemon juice
dash egg white
ice
lemon or orange peel

1 Shake all the ingredients well over ice until frosted.

2 Strain into a chilled cocktail glass and finish with a twist of lemon or orange peel.

413. Green Lady: Shake 2 measures gin, 1 measure green Chartreuse, and a dash of lime juice vigorously over ice until well frosted. Strain into a chilled cocktail glass. **Serves : 1**

414. Creole Lady: Pour 2 measures bourbon, 1 1/2 measures Madeira and 1 tsp grenadine over cracked ice in a mixing glass. Stir wellto mix, then strain into a chilled cocktail glass. Dress with cocktail cherries. **Serves : 1**

415. Lady: Shake 2 measures gin, 1 measure peach brandy, and 1 measure lemon juice over ice with 1 tsp egg white until well frosted. Strain into a chilled cocktail glass. **Serves : 1**

416. Blue Lady: Shake 2 1/2 measures blue Curaçao, 1 measure white crème de cacao, and 1 measure half and half cream over ice until well frosted. Strain into a chilled cocktail glass. **Serves : 1**

417. Shady Lady: Shake 3 measures tequila, 1 measure apple brandy, and 1 measure cranberry juice with a dash lime juice over ice until well frosted. Strain into a chilled cocktail glass. **Serves : 1**

418. Fair Lady: Shake 2 measures gin, 1 measure orange juice, 1 measure lime juice, and add 1 egg white with a dash strawberry liqueur vigorously until well frosted. Strain into a chilled cocktail glass. **Serves : 1**

(412)

White Lady

Simple, elegant, subtle, and much more powerful than appearance suggests, this is the perfect cocktail to serve before an al fresco summer dinner.

Serves : 1

2 measures gin
1 measure Triple Sec
1 measure lemon juice
cracked ice cubes

1 Shake the gin, Triple Sec and lemon juice vigorously over ice until well frosted.
2 Strain into a chilled cocktail glass.

Alexander

A creamy, chocolate-flavored, gin-based cocktail, decorated with grated nutmeg.

Serves : 1

1 measure gin
1 measure crème de cacao
1 measure half and half cream
cracked ice cubes
freshly grated nutmeg, to decorate

1 Shake the ingredients vigorously over ice until well frosted.
2 Strain into a chilled cocktail glass and dress with the nutmeg.

What the Hell

Cheer yourself up when you are at a loose end, or when everything seems to have gone wrong, with this simple but delicious concoction.

Serves : 1

cracked ice cubes
dash of lime juice
1 measure gin
1 measure apricot brandy
1 measure dry vermouth
twist of lemon peel

1 Put cracked ice cubes into a mixing glass.
2 Dash lime juice over the ice and pour in the gin, apricot brandy and vermouth.
3 Stir well to mix.
4 Strain into a chilled cocktail glass and dress with a twist of lemon peel.

421. Why Not: Put cracked ice cubes into a mixing glass. Dash lemon juice over the ice. Pour in 2 measures gin, 1 measure peach brandy, and 1 measure Noilly Prat. Stir to mix. Strain into a chilled cocktail glass. **Serves : 1**

422. Is This All: Shake 2 measures lemon vodka, 1 measure Triple Sec, 1 measure lemon juice, and 1 egg white over cracked ice until well frosted. Strain into a chilled cocktail glass. **Serves : 1**

423. What the Dickens: Pour 2 measures gin into a heatproof tumbler and stir in 1½ tsp icing sugar. Top up with hot water. **Serves : 1**

424. This Is It: Shake 2 measures gin, 1 measure Triple Sec, 1 measure lemon juice, and 1 egg white vigorously over cracked ice until well frosted. Strain the mixture into a chilled cocktail glass. **Serves : 1**

Silver Streak

This short drink can be made with either gin or vodka. Be sure both liquors are really cold and don't stir, just let the kümmel sink through the gin and then enjoy as a nightcap.

Serves : 1

1 measure gin or vodka, iced
1 measure kümmel, iced

1 Fill a small old-fashioned glass or tumbler with ice and pour in the gin or vodka.
2 Slowly pour on the kümmel and then drink before they become too mingled.

Vespers

A calming drink to enjoy in quiet solitude and repose and certainly not a drink to be rushed.

Serves : 1

1 1/2 measures iced gin
1 measure iced vodka
1/2 measure dry vermouth or Lillet
ice
lemon peel to garnish

1 Shake the first three ingredients over ice until frosted.
2 Strain into a frosted martini glass.
3 Add the lemon peel.

Balalaika

427

CLASSIC

A very lemony cocktail but it works well and you could always add the lemon gradually, to your taste.

Serves : 1

1/2 measure vodka, chilled
1/4 measure Cointreau, chilled
1/4 measure fresh lemon juice
piece of lemon
ice

1 Pour the three liquids into a small cocktail glass.
2 Stir gently, add a twist or piece of lemon and one ice cube.

Vodkatini

428

The celebrated 007 popularised the use of vodka as the base of the Martini, rather than gin, hence the Vodkatini is now widely accepted as an incredibly stylish and tasty alternative.

Serves : 1

1 measure vodka
ice
dash dry vermouth
a single olive or a twist of lemon

1 Pour the vodka over a handful of ice in a mixing glass.
2 Add the vermouth, stir well and strain into a cocktail glass.
3 Dress with a single olive or a twist of lemon.

Caiproska

429

This is a very fresh version of vodka and lime. If you find it too sharp, add a little more sugar to taste.

Serves : 1

1 lime, cut into 6 wedges
3 tsp powdered sugar
a really good slug of vodka
crushed or cubed ice

1 Put the lime wedges and sugar in a tumbler and mash them to release the juice and combine well with the sugar.
2 Pour on the vodka and add crushed ice to fill the glass. For maximum kick, drink through a straw!

1001 Cocktails

Peach Floyd

Shots look stunning in the right type of glass, but as they are for drinking down in one, keep them small and have everything really well chilled.

Serves : 1

1 measure peach schnapps, chilled
1 measure vodka, chilled
1 measure white cranberry and peach juice, chilled
1 measure cranberry juice, chilled

1 Stir all the ingredients together over ice and pour into an iced shot glass.

Vodka Zip

This mix relies on being really cold, so you could serve it over ice if you prefer.

Serves : 1

2 measures vodka
1 measure freshly squeezed lemon juice
scoop crushed ice
strip of lemon peel

1 Shake the vodka and lemon juice with half the crushed ice until well frosted.
2 Strain into an iced wine glass or large cocktail glass filled with more crushed ice.
3 Dress with a strip of lemon peel.

Metropolitan

The original Metropolitan was prepared with gin, but, in recent years, vodka has become the more fashionable short drink base. Cranberry is a new addition too.

Serves : 1

2 measures Kurrant vodka
1 measure Triple Sec
1 measure fresh lime juice
1 measure cranberry juice
orange peel

1 Shake all the ingredients over ice until well frosted.
2 Strain into a chilled cocktail glass.
3 Dress with a strip of orange peel.

Black Russian

History records only White and Red Russians. The omission of the Black Russian is a sad oversight. For a coffee liqueur, you can use either Tia Maria or Kahlua, depending on your personal taste – the latter is sweeter.

Serves : 1

2 measures vodka
1 measure coffee liqueur
4-6 cracked ice cubes

1 Pour the vodka and liqueur over cracked ice cubes in a small chilled highball glass.
2 Stir to mix.

Rule Britannia

Unusually pretty and clever, but it requires a few hours' forward planning to get these blue ice cubes ready in time. They melt quickly too.

Serves : 1

blue Curaçao
$^1/_4$ measure Campari
$^1/_2$ measure vodka
$^1/_4$ measure pink grapefruit juice
ice

1 Make two blue ice cubes with 1-2 tbsp water and 1-2 tsp Curaçao.
2 Freeze these well in advance.
3 Shake the rest of the ingredients together well over ice.
4 Strain into a chilled cocktail glass and add an ice cube at the last minute.

The AWOL

CLASSIC

As its name suggests, you won't last long drinking many of these in an evening!

Serves : 1

1 measure melon liqueur, iced
1/2 measure lime juice, chilled
1/2 measure vodka, iced
1/2 measure white rum, iced
ice

1 Stir all the ingredients briefly together over ice and strain into a chilled cocktail glass.

436

The Spray

If you can't find raspberry vodka, you can make your own simply by marinating about 10 berries in a bottle of vodka for only about 12 hours. Then remove the berries and the vodka is good enough on its own!

Serves : 1

1 measure raspberry vodka
1/2 measure framboise
1/2 measure Cointreau
3/4 measure cranberry juice
2 dashes orange bitters
1 dash lime cordial
ice
1 raspberry

1 Shake all the ingredients together over ice until frosted.
2 Strain into a chilled martini glass.
3 Dress with a fresh raspberry.

437

Silver Berry

This drink is perfect for one of those very special occasions – except that you really can't drink very many!

Serves : 1

1 measure raspberry vodka, iced
1 measure crème de cassis. iced
1 measure Cointreau, iced
edible silver paper or a frozen berry

1 Carefully and slowly layer the three liquors in the order listed, in a well-iced shot glass or tall thin cocktail or elgin glass.
2 They must be well iced first and may need time to settle into their layers.
3 Dress with the silver paper or a frozen berry.

438 Thunderbird

Enjoy the heady perfume of all these ingredients as you sip this iced delight.

Serves : 1

2 measures iced vodka
dash of Parfait Amour
dash of cassis
small piece of orange zest
one rose or violet petal

1 Pour the vodka into a frosted martini glass.
2 Add the other ingredients slowly and stir only once.

439 Full Monty

The expression "full monty" – meaning not holding anything back – has been around for a long time, but was given a new lease of life by the highly successful British film of the same title. However, you can keep your clothes on when drinking this.

Serves : 1

1 measure vodka
1 measure Galliano
cracked ice cubes
grated ginseng root (use root ginger if you can't find ginseng)

1 Shake the vodka and Galliano vigorously over ice until well frosted.
2 Strain into a chilled cocktail glass and sprinkle with grated ginseng root.

440. Back to the Future: Shake 2 measures gin, 1 measure slivovitz, and 1 measure lemon juice vigorously over ice until well frosted. Strain into a chilled cocktail glass. **Serves : 1**

441. Star Wars: Shake 2 measures gin, 2 measures lemon juice, 1 measure Galliano, and 1 measure crème de noyeau vigorously over ice until well frosted. Strain into a chilled cocktail glass. **Serves : 1**

442. Titanic: Shake 3 measures mandarin liqueur and 2 measures vodka vigorously over ice until well frosted. Half fill a chilled tumbler with cracked ice cubes and strain the cocktail over them. Top up with sparkling water. **Serves : 1**

443. Last Mango in Paris: Whizz 2 measures vodka, 1 measure framboise, 1 measure lime juice, 1/2 peeled, stoned and chopped mango, and 2 halved strawberries in a blender until slushy. Pour into a chilled goblet and dress with a slice of lime and a strawberry. **Serves : 1**

1001 Cocktails

Black Beauty

For a very different version, try it with one of the black vodkas which have recently appeared on the market. The dramatic color and subtle flavor are worth experiencing.

Serves : 1

2 measures vodka
1 measure black Sambuca
1 black olive

1 Stir the vodka and Sambuc with ice in a mixing glass until frosted.
2 Strain into an iced martini glass and add the olive.

Raspberrini

Wonderfully fresh tasting with a smell of summer that will take away all your cares...

Serves : 1

1 oz fresh or frozen raspberries
1 tbsp powdered sugar
1-2 drops fresh lemon juice
splash of framboise
ice cubes
2 measures vodka, well iced

1 Retain 2-3 raspberries to add later.
2 Crush the rest in a bowl with the sugar, lemon and framboise.
3 Strain well.
4 Pour the vodka into an iced martini glass and add the purée and reserved raspberries.

446. Strawberrini: As above, but use fraise instead of framboise and use lime juice. **Serves : 1**

447. Blackberrini: As above, but use cassis instead of fraise. **Serves : 1**

Spotted Bikini

A cheeky name for an amusing cocktail. It also tastes great, although you may like to add a little sugar to taste.

Serves : 1

2 measures vodka

1 measure white rum

1 measure cold milk

juice $^1/_2$ lemon

ice

1 ripe passion fruit

piece of lemon

1 Shake the first four ingredients over ice until well frosted.

2 Strain into a chilled medium cocktail glass and add the passion fruit, not strained, at the last minute so you see the black seeds.

3 Dress with a piece of lemon.

449

Perfect Love

This is the literal translation for an unusual purple liqueur flavored with rose petals, almonds and vanilla.

Serves : 1

1 measure vodka

$^1/_2$ measure Parfait Amour

$^1/_2$ measure maraschino

scoop crushed ice

1 Shake all the ingredients together over ice until frosted.

2 Strain into a chilled tall thin cocktail glass with more ice.

Ninetynine Park Lane

London's Park Lane was once a prestigious road of smart apartments, with only the very occasional bright neon light!

Serves : 1

1 measure vodka

1 measure Cointreau

2 measures orange juice

1 small egg white

few ice cubes

1/2 measure green crème de menthe

1 Shake the first four ingredients together over crushed ice.

2 Pour into a medium-sized cocktail glass or goblet over more crushed ice.

3 Shake or sprinkle on the crème de menthe.

Anouchka

Sambuca is liquorice flavored and therefore not to everyone's taste. However, used here with a dash of blackberry liqueur and the iced vodka, it's a great combination.

Serves : 1

1 measure vodka, iced

dash black Sambuca

dash crème de mure

a few blackberries

1 Pour the vodka into a chilled shot glass.

2 Add a dash of the Sambuca and then a dash of the crème de mure.

3 Dress with a few blackberries, fresh or frozen.

Crocodile

452

This is certainly a snappy cocktail with a bit of bite. However, it probably gets the name from its spectacular color – Midori, a Japanese melon-flavored liqueur, which is a startling shade of green.

Serves : 1

2 measures vodka
1 measure Triple Sec
1 measure Midori
2 measures lemon juice
cracked ice cubes

1 Pour the vodka, Triple Sec, Midori, and lemon juice over ice and shake vigorously until well frosted.
2 Strain into a chilled cocktail glass.

453. Alligator: Pour 2 measures vodka, 1 measure Midori, $1/2$ measure dry vermouth, and $1/4$ tsp lemon juice over ice and shake vigorously until well frosted. Strain into a chilled cocktail glass. **Serves : 1**

454. Melon Ball: Pour 2 measures vodka, 2 measures Midori, and 4 measures pineapple juice over ice and stir well to mix. Half fill a chilled tumbler with cracked ice cubes and strain the cocktail over them. Decorate with a melon wedge. **Serves : 1**

455. Melon State Ball: Pour 2 measures vodka, 1 measure Midori, and 2 measures orange juice over ice cubes and shake vigorously until well frosted. Strain into a chilled cocktail glass. **Serves : 1**

Golden Tang

456

Summery colors combine with the fall flavors of fruit and herbs to produce a delicious and refreshing mix.

Serves : 1

2 measures vodka
1 measures Strega
$1/2$ measure crème de banane
$1/2$ measure orange squash
cracked ice
cherry and orange slice

1 Shake first four ingredients together over ice until well frosted.
2 Strain into chilled glass and dress with a cherry and slice of orange.

Harvey Wallbanger

 CLASSIC

This well-known contemporary classic cocktail is a great party drink – mix it strong at first, then weaker as the evening goes by – or without alcohol for drivers and no one would know...!

Serves : 1

3 measures vodka
8 measures orange juice
2 tsp Galliano
ice cubes
cherry and slice of orange

1 Half fill a highball glass with ice, pour vodka and orange over the ice cubes, and float Galliano on top.
2 Garnish with a cherry and slice of orange.
3 For a warming variant, mix a splash of ginger wine with the vodka and orange.

Polynesian Pepper Pot

It may seem strange to make a sweet drink and then season it with pepper and spices, but there is a long and honorable culinary tradition of making the most of the slightly acerbic flavor of pineapple in this way.

Serves : 1

2 measures vodka
1 measure golden rum
4 measures pineapple juice
1/2 measure orgeat
1 tsp lemon juice
cracked ice cubes
1/4 tsp cayenne pepper
dash Tabasco sauce
pinch of curry powder

1 Pour the vodka, rum, pineapple juice, orgeat and lemon juice over ice in a shaker and add the cayenne and dash of Tabasco.
2 Shake vigorously until well frosted.
3 Strain into a chilled glass and sprinkle curry powder on top.

459. Polynesian Sour: Whiz 4-6 crushed ice cubes in a blender with 2 measures light rum, 1/2 measure guava juice, 1/2 measure lemon juice, and 1/2 measure orange juice until smooth. Pour the mixture into a chilled cocktail glass. **Serves : 1**

460. Polynesia: Shake 2 measures white rum, 2 measures passion fruit juice, 1 measure lime juice, and 1 egg white over cracked ice with a dash Angostura bitters until well frosted. Strain into a chilled cocktail glass. **Serves : 1**

(461)

Affinity

Some cocktails need to be stirred not shaken. Use a large glass with space for lots of ice to cool the cocktail quickly. Then strain immediately to avoid diluting the flavors.

Serves : 1

1 measure Scotch whiskey
1/2 measure dry vermouth
1/2 measure red vermouth
2 dashes Angostura bitters
few ice cubes

1 Pour the ingredients, in the order they are listed, over ice in a mixing glass.
2 Stir with a long-handled spoon.
3 Strain into a chilled cocktail glass.

(462)

Loch Lomond

Syrup de gomme was used long before we had mixers like ginger beer or tonic, so this may be where the idea stemmed from.

Serves : 1

1 1/2 measures Scotch whiskey
1 measure syrup de gomme
3 dashes Angostura bitters
ice

1 Shake well over ice and strain into a cocktail glass.

Barbican

CLASSIC

For a really stunning effect prepare these ice cubes well in advance. Simply put the black seeds from the passion fruit in a little lemon water and freeze overnight.

Serves : 1

2 measures Scotch whiskey
¹/₄ measure Drambuie
¹/₂ a passion fruit, strained to separate seeds from juice
seeds frozen in ice cubes

1 Shake the whiskey, Drambuie and passion fruit juice over ice until well chilled.
2 Strain into a chilled cocktail glass.
3 Finish with a passion fruit ice cube.

Highland Fling

Blended whiskey is best suited to cocktails – single malts should always be drunk neat or with a little added water. However, a throat-burning blend of whiskey will make a mixture closer to rocket fuel than a cocktail and no amount of additions will help.

Serves : 1

cracked ice cubes
dash Angostura bitters
2 measures Scotch whiskey
1 measure sweet vermouth
cocktail olive, to decorate

1 Put the cracked ice into a mixing glass.
2 Dash Angostura bitters over the ice.
3 Pour in the whiskey and vermouth.
4 Stir well to mix and strain into a chilled glass.
5 Dress with a cocktail olive.

465. Thistle: Put 4-6 cracked ice cubes into a mixing glass. Dash Angostura bitters over the ice and pour in 2 measures Scotch whiskey and 1¹/₂ measures sweet vermouth. Stir well to mix and strain into a chilled cocktail glass. **Serves : 1**

466. Beadlestone: Put 4-6 cracked ice cubes into a mixing glass. Pour 2 measures Scotch whiskey and 1¹/₂ measures dry vermouth over the ice. Stir well to mix and strain into a chilled cocktail glass. **Serves : 1**

467. Flying Scotsman: Put 4-6 crushed ice cubes into a blender, dash Angostura bitters over the ice and add 2 measures Scotch whiskey, 1 measure sweet vermouth, and ¹/₄ tsp sugar syrup. Blend until slushy and pour into a small chilled tumbler. **Serves : 1**

Rusty Nail

One of the great classic cocktails, so simple and very popular. It must be served on the rocks.

Serves : 1

cracked ice
1 measure Scotch whiskey
1 measure Drambuie

1 Fill an old-fashioned glass or low tumbler half full with ice.
2 Pour in the whiskey and Drambuie and stir well.

Robbie Burns

Don't just drink this on 25 January, it's far too good and should help you enjoy your haggis or other Scottish occasions!

Serves : 1

$^1/_2$ measure sweet vermouth
$^1/_2$ measure Scotch whiskey
$^1/_4$ measure Benedictine
finely grated lemon zest

1 Shake the liquids together gently and pour into a small unchilled liqueur glass or tiny tumbler.
2 Sprinkle with a little zest.

Whiskey Mac

This popular classic is enjoyed worldwide as a warming winter drink, so don't be tempted to chill the glass or the drinks.

Serves : 1

1¹/2 measures Scotch whiskey
1 measure ginger wine

1 Carefully pour ingredients into an old-fashioned glass and allow to mix but don't stir.

Godfather

Amaretto is an Italian liqueur, so perhaps the inspiration for this cocktail comes from Don Corleone, the protagonist in Mario Puzo's best-selling novel, unforgettably portrayed in the film by Marlon Brando.

Serves : 1

cracked ice cubes
2 measures Scotch whiskey
1 measure Amaretto

1 Fill a chilled highball glass with cracked ice cubes.
2 Pour in the whiskey and Amaretto and stir to mix.

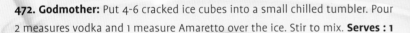

472. Godmother: Put 4-6 cracked ice cubes into a small chilled tumbler. Pour 2 measures vodka and 1 measure Amaretto over the ice. Stir to mix. **Serves : 1**

473. Godchild: Whizz 4-6 crushed ice cubes into a blender with 1¹/2 measures Amaretto, 1 measure vodka, and 1 measure half and half cream. Blend until smooth, then pour into a chilled champagne flute. **Serves : 1**

474. Goddaughter: Put 4-6 crushed ice cubes into a blender and add 2 measures apple brandy, 1 measure Amaretto, and 1 tbsp apple sauce. Blend until smooth, then pour the mixture, without straining, into a chilled goblet. Sprinkle with ground cinnamon and serve with a straw. **Serves : 1**

475. Godson: Put 4-6 cracked ice cubes into a chilled tumbler. Pour in 2 measures Amaretto and top up with orange juice. Stir well to mix and decorate with a slice of orange. **Serves : 1**

 # Los Angeles

The reason why this restorative potion is named for the City of Angels remains obscure. Perhaps because the earth quakes if too many are imbibed!

Serves : 1

2 measures Scotch whiskey

1 measure lemon juice

1 egg

dash sweet vermouth

cracked ice

1 Shake all the ingredients together over ice until well frosted.

2 Strain into a chilled cocktail glass.

 # Brooklyn

This mix gives an unusually bitter-sweet cocktail when finished off with the more unusual Amer Picon bitters.

Serves : 1

1 measure rye whiskey

1/2 measure sweet vermouth

dash maraschino

dash Amer Picon or Angostura bitters

cocktail cherry

1 Stir in a mixing glass with ice to chill, then strain into a chilled cocktail glass.

2 Add a cocktail cherrry to finish.

 # New Yorker

New York's favorite whiskey has seen the creation of many great cocktails – this is one of the quickest and best.

Serves : 1

2 measures Jack Daniels whiskey

1/2 measure fresh lime juice

1/2 measure grenadine

ice

orange peel

1 Shake the first three ingredients over ice well until frosted.

2 Pour into a chilled cocktail glass and serve with a twist of orange peel.

Alhambra

Even the smallest amount of apricot brandy adds an aromatic fruity finish to this full-bodied cocktail.

Serves : 1

1/2 measure Scotch whiskey
1/2 measure golden rum
1/4 measure sweet vermouth
1/8 measure apricot brandy
ice cubes
cherry

1 Mix the first four ingredients together in a mixing glass with ice.
2 Strain into a medium-size tumbler filled with ice and dress with a cherry.

Manhattan

Said to have been invented by Sir Winston Churchill's American mother, Jennie, the Manhattan is one of many cocktails named after places in New York.

Serves : 1

cracked ice cubes
dash Angostura bitters
3 measures rye whiskey
1 measure sweet vermouth
cocktail cherry, to decorate

1 Stir the liquids over cracked ice in a mixing glass and mix well.
2 Strain into a chilled glass and decorate with the cherry.

481. Manhattan Dry: Prepare as for the Manhattan but using dry vermouth and adding 2 dashes Curaçao. **Serves : 1**

482. Harlem: Shake 2 measures gin, 1 1/2 measures pineapple juice, and 1 tsp maraschino over ice, add 1 tbsp chopped fresh pineapple and shake vigorously until well frosted. Strain into a small chilled tumbler. **Serves : 1**

483. Broadway Smile: Pour 1 measure chilled Triple Sec into a small chilled tumbler. With a steady hand, pour 1 measure chilled cassis on top, without mixing, then pour 1 measure chilled Swedish Punsch on top, again without mixing. **Serves : 1**

484. Coney Island Baby: Shake 2 measures peppermint schnapps and 1 measure dark crème de cacao, vigorously over ice until well frosted. Fill a small chilled tumbler with cracked ice and strain the cocktail over it. Top up with soda water. **Serves : 1**

Twin Peaks

Bourbon, named after a county in Kentucky, must be made from at least 51 per cent corn mash and is the USA's most popular whiskey. It forms the basis of many more cocktails than its Scottish cousin.

Serves : 1

2 measures bourbon
1 measure Benedictine
1 measure lime juice
dash of Triple Sec
cracked ice cubes
slice of lime

1 Shake the bourbon, Benedictine, lime juice and a dash of Triple Sec vigorously over ice until well frosted.
2 Strain into a chilled highball glass and dress with a slice of lime.

486

Tricky Dicky

Bourbon fans may think this is a waste of good bourbon, but try this mix first – the result is quite different and a winner.

Serves : 1

1 measure bourbon whiskey
2 dashes white crème de menthe
2 dashes white Curaçao
1 dash Angostura bitters
1 dash syrup de gomme
ice cubes
mint leaves

1 Shake all the ingredients except the mint leaves over ice until frosted and strain into a chilled cocktail glass.
2 Dress with mint.

Black Bush

Bourbon whiskey has its own distinctive flavor, which is warm, rich and oaky.

Serves : 1
1/2 measure bourbon whiskey
1/2 measure sloe gin
ice
fresh cherry

1 Stir the ingredients together with ice.
2 Strain into a chilled cocktail glass and and dress with a fresh cherry.

488. Confederate Railroad: Shake 2 measures bourbon, 1 measure Southern Comfort, 1 measure orange juice, and a dash Triple Sec vigorously over ice until well frosted. Strain into a chilled cocktail glass. Dress with a slice of orange. **Serves : 1**

489. Queen of Memphis: Shake 2 measures bourbon, 1 measure Midori, 1 measure peach juice, and a dash maraschino vigorously over ice until well frosted. Strain into a chilled cocktail glass and dress with a wedge of melon. **Serves : 1**

490. Trashy Women: Shake 2 measures bourbon, 1 measure Pernod, 1 measure apple juice, and a dash Angostura bitters vigorously over ice until well frosted. Strain into a chilled cocktail glass and dress with a slice of apple. **Serves : 1**

491. Long Gone: Shake 2 measures bourbon, 1 measure Drambuie, 1 measure orange juice, and a dash orange bitters vigorously, until well frosted. Strain into a chilled cocktail glass. Dress with a slice of orange. **Serves : 1**

 # Blackberry Freeze

This cocktail does suit being really cold and adding the frozen berries in place of ice is quite a useful and attractive idea.

Serves : 1

1 measure bourbon whiskey

1 measure dry vermouth

$^1/_4$ measure lemon juice

$^1/_4$ measure blackberry liqueur

ice cubes or a few frozen blackberries

1 Shake all the ingredients except the berries together well over ice until frosted.

2 Strain into a cocktail glass and float in few frozen blackberries.

Dandy

CLASSIC

The fruit flavor added at the end is what gives this rich combination a special touch.

Serves : 1
$^1/_2$ measure rye whiskey
$^1/_2$ measure Dubonnet
dash Angostura bitters
3 dashes cassis
ice
few frozen berries

1 Mix the first four ingredients with ice and strain into an iced shot glass.
2 Dress with a berry or two.

Royalist

Presumably this drink derives its name from its bourbon base. Of the bourbon line of French kings, Louis XVI did not let it go to his head.

Serves : 1
1 measure bourbon
2 measures dry vermouth
1 measure Benedictine
dash peach bitters
cracked ice

1 Stir all ingredients together in a mixing glass until well frosted.
2 Strain into a cocktail glass.

Maple Leaf

One might expect a drink named for the national emblem of Canada to feature Canadian Club whiskey, but it owes its title to the maple syrup used as an ingredient.

Serves : 1

2 measures bourbon whiskey

1 measure lemon juice

1 tsp maple syrup

crushed ice

1 Shake all ingredients together over ice until well frosted.

2 Strain into a cocktail serving glass

Rolls-Royce

It's hardly surprising that several classic cocktails have been named after a famous marque. This version was created by author H E Bates in his popular novel *The Darling Buds of May*.

Serves : 1

cracked ice cubes

dash orange bitters

2 measures dry vermouth

1 measure dry gin

1 measure Scotch whiskey

1 Put the cracked ice cubes into a mixing glass.

2 Dash the bitters over the ice.

3 Pour the vermouth, gin and whiskey over the ice and stir to mix.

4 Strain into a chilled cocktail glass.

497. Rolls-Royce (second version): Put 4-6 ice cubes into a mixing glass. Pour 3 measures gin, 1 measure dry vermouth, 1 measure sweet vermouth, and $^{1}/_{4}$ tsp Benedictine over the ice. Stir well to mix, then strain into a chilled cocktail glass. **Serves : 1**

498. American Rolls-Royce: Shake 2 measures brandy, 2 measures orange juice and 1 measure Triple Sec over ice until well frosted. Strain into a chilled glass. **Serves : 1**

499. Golden Cadillac: Shake 1 measure Triple Sec, 1 measure Galliano, and 1 measure half and half cream vigorously over ice until well frosted. Strain the mixture into a chilled cocktail glass. **Serves : 1**

Old Fashioned

So ubiquitous is this cocktail that a small straight-sided tumbler is known as an old-fashioned glass. It is a perfect illustration of the saying, "Sometimes the old ones are the best."

Serves : 1

1 sugar cube
dash Angostura bitters
1 tsp water
2 measures bourbon or rye whiskey
cracked ice cubes
twist of lemon peel

1 Place the sugar cube in a small chilled old-fashioned glass, add a dash bitters and 1 tsp water.
2 Mash with a spoon until the sugar has dissolved, then pour in the whiskey and stir.
3 Add the cracked ice cubes and decorate with a twist of lemon.

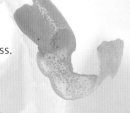

501. Brandy Old Fashioned: Make as above, replacing the whiskey with 3 measures brandy. **Serves : 1**

502. Old Etonian: Put cracked ice cubes into a mixing glass, add a dash of crème de noyeau and orange bitters, 1 measure gin and 1 measure Lillet. Stir to mix well, then strain into a chilled cocktail glass. Squeeze over a piece of orange peel. **Serves : 1**

503. Old Pal: Pour 2 measures rye whiskey over ice in a shaker with 1¹/₂ measures Campari and 1 measure sweet vermouth. Shake vigorously until well frosted, then strain into a chilled cocktail glass. **Serves : 1**

504. Old Trout: Pour 1 measure Campari and 2 measures orange juice over ice in a shaker. Shake vigorously until well frosted. Fill a tall glass with ice cubes and strain the cocktail over them. Top up with sparkling water and decorate with a slice of orange. **Serves : 1**

505 The Algonquin

Style and sophistication are the key to this drink from the famous Algonquin Hotel in New York.

Serves : 1

$^1/_2$ measure rye whiskey
$^1/_2$ measure dry vermouth
$^1/_4$ measure pineapple juice
ice cubes

1 Shake all the ingredients over ice until frosted.
2 Strain into an ice-filled old-fashioned glass.

506 Sazerac

Regarded by many people of New Orleans as the best cocktail in the world! Make it with cognac instead of rye for a truly spectacular drink.

Serves : 1

ice cubes
1 tsp sugar syrup or granulated sugar
3 dashes Angostura bitters
2 measures rye whiskey
$^1/_2$ tsp anise liqueur
strip of lemon peel

1 Fill a tumbler or cocktail glass with ice cubes to chill well.
2 Mix the syrup, bitters and whiskey until well blended.
3 Tip the ice out of the glass and swirl the anise liqueur round the inside of the glass to coat lightly and drain off any excess.
4 Pour in the whiskey mix.
5 Rub the strip of peel along the rim, add to the glass and then serve.

507 Commodore

This classic cocktail is short and sharp, with a good strong kick that will be sure to wake you up.

Serves : 1

4 measures rye whiskey
1 measure fresh lime juice
2 dashes orange bitters
sugar to taste
ice
strip of lime peel

1 Shake all the ingredients except the lime peel together over ice until well frosted.
2 Strain into a small tumbler or cocktail glass and dress with lime peel.

Cowboy

In movies, cowboys drink their rye straight, often pulling the cork out of the bottle with their teeth, and it is certainly difficult to imagine John Wayne or Clint Eastwood sipping delicately from a chilled cocktail glass.

Serves : 1

3 measures rye whiskey
2 tbsp half and half cream
cracked ice cubes

1 Pour the whiskey and cream over ice and shake vigorously until well frosted.
2 Strain into a chilled glass.

509. Cowgirl's Prayer: Pour 2 measures golden tequila and 1 measure lime juice over ice in a tall tumbler and top up with lemonade. Stir gently to mix and decorate with slices of lemon and lime. **Serves : 1**

510. OK Corral: Pour 2 measures rye whiskey, 1 measure grapefruit juice, and 1 tsp orgeat over ice and shake vigorously until well frosted. Strain into a chilled cocktail glass. **Serves : 1**

511. Navajo Trail: Pour 2 measures white tequila, 1 measure Triple Sec, 1 measure lime juice, and 1 measure cranberry juice over ice and shake vigorously until well frosted. Strain into a chilled cocktail glass. **Serves : 1**

512. Klondike Cooler: Put ¹/₂ tsp powdered sugar into a tall chilled tumbler and add 1 measure ginger ale. Stir until the sugar has dissolved, then fill the glass with cracked ice cubes. Pour 2 measures blended American whiskey over the ice and top up with sparkling water. Stir gently to mix and dress with a spiral of lemon peel. **Serves : 1**

Kicking Bull

Don't dilute with too much ice until you have tried this very interesting mix.

Serves : 1

1 measure tequila
1 measure rye whiskey
1 measure Kahlua
ice

1 Stir all the ingredients briskly in a large tumbler full of ice.
2 Serve immediately.

Vieux Carré

Originating in the old town of New Orlean's, this is a mean cocktail for serious occasions.

Serves : 1
1 measure rye whiskey
1 measure cognac
1 measure sweet vermouth or martini
4 dashes Angostura or Peychauds bitters
1 tsp Benedictine
ice

1 Mix all the ingredients in a cocktail shaker or tall glass.
2 Then pour into a small ice-filled tumbler or cocktail glass.

Baccarat

Cocktails have always been enjoyed at casinos and very much go hand in hand with the atmosphere of risk and gamble!

Serves : 1
1 measure Jack Daniels
1/2 measure Dubonnet
2 dashes cassis
ice

1 Shake all the ingredients well over ice until frosted.
2 Strain into a chilled cocktail glass.

 516

Irish Shillelagh

A shillelagh (pronounced shee-lay-lee) is a wooden cudgel, traditionally made from blackthorn. Undoubtedly, this is a cocktail that hits the spot.

Serves : 1
crushed ice cubes
2 measures Irish whiskey
1 measure lemon juice
¹/₂ measure sloe gin
¹/₂ measure white rum
¹/₂ tsp sugar syrup
¹/₂ peach, peeled, stoned and finely chopped
2 raspberries, to decorate

1 Put the crushed ice cubes into a blender and add the whiskey, lemon juice, sloe gin, rum, sugar syrup and chopped peach.
2 Blend until smooth. Pour into a small chilled highball glass and dress with raspberries.

517. Shillelagh: Shake 2 measures Irish whiskey, 1 measure dry sherry, 1 tsp golden rum, 1 tsp lemon juice, and a pinch of powdered sugar vigorously over ice until well frosted. Strain into a chilled cocktail glass and dress with a cocktail cherry. **Serves : 1**

518. Irish Eyes: Put 4-6 cracked ice cubes into a mixing glass. Pour 2 measures Irish whiskey and ¹/₂ measure green Chartreuse over the ice. Stir well. Strain into a chilled glass. **Serves : 1**

519. Colleen: Shake 2 measures Irish whiskey, 1 measure Irish Mist, 1 measure Triple Sec, and 1 tsp lemon juice vigorously over ice until well frosted. Strain into a chilled cocktail glass. **Serves : 1**

 520

Shamrock

Whether or not St Patrick was the inventor of Irish whiskey, this drink is a favorite on his feast day, 17 March.

Serves : 1
1 measure Irish whiskey
1 measure dry vermouth
3 dashes green Chartreuse
3 dashes crème de menthe
cracked ice

1 Stir all ingredients together in a mixing glass until well frosted.
2 Strain into a chilled cocktail glass.

Scarlett O'Hara

Appropriately a rich red covor with the warm undertones of Southern Comfort.

Serves : 1

2 measures Southern Comfort

2 measures cranberry juice

1 measure lime juice

ice

cranberry ice cubes

1 Prepare a few ice cubes in advance with cranberries frozen in them.

2 Shake the first three ingredients well over ice, then strain into a chilled cocktail glass.

3 Finish with a cranberry ice cube.

(522) # Rhett Butler CLASSIC

When Margaret Mitchell wrote her civil war epic, *Gone With the Wind*, she created an enduring romantic hero in Rhett Butler. His debonair charm and devil-may-care lifestyle were brought to life by the heart-throb film star Clark Gable.

Serves : 1

2 measures Southern Comfort

$1/2$ measure clear Curaçao

$1/2$ measure lime juice

1 tsp lemon juice

cracked ice cubes

twist of lemon peel

1 Shake the Southern Comfort, Curaçao, lime juice and lemon juice vigorously over ice until well frosted.

2 Strain into a chilled cocktail glass and dress with the lemon twist.

523. Ashley Wilkes: Crush 3 fresh mint sprigs and place in a chilled tumbler. Add 1 tsp sugar, a dash of lime juice, and 6 cracked ice cubes. Pour in 2 measures bourbon and 1 measure peach brandy and stir to mix. Dress with a fresh sprig of mint. **Serves : 1**

524. Melanie Hamilton: Shake 2 measures Triple Sec, 1 measure Midori, and 2 measures orange juice vigorously over ice until well frosted. Strain the mixture into a chilled cocktail glass. Dress with a wedge of cantaloupe melon. **Serves : 1**

Mount Etna

525

Not surprisingly this is a fairly explosive cocktail. It may not work first time but if it does handle with care!

Serves : 1

2 measures whiskey
2 measure pure orange juice
shell of $^1/_2$ lime, squeezed empty
$1^1/_2$ measures Cointreau

1 Mix the whiskey, orange, and lime juice in an old-fashioned glass.

2 Soak the lime shell in the Cointreau in a small pan for about 10 minutes.
3 Warm the Cointreau carefully over a low heat. Hold the lime shell in a large spoon, fill it with Cointreau and ignite carefully.
4 Lower immediately into the glass. Allow flames to finish and the glass rim to cool before drinking.

Whiskey Sour

526

Originating in the American South and using some of the best American whiskey, this classic can also be made with vodka, gin or other spirits.

Serves : 1

1 measure lemon or lime juice
2 measures blended whiskey
1 tsp powdered sugar or syrup de gomme
ice
slice of lemon or lime
maraschino cherry

1 Shake the first three ingredients well over ice and strain into a cocktail glass.
2 Finish with a slice of lemon or lime and a cherry.

527. Bourbon Sour: Substitute bourbon for the whiskey and decorate with an orange slice. **Serves : 1**

528. Brandy Sour: Substitute $2^1/_2$ measures brandy for the blended whiskey. **Serves : 1**

529. Boston Sour: Make a Whiskey Sour as above, add 1 egg white to the ingredients and decorate with a cocktail cherry and a slice of lemon. **Serves : 1**

530. Fireman's Sour: Shake 2 measures white rum, $1^1/_2$ measures lime juice, 1 tbsp grenadine and 1 tsp syrup de gomme over ice until well frosted. Strain into a cocktail glass and decorate with a cocktail cherry and a slice of lemon. **Serves : 1**

531. Strega Sour: Shake 2 measures gin, 1 measure Strega, and 1 measure lemon juice vigorously over ice until well frosted. Strain into a cocktail glass and decorate with a slice of lemon. **Serves : 1**

Bomb Squad

You could probably flambé this drink too, but enjoy the alcoholic tomatoes first.

Serves : 1

1 measure tequila

1 measure whiskey

1 measure vodka

few drops Tabasco sauce

ice

2 cherry tomatoes soaked in vodka

1 Mix the first four ingredients together and pour into an iced shot or cocktail glass.

2 Add an ice cube and finish with the tomatoes on cocktail sticks.

Whiskey Crusta

Crusta was the original word to mean crusting the rim of the glass. Tumblers and old-fashioned glasses are not often crusted but it works well with a short strong drink in a spacious glass.

Serves : 1

$^1/_2$ tsp powdered sugar

$^1/_2$ measure lemon juice

1 measure whiskey

1 tsp sugar syrup

1 tsp maraschino

dash orange bitters

slice of lemon or orange

1 Rub the rim of an old-fashioned glass with some of the lemon juice and then dip in sugar.

2 Stir all the ingredients over ice until well iced and strain into the crusted glass.

3 Dress with fruit.

Tartan Breeze

This will put some fire in your sporran ready for real Scottish Highland ice and winds.

Serves : 1

1 $^1/_2$ measures Scotch whiskey

$^1/_2$ measure apricot brandy

1 measure orange juice

dash Angostura bitters

ice cubes

1 Shake all the ingredients together well over ice.

2 Strain into a large cocktail glass with more ice and drink through a straw.

535 The Bacardi Cocktail

White rum, synonymous with the name Bacardi, is the base of many well-known cocktails. This one, of course, must be made with Bacardi.

Serves : 1

2 measures Bacardi rum
2 tsp fresh lime juice
dash grenadine
powdered sugar or sugar syrup to taste
ice

1 Shake the ingredients over ice until well frosted.
2 Strain into a shallow cocktail glass.
3 Drink with a straw.

536 Bacardi Crusta

Experienced cocktail makers will know that absinthe is an extra strong spirit – making this cocktail especially daring.

Serves : 1

1/2 measure lime juice
1 tsp granulated sugar
1 tsp absinthe
11/2 measures white rum
slice or wedge of lime

1 Rub a little lime round the rim of a cocktail glass and dip into the sugar to lightly crust the glass.
2 Set aside to harden. Stir the rest of the lime juice with the remaining ingredients over ice until well frosted.
3 Strain into the prepared glass and dress with lime.

537 Blue Hawaiian

An eye-catching drink with a tropical flavor. Be flamboyant with the fruit finish if you like – certainly on special occasions – or just leave this drink to stand out from the crowd.

Serves : 1

ice
2 measures Bacardi rum
1/2 measure blue curaçao
1 measure pineapple juice
1/2 measure coconut cream
small wedge of pineapple

1 Place a handful of ice into the cocktail shaker and pour in the liquids.
2 Shake all the ingredients vigorously over ice and strain into a cocktail glass or wine goblet.
3 Garnish with a small wedge of pineapple.

Casablanca

(538)

Named after the movie in 1942 and most probably enjoyed by its hero, the unforgettable Humphrey Bogart.

Serves : 1

3 measures white rum

4 measures pineapple juice

2 measures coconut cream

2 scoops crushed ice

pineapple to finish

1 Shake all the ingredients except the fruit together over ice and strain into a large cocktail glass with more ice if you wish.

2 Dress with pineapple.

Acapulco

(539)

This is one of many cocktails that has changed over the years. Originally, it was always rum-based and did not include any fruit juice. Nowadays, it is increasingly made with tequila, since this has become better known outside its native Mexico.

Serves : 1

2 measures white rum

1/2 measure Triple Sec

1/2 measure lime juice

1 tsp sugar syrup

1 egg white

10-12 cracked ice cubes

sprig of fresh mint, to decorate

1 Shake all the ingredients except the mint vigorously over ice until frosted.

2 Half fill a chilled highball glass with cracked ice cubes and strain in the cocktail.

3 Dress with mint.

Cuba Special

(540)

This is short, strong and sweet. Serve with plenty of ice to enhance all the flavors and sip slowly.

Serves : 1

1 1/2 measures white rum

1 1/2 measures pineapple juice

juice 1/2 fresh lime

1 measure Cointreau

crushed ice

cherries and a piece of pineapple

1 Shake all the ingredients together except the fruit over ice until well frosted.

2 Pour into a chilled medium cocktail glass or tumbler and finish with cherries and a piece of pineapple.

Cinderella

(541)

If the fairy-story heroine had been knocking back cocktails until the clock struck midnight, it's hardly surprising that she forgot the time and lost her shoe on the way home.

Serves : 1

3 measures white rum
1 measure white port
1 measure lemon juice
1 tsp sugar syrup
1 egg white
cracked ice cubes

1 Shake the rum, port, lemon juice and sugar syrup over ice with the egg white until well frosted.

2 Strain into a chilled glass.

542. Glass Slipper: Shake 3 measures gin and 1 measure blue Curaçao over ice until well frosted. Strain into a chilled cocktail glass. **Serves : 1**

543. Prince Charming: Shake 2 measures vodka, 1 measure apricot brandy, 1 measure apple brandy, and 1 tsp lemon juice over ice until well frosted. Strain into a chilled cocktail glass. **Serves : 1**

544. Peter Pan: Shake 1 measure gin, 1 measure dry vermouth, 1 measure peach brandy, and 1 measure orange juice over ice until well frosted. Strain into a chilled cocktail glass. **Serves : 1**

545. Tinkerbell: Shake 2 measures vodka, 1 measure cherry brandy, 1 egg white, and a dash grenadine over ice until well frosted. Strain into a chilled cocktail glass. **Serves : 1**

Bishop

(546)

It is strange how men of the cloth have gained a reputation for being enthusiastic about the good material things in life. Even Rudyard Kipling wrote about smuggling "brandy for the parson." It goes to show that spirituality is no barrier to spirits.

Serves : 1

dash of lemon juice
1 measure white rum
1 tsp red wine
pinch of powdered sugar
cracked ice cubes

1 Splash the lemon juice over the ice, pour in the white rum and red wine, and add a pinch of sugar.

2 Shake vigorously until frosted.

3 Strain into a chilled wine glass.

Fox Trot

Such a quick and easy cocktail should be made and enjoyed more often, just like the old-fashioned dance itself!

Serves : 1

juice of $^1/_2$ lemon or 1 lime
2 dashes orange Curaçao
2 measures white rum
ice
orange peel

1 Shake the first three ingredients well over ice and strain into a cocktail glass.
2 Add more ice if you wish and dress with a strand of orange peel.

Daiquiri

Daiquiri is a town in Cuba, where this drink was said to have been invented in the early part of the twentieth century. A businessman had run out of imported gin and so had to make do with the local drink – rum – which, at that time, was often of unreliable quality.

Serves : 1

2 measures white rum
$^3/_4$ measure lime juice
$^1/_2$ tsp sugar syrup
cracked ice

1 Pour the rum, lime juice, and sugar syrup over ice and shake vigorously until well frosted.
2 Strain into a chilled cocktail glass.

549. Derby Daiquiri: Blend 2 measures white rum, 1 measure orange juice, $^1/_2$ measure Triple Sec, and $^1/_2$ measure lime juice. Blend with ice until smooth, then pour, without straining, into a chilled cocktail glass. **Serves : 1**

550. Banana Daiquiri: Blend 2 measures white rum, $^1/_2$ measure Triple Sec, $^1/_2$ measure lime juice, $^1/_2$ measure half and half cream, 1 tsp sugar syrup, and $^1/_4$ peeled and sliced banana. Blend until smooth, then pour the mixture, without straining, into a chilled goblet and dress with a slice of lime. **Serves : 1**

551. Peach Daiquiri: Blend 2 measures white rum, 1 measure lime juice, $^1/_2$ tsp sugar syrup, and $^1/_2$ peeled, stoned and chopped peach. Blend until smooth, then pour, without straining, into a chilled goblet. **Serves : 1**

552. Passionate Daiquiri: Pour 2 measures white rum, 1 measure lime juice, and $^1/_2$ measure passion fruit syrup over ice and shake vigorously until well frosted. Strain into a chilled cocktail glass and decorate with a cocktail cherry. **Serves : 1**

Frozen Daiquiri

(553)

One of the great classic cocktails, the Daiquiri has moved on. It's not just mixed with fresh fruit or unusual ingredients, it's entered the twenty-first century with a whole new future as slushes take on a leading role in fashionable cocktail bars.

Serves : 1
crushed ice cubes
2 measures white rum
1 measure lime juice
1 tsp sugar syrup
slice of lime

1 Whizz the crushed ice, rum, lime juice and sugar syrup in a small blender until slushy.
2 Pour into a chilled champagne flute and decorate with the lime slice.

554. Frozen Pineapple Daiquiri: Whizz crushed ice in a small blender with 2 measures white rum, 1 measure lime juice, $1/2$ tsp pineapple syrup, and 2oz/60g finely chopped fresh pineapple until slushy. Pour into a chilled cocktail glass. Dress with pineapple wedges. **Serves : 1**

555. Frozen Strawberry Daiquiri: Whizz crushed ice cubes in a blender and add 2 measures white rum, 1 measure lime juice, 1 tsp sugar syrup, and 6 fresh or frozen strawberries. Blend until slushy. Pour into a chilled cocktail glass and dress with a strawberry. **Serves : 1**

556. Frozen Peach Daiquiri: Whizz crushed ice in a blender with 2 measures white rum, 1 measure lime juice, 1 tsp sugar syrup, and $1/2$ a peeled, stoned and chopped peach until slushy. Pour into a chilled cocktail glass and dress with a slice of peach. **Serves : 1**

X Y Z

(557)

Ice cool, this beautifully simple cocktail is very refreshing and morish.

Serves : 1
$1/2$ measure fresh lemon juice
$1/2$ measure white rum
$1/2$ measure Cointreau
cracked ice
slice of lime

1 Shake all the ingredients together over ice until well frosted.
2 Strain into a chilled cocktail glass and dress with a slice or twist of lime.

Peach Dreamer

Orange juice with a dangerous kick and a tantalising pink ripple.

Serves : 1

1 measure white rum
1 measure peach schnapps
3 measures fresh orange juice
1 measure grenadine
ice cubes and crushed ice

1 Shake the first three ingredients well over ice and pour on to crushed ice in a chilled cocktail glass.
2 Slowly pour a little grenadine into the glass before serving.

Palm Breeze

If only making one cocktail use fresh pineapple, then grate and sieve a little flesh to make real juice, the flavor is much nicer – although perhaps not quite as sweet.

Serves : 1

1 measure white rum
1 measure gin
2-3 measures pineapple juice
ice
slice of fresh pineapple

1 Shake all ingredients well over ice and strain into a cocktail glass.
2 Finish with a slice of fresh pineapple.

The Kicker

There is certainly some kick in this cocktail, but it will be best enjoyed if you ice all the ingredients well first.

Serves : 1

2 dashes sweet vermouth
$^{1}/_{3}$ measure Calvados
$^{2}/_{3}$ measure white rum
strip of apple peel

1 Shake the liquids well over ice and strain into a cocktail glass.
2 Dress with a curl of apple peel.

Port Flip

The sailor's favorite is a great winter warmer for anyone anytime, but be warned, it has a fair kick!

Serves : 1
1 egg
2 tsp powdered sugar
grated nutmeg or ground ginger
1 1/4 cups rum, port, brandy
or whiskey

1 Whisk the egg, sugar and nutmeg together.
2 Warm the rum slightly in a pan over a low heat and whisk in the egg mixture.
3 Serve when frothy and as warm or hot as you wish (do not heat too much or the egg may curdle).

Rum Swizzle

Cocktails were originally blended with swizzle sticks until the glass became frosted – hard work on the arms!

Serves : 1
2 measures dark rum
1 measure fresh lime juice
1/2 measure syrup de gomme
2-3 dashes Angostura bitters
1/2 cup crushed ice

1 Blend all the ingredients slowly in a blender until frothy and part frozen.
2 Pour into an iced tumbler with more ice to taste.
3 Serve with a swizzle stick.

Tongue Twister

Light or golden rum has a subtler taste than the dark rum, so it doesn't mask other liqueur flavors.

Serves : 1

1 measure light rum
$^1/_2$ measure coconut cream liqueur
$^1/_2$ measure orange Curaçao
1 measure lemon juice
ice
little grated nutmeg or cocoa powder

1 Shake the first four ingredients well over ice.
2 Strain into a chilled cocktail glass and sprinkle with grated nutmeg or cocoa powder to finish.

Contrary Mary

The type of rum makes all the difference to any cocktail, but especially here, where the result should be quite soft, not knock-out! So use a white or golden rum.

Serves : 1

$1^1/_2$ measures light rum
$1^1/_2$ measures pineapple juice
2 dashes grenadine
1 dash maraschino
ice
cherries

1 Shake the ingredients well together and strain into a cocktail glass.
2 Add ice to taste and dress with cherries.

St Lucy Smash

 CLASSIC

Not only does this taste wonderful, it also smells like a tropical island.

Serves : 1

2 segments lime
2 measures Mount Gay rum
$^1/_2$ measure raspberry liqueur
1 measure apple juice
few mint leaves, crushed
raspberries and slice of lime

1 Rub lime around the rim of an old-fashioned tumbler, then chill it.
2 Shake the lime and remaining ingredients over ice.
3 Pour into the chilled tumbler, adding more ice to taste.
4 Finish with a raspberries and a slice of lime.

Shanghai

(566)

Dark rum, with its stronger sweeter taste, perfectly suits the dryness of the anise flavored pastis.

Serves : 1

4 measures dark rum

1 measure pastis

3 measures lemon juice

2 dashes grenadine

cracked ice

lemon slice and maraschino cherry

1 Shake all the ingredients together except the fruit over ice until well frosted.

2 Strain into a chilled glass and dress with a slice of lemon and a cherry.

(567)

Apricot Lady

The mellow flavor of this cocktail is matched by its rich golden color, with all the fragrance of a tropical sunrise.

Serves : 1

2 measures golden rum

2 measures apricot brandy

1 measure fresh lime juice

3 dashes orange Curaçao

1 tsp egg white

small scoop crushed ice

apricot slice

1 Whizz all the ingredients except the fruit in a blender until slushy.

2 Strain into a chilled glass.

3 Dress with a slice of apricot and drink with a straw.

(568)

Green Devil

This mix of blue Curaçao and orange juice produces a truly wicked shade of green – but a great taste!

Serves : 1

lime juice
powdered sugar
1 measure light rum
¹/₂ measure blue Curaçao
1 measure orange juice
ice
slice of lime

1 Dip the rim of a large cocktail glass into lime juice and then into sugar to create sugar frosting. Set aside to dry.
2 Shake the ingredients well over ice.
3 Pour into the frosted glass and finish with a slice of lime.

(569)

The Devil

It doesn't taste quite as wicked as it sounds, but it has got a black streak in it that you may want to change to something sweeter, like a twist of fruit.

Serves : 1

1 measure dark rum
¹/₂ measure red vermouth
ice
black olive

1 Stir the ingredients together over ice.
2 Strain into a chilled cocktail glass and dress with a black olive.

(570)

Jamaica Joe

Rich and pungent Jamaica rum will mix surprisingly well with the sweetness of the Tia Maria and advocaat (an egg-and-brandy liqueur).

Serves : 1

1 measure Jamaica rum
1 measure Tia Maria
1 measure advocaat
cracked ice
dash grenadine
nutmeg to finish

1 Shake the rum, Tia Maria and advocaat together over ice until well frosted.
2 Add the grenadine.
3 Pour into a chilled cocktail glass and dust lightly with freshly grated nutmeg.

The Digger

This refreshing mix of citrus flavors has quite a kick so add plenty of crushed ice.

Serves : 1

2 measures brandy
1 measure Van der Hum or orange liqueur
1 measure syrup de gomme
3-4 grapefruit segments
crushed ice
long twist grapefruit peel

1 Whizz all the ingredients except the peel in al blender for 10-15 seconds.
2 Pour into a medium-size cocktail glass with extra ice.
3 Dress with peel and drink with a straw.

American Beauty

This sumptuous drink packs quite a punch, so beware of too many beauties – appreciate them slowly.

Serves : 1

1 measure brandy
1 measure dry vermouth
1 measure grenadine
1 measure orange juice
1 dash white crème de menthe
ice
2-3 dashes port

1 Shake all the ingredients except the port together over ice until well frosted.
2 Strain into a chilled cocktail glass and gently add the port so that it floats on top.
3 Drink immediately.

573

Millionaire

There are many versions of this cocktail, mainly dependent on the unusual contents of your cocktail cabinet.

Serves : 1
²/₃ measure apricot brandy
²/₃ measure sloe gin
²/₃ measure Jamaican rum
dash grenadine
juice ¹/₂ lemon or lime
ice
few blueberries

1 Shake all the ingredients except the berries well over ice and strain into an ice-filled cocktail glass.
2 Add a few blueberries at the last minute.

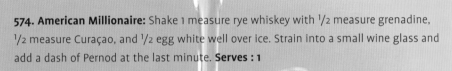

574. American Millionaire: Shake 1 measure rye whiskey with ¹/₂ measure grenadine, ¹/₂ measure Curaçao, and ¹/₂ egg white well over ice. Strain into a small wine glass and add a dash of Pernod at the last minute. **Serves : 1**

575. French Millionaire: Shake 1 measure brandy with ¹/₅ measure orgeat, ¹/₅ measure orange Curaçao, ¹/₅ measure crème de noyeau, and 2 dashes Angostura bitters over ice. Strain into cocktail glass. **Serves : 1**

576. Millionaire Cocktail: Shake ²/₃ measure bourbon with ¹/₃ measure Cointreau, 2 dashes grenadine, and 1 egg white over ice and strain into a cocktail glass. **Serves : 1**

577

First Night

A rich and warming concoction, ideal to calm the nerves before a first night – or to celebrate after...

Serves : 1
2 measures brandy
1 measure Van der Hum
1 measure Tia Maria
1 tsp cream
ice
grated or flaked chocolate

1 Shake all the ingredients except the chocolate together over ice.
2 Strain into a chilled cocktail glass and dress with a little grated chocolate.

Bosom Caresser

It would probably be unwise to investigate the provenance of this oddly-named cocktail – perhaps it is so called because it creates a pleasantly warm glow in the cockles of the heart.

Serves : 1

dash Triple Sec
cracked ice cubes
1 measure brandy
1 measure Madeira

1 Dash Triple Sec over cracked ice in a mixing glass.
2 Pour in the brandy and Madeira.
3 Stir well to mix, then strain into a chilled cocktail glass.

Roller Coaster

Perhaps not the cocktail to use your best vintage brandy in, as there are so many things added.

Serves : 1

2 dashes fresh lemon juice
powdered sugar
spiral of orange peel
1 measure brandy
1/2 measure dry orange Curaçao
3 dashes maraschino
1 dash Angostura bitters

1 Rub the rim of the glass with lemon juice and then dip it into sugar.
2 Leave to dry.
3 Place a long twist or curl of orange peel in the base of the glass and fill with ice.
4 Stir all the ingredients, except Angostura bitters, in a small glass of ice and strain into the prepared glass.
5 Top with the bitters at the last moment.

Between the Sheets

 CLASSIC

As the name of this cocktail always seems to imply romance and hints that the sheets in question are, at the very least, satin, make it for two people. Certainly, this delicious concoction is as smooth as silk.

Serves : 2

cracked ice

4 measures brandy

3 measures white rum

1 measure clear Curaçao

1 measure lemon juice

1 Put the cracked ice into a cocktail shaker.

2 Pour the brandy, rum, Curaçao, and lemon juice over and shake vigorously until frosted.

3 Strain into two chilled wine goblets.

581

Corpse Reviver

 CLASSIC

Not a morning-after reviver, more an end-of-a-hectic-day pick-me-up and one to get you in the mood for a party!

Serves : 1

cracked ice

2 measures brandy

1 measure apple brandy

1 measure sweet vermouth

1 Put the cracked ice into a mixing glass.

2 Pour the brandy, apple brandy, and vermouth over the ice.

3 Stir gently to mix.

4 Strain into a chilled cocktail glass.

582

Adam's Apple

Applejack in the USA, Calvados in France and apple brandy as a generic term – whatever you call it, it provides a delicious fruit flavor and a tempting aroma to this cocktail.

Serves : 1

2 measures apple brandy

1 measure gin

1 measure dry vermouth

dash yellow Chartreuse

ice

1 Pour the ingredients over ice in a mixing glass.

2 Stir well and strain into a chilled glass.

Antonio

(583)

This is mint with power! Serve it on the rocks to lessen the blow, or sip slowly and leisurely.

Serves : 1

¹/₃ measure brandy

¹/₃ measure gin

¹/₆ measure maraschino

¹/₆ measure crème de menthe

ice

1 Chill a small cocktail glass.

2 Mix all four ingredients together over ice and strain into the chilled glass.

3 Add more ice to taste

4 Serve with a straw.

Golden Medallion

(584)

Orange juice and Galliano bring out the rich fruitiness of the brandy.

Serves : 1

1 measure brandy

1 measure Galliano

1 measure fresh orange juice

dash egg white

cracked ice

grated orange zest

1 Shake the ingredients excetp the zest together over ice until well frosted.

2 Strain into a cocktail glass.

3 A little finely grated zest of orange peel sprinkled on top will set off the glowing color.

Tip: For an alternative garnish, pare a strip of peel from the orange – taking care to remove any white pith – fold the strip into a concertina and spear it on a cocktail stick.

Brasilica

(585)

This bright and cheeky little cocktail has a serious kick disguised by fresh fruity flavors.

Serves : 1

¹/₂ measure brandy

¹/₄ measure port

1 measure orange juice

ice

¹/₂ measure framboise or a few drops raspberry syrup

1 Shake the brandy, port, and orange juice well over ice.

2 Pour into a chilled glass and then slowly pour in the fruit liqueur or raspberry syrup so that some sits at the base of the glass.

3 Serve with a stirrer.

Which Way?

Aniseed-flavored pastis, such as Pernod, are firm favorites in today's cocktail bars and often form the basis of almost lethally strong drinks.

Serves : 1

1 measure Pernod

1 measure anisette

1 measure brandy

cracked ice cubes

1 Shake the Pernod, anisette and brandy vigorously over ice until well frosted.
2 Strain into a chilled wine glass.

587. TNT: Put 4-6 cracked ice cubes into a mixing glass. Pour 1 measure Pernod and 1 measure rye whiskey over the ice and stir well to mix. Strain into a chilled cocktail glass. **Serves : 1**

588. Victory: Shake 2 measures Pernod and 1 measure grenadine vigorously over ice until well frosted. Strain into a chilled tumbler and top up with sparkling mineral water. **Serves : 1**

589. Blanche: Shake 1 measure Pernod, 1 measure Triple Sec and $^1/_2$ measure clear Curaçao vigorously over ice until well frosted. Strain into a chilled cocktail glass. **Serves : 1**

590. Nineteen Pick-me-up: Shake 2 measures Pernod, 1 measure gin, $^1/_4$ tsp sugar syrup, and dash Angostura bitters vigorously over ice until well frosted. Half fill a tumbler with cracked ice cubes and strain the cocktail over them. Top up with sparkling water. **Serves : 1**

Brandy Alexander

A lovely creamy concoction that is popular as an after-dinner cocktail. The original was the Alexander, a gin-based drink.

Serves : 1

1 measure brandy

1 measure dark crème de cacao

1 measure heavy cream

ice

grated nutmeg

1 Shake the brandy, crème de cacao and cream vigorously over ice until well frosted.
2 Strain into a chilled cocktail glass and dress with a sprinkling of grated nutmeg.

B & B

(592)

Although elaborate concoctions are great fun to mix – and drink – some of the best cocktails are the simplest. B & B – brandy and Benedictine – couldn't be easier, but it has a superbly subtle flavor.

Serves : 1

1 measure brandy
1 measure Benedictine
cracked ice cubes

1 Pour the brandy and Benedictine over the ice in a mixing glass and stir to mix.
2 Strain into a chilled cocktail glass.

(593)

Moonraker

A powerful mix, this cocktail is more likely to fire you into orbit than to reduce you to trying to rake the moon's reflection out of a pond.

Serves : 1

cracked ice cubes
dash Pernod
1 measure brandy
1 measure peach brandy
1 measure quinquina (aperitif wine)

1 Put the cracked ice cubes into a mixing glass.
2 Dash Pernod over the ice and pour in the brandy, peach brandy, and quinquina.
3 Stir well to mix, then strain into a chilled highball glass.

594. Moonshot: Put cracked ice cubes into a mixing glass. Dash Tabasco sauce over the ice and pour in 2 measures gin and 3 measures clam juice. Stir well to mix, then strain into a chilled tumbler. **Serves : 1**

595. Moon Landing: Shake 1 measure vodka, 1 measure Tia Maria, 1 measure Amaretto, and 1 measure Baileys Irish Cream over ice until well frosted. Strain into a chilled shot glass. **Serves : 1**

596. Moonlight: Shake 2 measures apple brandy, 2 measures lemon juice, and 1/2 tsp sugar syrup vigorously over ice until well frosted. Half fill a small chilled tumbler with cracked ice cubes and strain the cocktail over them. **Serves : 1**

597. Moonrise: Put 1 1/4 cups medium dry cider into a saucepan with 1 tbsp brown sugar, a pinch of ground cinnamon and a pinch of freshly grated nutmeg. Heat gently, stirring until the sugar has dissolved. Pour into a warmed punch glass and stir in 1 measure apple brandy. Float 2 tsp half and half cream on top by pouring it gently over the back of a teaspoon. **Serves : 1**

Sangaree

Like Sangria, the name of this cocktail is derived from the Spanish word for blood and it was originally made with wine. Nowadays, it is more usually made with a spirit base, but whatever is used, it is invariably flavored with fresh nutmeg.

Serves : 1

6 cracked ice cubes

2 measures brandy

1 measure sugar syrup

soda water

1 tsp port

pinch of freshly grated nutmeg

1 Put ice cubes into a chilled highball glass.
2 Pour over the brandy and sugar syrup, then top up with soda water.
3 Stir gently to mix.
4 Float the port on top by pouring it gently over the back of a teaspoon and sprinkle with nutmeg.

599. Savoy Sangaree: Put 6 cracked ice cubes into a mixing glass, pour in 1 measure port, 1 tsp powdered sugar, and stir until dissolved. Strain into a chilled cocktail glass and sprinkle with freshly grated nutmeg. **Serves : 1**

600. Whiskey Sangaree: Put cracked ice into a chilled tumbler. Pour on 2 measures bourbon and 1 tsp sugar syrup and top up with soda water. Stir gently to mix, then float 1 tbsp ruby port on top. Sprinkle with freshly grated nutmeg. **Serves : 1**

601. Scotch Sangaree: Put 1 tsp clear honey in a chilled tumbler with a little sparkling water. Stir until dissolved. Add cracked ice, 2 measures Scotch whiskey and top up with sparkling water. Stir gently to mix, then decorate with a lemon twist and sprinkle with freshly grated nutmeg. **Serves : 1**

602. Gin Sangaree: Put cracked ice cubes into a chilled tumbler. Pour 2 measures gin and $1/2$ tsp sugar syrup over the ice, top up with sparkling water. Stir gently to mix, then float 1 tbsp port on top. Sprinkle with freshly grated nutmeg. **Serves : 1**

(603)

Tuscan Dessert

Italian brandies have their own character and delicious flavor, like this Tuscan speciality.

Serves : 1

2 measures Tuaca brandy

4 measures apple juice

1/2 measure lemon juice

1 tsp brown sugar

ice

pinch cinnamon

1 Shake all the ingredients except the cinnamon well over ice and strain into a chilled tumbler.

2 Add more ice to taste and sprinkle with cinnamon.

(604)

FBR

A number of cocktails are known simply by initials. In this case, FBR stands for Frozen Brandy and Rum. Others seem to be quite obscure and, in one or two instances, slightly naughty.

Serves : 1

6–8 crushed ice cubes

2 measures brandy

1^1/2 measures white rum

1 tbsp lemon juice

1 tsp sugar syrup

1 egg white

1 Put the crushed ice, brandy, rum, lemon juice, sugar syrup and egg white into a blender.

2 Blend until slushy and pour into a chilled highball glass.

605. KGB (presumably, Komityet Gosudarstvyennoi Byezopasnosti): Shake 1^1/2 measures gin and 1/2 measure Kummel over ice with a dash of apricot brandy vigorously until well frosted. Strain into a chilled cocktail glass. **Serves : 1**

606. MQS (Mary Queen of Scots): Rub the rim of a chilled cocktail glass with a wedge of lemon, then dip into powdered sugar to frost. Put 4-6 cracked ice cubes into a mixing glass. Pour 2 measures Scotch whiskey, 1 measure Drambuie and 1 measure green Chartreuse over the ice and stir to mix. Strain into the prepared glass. **Serves : 1**

607. BVD (Brandy, Vermouth and Dubonnet): Put 4-6 cracked ice cubes into a mixing glass. Pour 1 measure each of brandy, dry vermouth and Dubonnet over the ice. Stir to mix and strain into a chilled cocktail glass. Although it retains the same name, a modern BVD contains 1 measure each of white rum, gin and dry vermouth. **Serves : 1**

Golden Galleon

The deep yellows of Galliano and passion fruit make sure this cocktail is both a rich golden color and good fruity flavor.

Serves : 1
1 measure brandy
1 measure Galliano
1 measure passion fruit juice
dash lemon juice
ice cubes

1 Stir all the ingredients together well in a stirring glass.
2 Strain into an ice-filled tumbler and add a stirrer.

Princess

No particular princess is specified, although a number of other cocktails are named after queens and princes. Perhaps drinking this makes everyone feel like royalty.

Serves : 1
2 tsp chilled half and half cream
1 tsp powdered sugar
2 measures chilled apricot brandy

1 Pour the cream into a tiny bowl and stir in the sugar.
2 Pour the apricot brandy into a chilled liqueur glass and float the sweetened cream on top by pouring it over the back of a teaspoon.

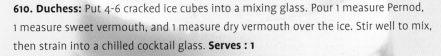

610. Duchess: Put 4-6 cracked ice cubes into a mixing glass. Pour 1 measure Pernod, 1 measure sweet vermouth, and 1 measure dry vermouth over the ice. Stir well to mix, then strain into a chilled cocktail glass. **Serves : 1**

611. Duke: Shake 1 measure Triple Sec, $1/2$ measure lemon juice, and $1/2$ measure orange juice with 1 egg white and a dash of maraschino vigorously over ice until well frosted. Strain into a chilled wine glass. Top up with chilled champagne or sparkling wine. **Serves : 1**

612. Grand Duchess: Put 4-6 cracked ice cubes into a mixing glass. Pour 2 measures vodka, 1 measure Triple Sec, 3 measures cranberry juice, and 2 measures orange juice over the ice. Stir well to mix. Half fill a small chilled tumbler with cracked ice cubes and strain the cocktail over them. **Serves : 1**

 (613)

Santa Maria

This combination is sharp and sweet, so serve well iced or over ice if you like to soften the sharpness.

Serves : 1

1 measure brandy
1 measure Triple Sec
1 measure lemon juice
ice
twist of orange peel

1 Shake all the ingredients except the peel together over ice until frosted.
2 Pour into a chilled cocktail glass and finish with a twist of orange peel.

 (614)

Classic Cocktail

 CLASSIC

It cannot lay claim to being the first or even the only classic, but it has all the characteristic hallmarks of sophistication associated with cocktails.

Serves : 1

wedge of lemon
1 tsp powdered sugar
4-6 cracked ice cubes
2 measures brandy
1/2 measure clear Curaçao
1/2 measure maraschino
1/2 measure lemon juice
lemon peel twist, to decorate

1 Rub the rim of a chilled cocktail glass with the lemon wedge and then dip in the sugar to frost.
2 Shake the brandy, Curaçao, maraschino and lemon juice vigorously over ice until well frosted.
3 Strain into the frosted glass and decorate with the lemon twist.

615. Tequila Cocktail: Put cracked ice into a cocktail shaker with a dash Angostura bitters, 3 measures golden tequila, 1 measure lime juice and 1/2 measure grenadine. Shake vigorously until well frosted, then strain into a chilled cocktail glass. **Serves : 1**

616. Brandy Cocktail: Put cracked ice into a cocktail shaker with a dash Angostura bitters, 2 measures brandy and 1/2 tsp sugar syrup. Shake vigorously until well frosted, then strain into a chilled cocktail glass and decorate with a twist of lemon. **Serves : 1**

Sidecar

Cointreau is the best-known brand of the orange-flavored liqueur, or you could use Triple Sec. It is drier and stronger than Curaçao and is always colorless.

Serves : 1

2 measures brandy

1 measure Triple Sec

1 measure lemon juice

4-6 cracked ice cubes

orange peel twist, to decorate

1 Put the ice into a cocktail shaker.

2 Pour the brandy, Triple Sec and lemon juice over ice and shake vigorously until a frost forms.

3 Strain into a chilled glass and dress with twist of orange peel .

618. Champagne Sidecar: Make as above but strain into a chilled flute and top it up with chilled champagne. **Serves : 1**

619. Chelsea Sidecar: Pour 2 measures gin, 1 measure Triple Sec, and 1 measure lemon juice over ice and shake vigorously until well frosted. Strain into a chilled cocktail glass. Dress with a twist of lemon peel. **Serves : 1**

620. Boston Sidecar: Pour 1 1/2 measures white rum, 1/2 measure brandy, 1/2 measure Triple Sec, and 1/2 measure lemon juice over ice and shake vigorously until well frosted. Strain into a chilled cocktail glass and decorate with twist of orange peel. **Serves : 1**

621. Polish Sidecar: Pour 2 measures gin, 1 measure blackberry brandy, and 1 measure lemon juice over ice, shake vigorously until well frosted. Strain into a chilled cocktail glass. Decorate with a fresh blackberry. **Serves : 1**

Caesarini

Eggs are often used in cocktails, the yolks to enrich and give thickness to the drink, and the whisked up whites to give a stunning frothy effect.

Serves : 1

1 1/2 measures brandy

1/2 measure orange Curaçao

1 egg yolk

2 dashes grenadine

1 Shake the ingredients well over ice and strain into a medium-size cocktail glass.

623 Cherry Blossom

Cherry blossom is used to make a pretty, pink scented liqueur in Japan. This is not quite so subtle or scented, but well worth trying.

Serves : 1
2/3 measure brandy
3/5 measure cherry brandy
dash grenadine
dash Curaçao
dash lemon juice
ice

1 Shake all the ingredients together over ice and strain into a frosted cocktail glass.

624 Cherry Brandy Fix

A fix is quick and easy to prepare directly in the glass. Be sure to use plenty of ice for best effect.

Serves : 1
1 tsp powdered sugar
1 tsp water
juice of 1/2 lemon
1/2 measure cherry brandy
1 measure brandy
ice
slice of lemon

1 Mix the sugar and water in the base of a small tumber.
2 Stir in the lemon juice and brandies. Fill up with ice and stir slowly.
3 Dress with lemon.

Huntsman

If you're in need of Dutch courage, this will do the trick, and revive you at the end of the day, too.

Serves : 1
2 measures cognac
cracked ice
splash Benedictine
soda water

1 Stir the cognac over ice in an old-fashioned tumbler until well chilled.
2 Add a splash of Benedictine and soda water to taste.

626

Pisco Sour

This is the national drink of Chile and Peru – a cooling drink ideal for the heat of South American summers, but deceptively strong.

Serves : 1
2 measures Pisco
1 measure lemon juice
1 tsp powdered sugar
dash orange bitters (optional)
egg white (optional)
cracked ice

1 Shake all ingredients well over ice until frosted and strain into glasses.
2 The egg white is optional, but it does help to bind the flavors together and also improves the drink's appearance.

Tip: Gran Pisco, the driest (and strongest) version, is recommended.

 # Grandma's Surprise

We all know Grandma loves sherry, especially on the quiet, so this one hidden in fresh orange juice will really please her!

Serves : 1

1/2 measure cream sherry
1/2 measure medium dry vermouth
dash Angostura bitters
squeeze fresh orange juice
strip of peel

1 Stir the sherry and vermouth together with ice in a small tumbler.
2 Add a dash of Angostura bitters.
3 Top up with orange juice and a piece of peel.

 # Bamboo

This combination of sherry and vermouth produces a drink that really is almost bamboo or straw colored. It is also a light and easy cocktail, especially if well chilled.

Serves : 1

1 1/2 measures sherry
1 1/2 measures dry vermouth
1 dash orange bitters
ice
twist lemon peel

1 Chill a mixing glass.
2 Stir in the ingredients with a few ice cubes until chilled.
3 Strain into a chilled cocktail glass and dress with a twist of lemon.

 # Greenbriar

The origin of this potion is obscure. It may be named from the Greenbrier district of West Virginia, USA, one of the homes of the Mint Julep.

Serves : 1

2 measures dry sherry
1 measure dry vermouth
dash peach bitters
cracked ice
sprig of mint to garnish

1 Stir the ingredients together over ice in a wine glass until well chilled.
2 Dress with the mint.

Santa Vittoria

Dedicate this to any victorious match you have recently watched and enjoy the success all over again.

Serves : 1

1 measure Cinzano rosso

1 measure gin

1 measure fresh orange juice

1/4 measure Cointreau

ice

rose petals

1 Shake the first four ingredients well over ice and strain into a chilled cocktail glass.
2 Top with petals.

Raffles

A popular cocktail from colonial days, before tonic stole the show.

Serves : 1

1 measure white vermouth

1/4 measure gin

1/4 measure Campari

ice

slice of orange

1 Stir the ingredients over ice in a chilled medium tumbler.
2 Squeeze in a slice of orange and leave it in the glass.

632 Adonis

The sherry you choose makes all the difference to this drink, be it dry, sweet or the slightly nutty medium-sweet amontillado

Serves : 1

1 measure sherry

1/2 measure red vermouth

ice

dash orange bitters

orange peel

1 Stir the ingredients over ice in a chilled medium tumbler.

2 Dress with the orange peel.

633 Washington DC

This is a surprisingly dry drink until the sugar from the rim kicks in, but you may prefer it without.

Serves : 1

few drops cherry brandy

1 tbsp powdered sugar

2 dashes Angostura bitters

2 dashes syrup de gomme

1 measure dry vermouth

1/2 measure brandy

ice

maraschino cherry

1 Brush the rim of a shallow cocktail glass with the cherry brandy and dip in sugar.

2 Leave to dry.

3 Shake ingredients well together, strain into cocktail glass and finish with a large cube of ice and a cherry.

Bullfrog

Fresh lemon is so important in cocktails, especially when it is one of the key ingredients, so look for really fresh unwaxed lemons and keep them in a warm place to encourage easier juicing.

Serves : 1

1 measure dry vermouth

1 measure Triple sec

1 measure lemon juice

ice

green cherry and slices of lime

1 Shake all the ingredients except the fruit well over ice until frosted.

2 Strain into a chilled cocktail glass and finish with a green cherry and slices of lime.

Sherry Cobbler

A long drink made with syrup and fresh fruit garnishes, Sherry Cobbler is the original, but there are now numerous and often more potent variations.

Serves : 1
crushed ice
¹/₄ tsp sugar syrup
¹/₄ tsp clear Curaçao
4 measures amontillado sherry
pineapple wedges and twist of lemon peel

1 Fill a wine glass with crushed ice.
2 Add the sugar syrup and Curaçao and stir until frosted.
3 Pour in the sherry and stir well.
4 Dress with pineapple wedges and a twist of lemon peel.

636. Port Wine Cobbler: Put 1 tsp powdered sugar into a chilled wine glass and add 2 measures sparkling water. Stir until the sugar has dissolved. Fill the glass with cracked ice and pour in 3 measures ruby port. Dress with a slice of orange and a cocktail cherry. **Serves : 1**

637. Bourbon Cobbler: Put 1 tsp powdered sugar into a tall, chilled glass and dash lemon juice over it. Add 6 cracked ice cubes and pour in 2 measures bourbon and 2 measures Southern Comfort. Top up with soda water and stir to mix. Dress with a peach slice. **Serves : 1**

638. Brandy Cobbler: Put 1 tsp powdered sugar into a small chilled tumbler and add 3 measures sparkling water. Stir until the sugar has dissolved, then fill the glass with cracked ice. Pour in 2 measures brandy and stir well. Dress with a slice of lemon and a cocktail cherry. **Serves : 1**

639. Rum Cobbler: Put 1 tsp powdered sugar into a chilled goblet. Add 2 measures sparkling water and stir until the sugar has dissolved. Fill the glass with cracked ice and pour in 2 measures white rum. Stir well and dress with a lime slice and an orange slice. **Serves : 1**

Rembrandt

A quick and simple drink to rival Kir any day, but it may be quite sweet for some, so a drop of lemon juice will help.

Serves : 1
lemon juice
powdered sugar
1/2 measure apricot brandy
few drops of lemon juice (optional)
1 glass dry white wine, chilled

1 Dip the rim of a wine glass into a little lemon juice, then into the sugar. Set aside to dry.
2 Pour the brandy into base of the glass and add lemon juice to taste.
3 Top with wine so the brandy swirls round the glass.

Sherry Nights

Sherry is not often used in cocktails – perhaps there was never any to spare. Now, however, it is drunk less neat but mixed more in intriguing combinations like this one.

Serves : 1
dash egg white or fruit juice
powdered sugar
1 tsp finely grated zest of orange
1 measure medium sherry
1/2 measure whiskey
1 measure orange juice
2 dashes orange Curaçao
ice cubes

1 Dip the rim of a medium-size cocktail glass into a little beaten egg white, or lemon juice, then into the sugar and orange zest mixed. Put aside to set.
2 Whizz all the rest of the ingredients together in a blender for 10 seconds.
3 Pour into the prepared cocktail glass with more ice and serve with a straw.

Margarita

This cocktail, attributed to Francisco Morales and invented in 1942 in Mexico, is a more civilised version of the original way to drink tequila – lick of salt from the back of your hand, suck of lime juice and a shot of tequila!

Serves : 1

lime wedge

coarse salt

3 measures white tequila

1 measure Triple Sec or Cointreau

2 measures lime juice

cracked ice cubes

slice of lime, to decorate

1 Rub the rim of a chilled cocktail glass with the lime wedge and then dip in a saucer of coarse salt to frost.

2 Shake the tequila, Triple Sec and lime juice vigorously over cracked ice until well frosted.

3 Strain into the prepared glass and dress with lime.

 643

Tequila Steeler

Rich creamy coconut helps to smooth this fiery combination, but don't be fooled by the soft baby pink color!

Serves : 1

1 measure tequila

1/2 measure white rum

1/2 measure vodka

1/4 measure coconut cream

dash lime juice

few drops grenadine

ice

flower or petals

strips of lime peel

1 Shake the first six ingredients well together over ice.

2 Pour into a chilled glass and finish with a flower or petals and a strip of lime peel.

(644)

Tequila Shot

 CLASSIC

According to custom this is the only way to drink neat tequila. It is often described as being smooth and tart, so adding lime juice and salt may sound contradictory, but it works!

Serves : 1
pinch salt
1 measure gold tequila
wedge of lime

1 Put the salt at the base of your thumb, between thumb and forefinger.
2 Hold the lime wedge in the same hand.
3 Hold the shot in the other hand.
4 Lick the salt, down the tequila and suck the lime.

(645)

Bombshell

Tequila will give any cocktail a good kick, but this concoction is really not as strong as its name implies!

Serves : 1
2 measures dry Marsala
1 measure tequila
splash Campari
splash cherry brandy
piece of lemon

1 Mix the ingredients straight into a small tumbler or cocktail glass with ice.
2 Finish with a piece of lemon.

Teaser

Don't be tempted into thinking this looks like a refreshing glass of frosted juice!

Serves : 1
1 measure tequila
1 measure orange liqueur
1 measure fresh lime juice
1 dash egg white
ice
lime slice or twist

1 Shake all the ingredients together except the lime slice well over ice until frosted.
2 Pour into a chilled cocktail glass and finish with a twist or slice of lime and an ice cube.

Brave Bull

Spain's historical associations with Mexico has left many legacies – not least a taste for bullfighting – although whether this cocktail is named in tribute to the animal or because it makes the drinker proverbially brave is anyone's guess.

Serves : 1
2 measures white tequila
1 measure Tia Maria
cracked ice cubes
spiral of lemon peel

1 Pour the tequila and Tia Maria over cracked ice in mixing glass and stir well to mix.
2 Strain into a chilled goblet and dress with lemon peel.

648 Carolina

Some cocktails, such as this, require the mellow flavor of the golden, aged tequilas.

Serves : 1

3 measures golden tequila
1 tsp grenadine
1 tsp vanilla essence
1 measure half and half cream
cracked ice cubes
1 egg white
cinnamon
cocktail cherry

1 Pour the tequila, grenadine, vanilla, and cream over ice in a shaker and add the egg white.
2 Shake vigorously until frosted. Strain into a chilled cocktail glass.
3 Sprinkle with cinnamon and dress with a cocktail cherry.

649 Mad Dog

You will soon be in the dog-house if you have too many of these. Make it longer with plenty of ice if you do not wish to lap it up too quickly.

Serves : 1

1 measure white tequila
1 measure crème de banane
1 measure white crème de cacao
1/2 measure lime juice
lime, banana and cocktail cherry
cracked ice cubes

1 Shake the tequila, crème de banane, crème de cacao and lime juice vigorously over ice until well frosted.
2 Strain into a chilled cocktail glass and dress with a lime slice, banana slice and cocktail cherry.

650. Beagle: Put cracked ice cubes into a mixing glass. Dash kümmel and lemon juice over the ice and pour in 2 measures brandy and 1 measure cranberry juice. Stir well to mix and strain into a chilled cocktail glass. **Serves : 1**

651. Great Dane: Shake 2 measures gin, 1 measure cherry brandy, 1/2 measure dry vermouth, and 1 tsp kirsch vigorously over ice until well frosted. Strain into a chilled cocktail glass. Dress with a twist of lemon peel. **Serves : 1**

652. Bulldog Breed: Half fill a chilled tumbler with cracked ice cubes. Pour 1 measure gin and 2 measures orange juice over and top up with chilled ginger ale. Stir. **Serves : 1**

653. Bloodhound: Whizz 2 measures gin, 1 measure sweet vermouth, 1 measure dry vermouth, and 3 strawberries in a small blender with little crushed ice until smooth. Strain into a chilled cocktail glass. **Serves : 1**

Kokoloko

For a stunning party effect, quickly dip the rim of the glass first in one of the liqueurs, then into a mixture of cocoa and powdered sugar.

Serves : 1

cocoa powder
powdered sugar
1 measure coconut cream
1 measure coconut rum
1 measure crème de cacao
1 measure milk
ice cubes

1 Frost the rim of the glass using a little liqueur, cocoa powder and sugar. Set aside to dry.
2 Mix the first four ingredients together and pour over ice in a tumbler.
3 Top with chocolate curls.

Banshee

A surprising number of cocktails are named after ghouls, ghosts and things that go bump in the night. It seems unlikely that this one will get you wailing (except with delight), but it might make your hair stand on end.

Serves : 1

2 measures crème de banane
1 measure crème de cacao
1 measure half and half cream
cracked ice cubes

1 Shake the crème de banane, crème de cacao and half and half cream vigorously over ice until a frost forms.
2 Strain into a chilled wine glass.

Candy Floss

Banana freezes well, so it is great to use as a stirrer or finish to banana cocktails. Cut the fruit into long thin strips or diagonal slices and freeze briefly.

Serves : 1

1 measure peach schnapps
1 measure banana liqueur
1 measure apricot brandy
1-2 measures orange juice
ice
banana

1 Mix the first three ingredients well with orange juice to taste.
2 Pour into a tumbler full of ice and finish with a few pieces of banana, fresh or frozen.

(657)

Honeymoon

The traditional nuptial journey is so called because the first month of marriage was thought to be sweet. If you are sick of the sight of champagne following the wedding, why not share this sweet concoction?

Serves : 2
4 measures apple brandy
2 measures Benedictine
2 measures lemon juice
2 tsp Triple Sec
cracked ice cubes

1 Shake the brandy, Benedictine, lemon juice and Triple Sec vigorously over ice until well frosted.
2 Strain into two chilled cocktail glasses.

658. Bachelor's Bait: Shake 2 measures gin, 1 tsp grenadine, and 1 egg white over ice with a dash orange bitters until well frosted. Strain into a chilled cocktail glass. **Serves : 1**

659. Cupid: Shake 2 measures dry sherry, 1 tsp sugar syrup, 1 egg, and a dash Tabasco sauce vigorously over ice until well frosted. Strain into a chilled cocktail glass. **Serves : 1**

660. Kiss Kiss: Put 4-6 cracked ice cubes into a mixing glass. Pour 1 measure cherry brandy, 1 measure gin, and 1 measure sweet vermouth over the ice. Stir well, then strain into a chilled cocktail glass. **Serves : 1**

661. Wedding Bells: Put 4-6 cracked ice cubes into a mixing glass. Dash orange bitters over the ice and pour in 2 measures rye whiskey, 1 measure Triple Sec, and 2 measures Lillet. Stir well to mix, then strain into a chilled cocktail glass. **Serves : 1**

Panda

Slivovitz is a colorless plum brandy, usually made from Mirabelle plums. It is often drunk straight but can add a fruity note to cocktails. You can use apricot, peach or cherry brandy in its place if not available, but the cocktail will be a different color.

Serves : 1

1 measure slivovitz
1 measure apple brandy
1 measure gin
1 measure orange juice
cracked ice cubes
dash sugar syrup

1 Shake the slivovitz, apple brandy, gin, and orange juice vigorously over ice with a dash of sugar syrup until well frosted.
2 Strain into a chilled cocktail glass.

White Cosmopolitan

Nothing like its pink cousin the Cosmopolitan, for this is far more fruity and instead of vodka, it is based on a punchy lemon-flavored liqueur.

Serves : 1

1¹/₂ measures Limoncello
¹/₂ measure Cointreau
1 measure white cranberry and grape juice
ice
dash orange bitters
few red cranberries

1 Shake all except the bitters and cranberries over ice until frosted.
2 Strain into a chilled cocktail glass.
3 Add a dash of bitters and dress with cranberries.

Frozen Apples

Like vodka, schnapps can be kept in the freezer as it never completely freezes and is ready iced for use.

Serves : 1

1 measure apple schnapps, iced
1 measure white cranberry and apple juice
ice

1 Stir all ingredients well over ice and strain into a chilled cocktail glass.

Orange Bitter-Sweet

Izarra is a French floral liqueur based on armagnac and eaux de vie. The green is stronger than the yellow and its sweetness balanced here by the citrus and the Campari.

Serves : 1

1 measure yellow Izarra
1 measure Campari
juice 1 orange
ice
slice of orange

1 Shake all the ingredients, except the orange slices, until well frosted.
2 Strain into a chilled cocktail glass and dress with a slice of orange.

Hazy Lady

The bright pink grenadine soon trickles through these rich nutty flavored liqueurs to give a pretty base layer.

Serves : 1

$^1/_2$ measure crème de noyeau

$^1/_2$ measure coffee liqueur

$^1/_2$ measure brandy

$^1/_2$ measure orange juice

dash egg white

dash grenadine

grated nutmeg

1 Shake the first five ingredients together over ice until frosted.

2 Strain into an iced cocktail glass and dress with a dash of grenadine and sprinkling of nutmeg.

667

Paradiso

As with most short cocktails, the best results come from using iced drinks. The very high-sugar liqueurs and spirits can be kept in the refrigerator without freezing.

Serves : 1

1 measure Parfait Amour

1 measure Cointreau or Triple Sec

ice cubes

twist of orange peel

1 Pour the liqueurs into a small chilled liqueur glass with ice.

2 Add a twist of orange peel and a stirrer.

Last Tango

Use the mango slices here as added ice cubes. They look and taste great and do a good job.

Serves : 1

2-3 thin slices ripe mango, part-frozen
1¹/₂ measures Mandarine Napoleon
¹/₂ measure kirsch
crushed ice

1 Put the thin slices of peeled mango in to freeze 40-50 minutes before you need them.
2 Shake the liqueurs well over ice until frosted. Pour into a chilled cocktail glass with and add the slices of mango.

Mudslide

Despite its ominous-sounding name, this is a richly-flavored creamy concoction that is delicious whatever the weather.

Serves : 1

1¹/₂ measures Kahlua
1¹/₂ measures Baileys Irish Cream
1¹/₂ measures vodka
cracked ice cubes

1 Shake the Kahlua, Baileys Irish Cream and vodka vigorously over ice until well frosted.
2 Strain into a chilled goblet.

African Mint

CLASSIC

Amarula is a very rich and exotic liqueur, which is best served and drunk really cold – but not on ice as that will dilute its real character.

Serves : 1

3/4 measure crème de menthe, chilled
3/4 measure Amarula, chilled

1 Pour the crème de menthe into the base of a slim cocktail glass or shot glass, saving a few drops.
2 Pour the Amarula slowly over the back of a spoon to create a layer over the mint.
3 Drizzle any remaining drops of mint over the creamy liqueur to finish.

671

Crusted Green Monster

If you see the word crusted on a cocktail, it generally means the rim has been sugared as in this one. It is good with sharp-flavored mixes and makes very elegant looking cocktails.

Serves : 1

1/3 measure lemon juice
1 tsp powdered sugar
1/3 measure kümmel
1/3 measure green crème de menthe
1/2 measure gin
4 dashes peach bitters
ice

1 Rub a little lemon round the rim of a chilled cocktail glass and then dip in sugar.
2 Shake all the ingredients over ice until well frosted and strain into the chilled crusted glass.

672

Mint Imperial

This is a strong combination with a long-lasting effect, so enjoy with caution or add lots of ice to cool it down.

Serves : 1

1 measure green crème de menthe
1/2 measure Drambuie
dash of Pernod
2 dashes syrup de gomme
ice

1 Rub a little Pernod round the rim of a chilled cocktail glass and then dip in sugar.
2 Shake the ingredients together well over ice.
3 Strain into the frosted glass and add one ice cube.

1001 Cocktails

Foggy London Town

The anise will only turn cloudy once you start stirring over ice and if you use clear crème de menthe you could have a simple white fog.

Serves : 1

1/2 measure anisette
1/2 measure crème de menthe
few drops Angostura bitters
crushed ice

1 Stir the three ingredients over ice and pour into a cocktail class filled with ice.

Katrina

You can use green mint liqueur if you prefer, but this one is prettier and tastes just as good.

Serves : 1

1 measure Galliano
1/2 measure white crème de menthe
1/2 measure brandy
ice

1 Shake the first three ingredients well over ice.
2 Strain into chilled liqueur glasses.

The Charleston

A real mix of flavors with a lively kick!

Serves : 1

1/6 measure dry gin
1/6 measure kirsch
1/6 measure Curaçao
1/6 measure dry vermouth
1/6 measure sweet vermouth
lemon peel

1 Shake all the ingredients except the peel together and strain into a cocktail glass.
2 Top with lemon peel.

Pink Squirrel

676

Pink Squirrel

Crème de noyeau has a wonderful, slightly bitter, nutty flavor, but is, in fact, made from peach and apricot kernels. It is usually served as a liqueur, but does combine well with some other ingredients in cocktails.

Serves : 1

2 measures dark crème de cacao
1 measure crème de noyeau
1 measure half and half cream
cracked ice cubes

1 Shake the crème de cacao, crème de noyeau and half and half cream vigorously over ice until well frosted.
2 Strain into a chilled cocktail glass.

677. Pink Almond: Shake 2 measures blended American whiskey, 1 measure Amaretto, 1/2 measure crème de noyeau, 1/2 measure cherry brandy, and 1 measure lemon juice vigorously over ice until well frosted. Strain into a chilled goblet and dress with a slice of lemon. **Serves : 1**

678. Pink Pussycat: Half fill a chilled tumbler with cracked ice cubes. Dash grenadine over the ice and pour in 2 measures gin. Top up with pineapple juice and dress with pineapple. **Serves : 1**

679. Pink Heather: Pour 1 measure Scotch whiskey and 1 measure strawberry liqueur into a chilled champagne flute. Top up with chilled sparkling wine. Dress with a strawberry. **Serves : 1**

680. Pink Whiskers: Shake 2 measures apricot brandy, 1 measure dry vermouth, 2 measures orange juice and a dash of grenadine vigorously over ice until well frosted. Strain the mixture into a chilled cocktail glass. **Serves : 1**

681

Sand Martin

This looks rather dangerous and slips down very easily.

Serves : 1
1/2 measure green Chartreuse
1/2 measure sweet vermouth
1/2 measure gin
ice

1 Shake all the ingredients well over ice and strain into a cocktail glass.

Firewire

This delicate and refreshing-looking drink will set you alight, ready for an eventful evening or some serious foot stomping.

Serves : 1

1 measure pastis or Pernod
1 measure Cointreau
1/2 measure fresh lemon juice
crushed ice
twist of lemon peel

1 Shake the first three ingredients well with crushed ice until frosted.
2 Strain into a chilled cocktail glass and dress with a piece of lemon peel.

Firelighter

If you are really looking for a cocktail to give you a kick, this is it. The infamous absinthe is a seriously strong spirit and not to be treated lightly!

Serves : 1

1 measure absinthe, iced
1 measure lime juice cordial, iced

1 Ice a shot glass.
2 Shake the absinthe and lime over ice and, when well frosted, strain into the shot glass.

Black Hole

(684)

Get yourself out of a hole when you need something really unusual. This black Sambucca is certainly different and will intrigue your friends.

Serves : 1

2 measures black Sambuca, iced
2 measures dry vermouth, iced
cracked ice
soda water

1 Stir the two liquors over ice until frosted.
2 Strain into an old-fashioned glass and top up with soda to taste.

Prince Charles

The perfect drink after a day on the grouse moors?

Serves : 1

½ measure Drambuie
½ measure cognac
½ measure fresh lemon juice
ice

1 Stir all three drinks together over ice in a mixing glass until really cold.
2 Strain into an iced cocktail glass.

Triple Champion

Pink or ruby grapefruit juices are sweeter and gentler flavors than classic white grapefruit juices, so are very good mixers in cocktails.

Serves : 1

1 measure Cinzano bianco
1 measure Triple Sec
1-2 measures pink or ruby grapefruit juice
½ measure ruby port
ice

1 Mix all the ingredients in a tall tumbler with ice.

Yellow Quiver

Three fruits mixed with three different alcoholic drinks certainly makes for an exciting cocktail – top it with a swirl of blue Curaçao for a glamorous touch.

Serves : 1

¹/₂ measure Mandarine Napoleon
¹/₂ measure vodka
¹/₄ measure Galliano
¹/₂ measure pineapple juice
¹/₄ measure lemon juice
¹/₂ egg white
crushed ice
dash blue Curaçao

1 Shake all but the Curaçao over crushed iced until well frosted.
2 Pour into an iced cocktail glass and spoon the Curaçao on top at the last moment.

---

(688) # Pussyfoot

A pretty cocktail, reputed to have been created during the Prohibition era.

Serves : 1
cracked ice
juice ¹/₂ orange
juice ¹/₂ lemon
juice ¹/₂ lime
¹/₂ egg yolk
dash grenadine
slice of orange and sprig of mint

1 Shake all the ingredients vigorously over ice and strain into a chilled highball glass.
2 Dress with a slice of orange and a sprig of fresh mint.

Fruity Cocktails

Teardrop

The gin, fruit and cream makes a nice long cocktail and the pink syrup gently sinking through just gives it that final touch of the exotic.

Serves : 1
1 measure gin
2 measures apricot or peach nectar
1 measure half and half cream
crushed ice
1/2 measure strawberry syrup

1 Whizz all the ingredients except the syrup in a blender for 5-10 seconds until thick and frothy.
2 Pour into a long glass filled with crushed ice.
3 Splash or shake the strawberry syrup on the top.

Mississippi Fizz

This fizz is packed with fruity flavors and a subtle taste of frozen gin.

Serves : 1
2 measures gin
1 measure fresh lime juice
1 measure passion fruit juice
1/4 measure syrup de gomme
3 dashes orange flower water
1 measure soda water
crushed ice

1 Whizz all the ingredients together in a blender on fast for a few seconds or until really frothy.
2 Pour into a large iced cocktail glass or highball glass, iced and serve with straws.

 (691)

Fruit Crazy

Melon and mango both have powerful flavors and perfumes, making this an exotic and delicious concoction.

Serves : 1

1 measure gin

$^1/_2$ measure melon liqueur

1 measure mango nectar

1 measure grapefruit juice

1 small egg white

ice cubes

slices of mango

1 Shake the first six ingredients together over ice until frosted.

2 Strain into a chilled long glass with more ice to top up and finish with a slice of mango.

Seabreeze

Pink grapefruit juice is much sweeter and subtler than its paler cousin, so it is ideal to mix in cocktails where you want just a slight sharpness.

Serves : 1
1 1/2 measure vodka
1/2 measure cranberry juice
ice
pink grapefruit juice to taste

1 Shake the vodka and cranberry juice over ice until frosted.
2 Pour into a chilled tumbler or long glass and top up with grapefruit juice to taste.
3 Serve with a straw.

Bird of Paradise

This is sometimes made with blue Curaçao, but orange Curaçao gives a much more appetising finishing color. However, it's up to you, so try them both!

Serves : 1
1 measure gin, chilled
1 measure passion fruit nectar, chilled
1/2 measure orange Curaçao, chilled
crushed ice
1 thick slice watermelon – save a piece to decorate

1 Deseed the watermelon.
2 Blend all the ingredients together with the ice until partly frozen.
3 Pour into a tumbler or large cocktail glass and dress with a wedge of melon. You may need a spoon!

694 Seeing Red

There is a real kick to this cocktail and the vivid color comes from the cranberry juice.

Serves : 1

1 measure red vodka
1 measure peach schnapps
3 measures cranberry juice
crushed ice
soda water
frozen cranberries

1 Shake the first three ingredients over ice until well frosted.
2 Strain into a tall chilled cocktail glass, top up with soda water and float a few frozen cranberries on the top.

695 High Tea

A variation on the classic Pimm's that is a little stronger and more appley, yet still a great summer cocktail for special occasions.

Serves : 1

1 measure vodka
1 measure Pimm's No. 1
1 measure apple juice
ice
lemonade
cucumber strips and apple slices

1 Shake the first three ingredients over ice until frosted.
2 Strain into a chilled highball glass and top up with lemonade.
3 Finish with cucumber strips and apple slices.

Cranberry Collins

The classic Collins drink is made with gin, but its many variations are made with other spirits so try this one on for size...

Serves : 1

2 measures vodka

3/4 measure elderflower cordial

3 measures white cranberry and apple juice or to taste

soda water

cranberries and slice of lime

1 Shake the first three ingredients over ice until well frosted.

2 Strain into a highball glass with more ice and top up with soda to taste.

3 Dress with cranberries and a slice of lime.

Chica Chica

You can buy most flavored vodkas, but you can also make your own. Add a small quantity of the flavoring – a piece of lime or lemon peel, a few raspberries, blackcurrants, one or two dried apricots, or even a piece of chilli – to a bottle of vodka and leave for 12 hours.

Serves : 1

2 measures raspberry vodka

1 measure Chambery

2 measures cranberry and raspberry juice

crushed ice

1 measure apple juice

lemonade

apple slices

1 Mix the first three ingredients well with crushed ice in a chilled highball glass.

2 Stir in the apple juice and top up with lemonade to taste.

3 Finish with slices of apple.

On the Beach

Holiday drinks are often long and fruity and this refreshing cocktail is reminiscent of happy days in the sun.

Serves : 1

1 measure peach schnapps

1 measure vodka

2 measures fresh orange juice

3 measures cranberry and peach juice

dash of lemon juice

crushed ice

piece of orange peel

1 Shake the first four ingredients over ice until well frosted.

2 Strain into a highball glass filled with crushed iced and squeeze on the lemon juice.

3 Dress with orange peel.

(699) Cinnamon Park

Hints of cinnamon or other spices can make all the different to fruit-based cocktails. Add to taste or sprinkle more on the top before drinking.

Serves : 1

1 measure vodka
2 measures pink grapefruit juice
¹/₂ measure Campari
1 dash syrup de gomme
pinch or two cinnamon
1 egg white
ice

1 Shake all the ingredients well over ice and strain into a chilled medium-size cocktail glass.

(700) Mimi

This is a delicious mix without the kick of the vodka, so make a batch for non-alcohol drinkers and add the vodka for yourself!

Serves : 1

2 measures vodka
¹/₂ measure coconut cream
2 measures pineapple juice
crushed ice
slice or fan of fresh pineapple

1 Whizz the first four ingredients in a blender for a few seconds until frothy.
2 Pour into a chilled cocktail glass and finish with a piece of pineapple.

(701) The Blood Orange Cocktail

Although only available briefly, early in the Spanish orange season, blood oranges are ideal to enhance the fruity bittersweet of Campari. Mind you, it might be too bitter for some, so you could sugar-crust the rim to sweeten the first taste.

Serves : 1

powdered sugar
juice of 1 blood orange
1 measure red vodka
1 measure Campari
cracked ice
straws

1 Rub the rim of an old-fashioned or a large cocktail glass with a little orange juice and dip into sugar. Set aside to dry.
2 Shake the ingredients over ice until well frosted.
3 Fill the glass with ice and pour in the mixture. Serve with a stirrer.

1001 Cocktails

The Seducer

This combination of almond and herb spirits and ripe fresh peach makes a very aromatic and seductive drink.

Serves : 1

1 measure vodka
1/2 measure Amaretto
1/2 measure white vermouth
flesh of half ripe peach, peeled
ice

1 Whizz all the ingredients with 1/2 cup crushed ice in a blender on slow speed for about 10 seconds until slushy.
2 Pour into a large cocktail glass and add more ice if you wish.

703

William Tell

Any schnapps would do, but pear is the best flavor combination here.

Serves : 1

2 measures pear schnapps
1 measure maraschino
ice
2 measures apple juice
soda water

1 Stir the first two ingredients with ice in a tumbler or highball glass.
2 Add the apple juice and top up with soda to taste.

704

What a Peach

Vermouth is a popular light spirit and, mixed with fruit and sparkling water, makes many interesting long and refreshing drinks.

Serves : 1

1 measure dry vermouth
1/2 measure Amaretto
2 measures peach nectar
ice
peach-flavored sparkling water
flowers or petals

1 Shake the first three ingredients together over ice until frosted.
2 Strain into a chilled tall glass and top up with water to taste.
3 Float flowers or petals on the top.

Autumn Apple Cup

Perfect for late summer and hot weather entertaining in the garden, so have all the ingredients well chilled in advance.

Serves : 6

juice 3 small orange

5-6 measures (or to taste) Calvados or brandy

few drops vanilla essence

3 cups apple juice or cider, chilled

ice

slices of apple or orange

1 Mix the first four ingredients in a jug and top up with lots of ice.

2 Serve each cupful with a slice of orange or apple.

3 For a longer drink, add sparkling water, or an apple-flavored water, to taste.

Fuzzcaat

Holland is the home of advocaat, so it features in many adventurous Dutch cocktails.

Serves : 1

1 measure brandy

1/2 measure advocaat

1/2 measure peach brandy

flesh of 1/2 ripe peach, peeled

dash lime cordial

crushed ice

lemonade

slice of orange

1 In a blender, whizz the first five ingredients over ice until slushy and well frosted.

2 Pour into a tall glass with more ice, add lemonade to taste and finish with a slice of orange.

Deauville Passion

Deauville was elegant, extravagant and very fashionable during the cocktail era early last century and no doubt many great cocktails were created there.

Serves : 1

1 3/4 measures cognac

1 1/4 measures apricot Curaçao

1 1/4 measures passion fruit juice

bitter lemon to taste

mint leaves

1 Shake all but the bitter lemon and fruit over ice until well frosted.

2 Strain into a chilled highball glass and dress with mint leaves.

Christmas Punch

In the bleak midwinter a glass of this piping hot punch will warm the cockles of anyone's heart. Just don't let it simmer or heat for too long.

Serves : 8

4 cups red wine

4 tbsp sugar

1 cinnamon stick

1¹/₂ cups boiling water

¹/₃ cup brandy

¹/₃ cup sherry

¹/₃ cup orange liqueur, such as Cointreau

2 seedless oranges, cut into wedges

2 dessert apples, cored and cut into wedges

1 Put the wine, sugar and cinnamon into a large saucepan and stir together well.

2 Warm over a low heat, stirring, until just starting to simmer, but do not allow it to boil.

3 Remove from the heat and strain.

4 Discard the cinnamon stick.

5 Return the wine to the pan and stir in the water, brandy, sherry and orange liqueur.

6 Add the orange and apple wedges and warm gently over a very low heat, but do not allow it to boil.

7 Remove from the heat and pour into a large, heatproof punchbowl.

8 Ladle into heatproof glasses and serve hot.

Beach Bum

Like puréed mango on the rocks, this cocktail is fruit with a kick.

Serves : 1

1 measure dark rum

1 measure peach brandy

1 measure lime juice

flesh of half mango

ice

lime slice

1 Whizz all the ingredients in a blender at a slow speed for about 10 seconds.

2 Pour into a large glass filled with ice and dress with a slice of lime.

Atomic

Decliciously flavored with orange and mandarin, but topped with exotic fruits and kiwi, this rather eerie-looking drink tastes wonderful.

Serves : 1

1¼ measures cognac
¾ meaure Grand Marnier
¼ measure blue Curaçao
ice
3 measures exotic fruit juice
1 tsp fraise
kiwi slices

1 Shake the first three ingredients together over ice until frosted.
2 Strain into a chilled highball glass and top up with fruit juice.
3 Float in a few drops of fraise and dress with slices of kiwi.
4 Drink through a straw.

BBC

All you need with this is the sunshine, the beach and the warm sea lapping at your toes.

Serves : 1

1 measure dark rum
1 measure Baileys Irish Cream
½ measure coconut cream
½ ripe banana
crushed ice

1 Whizz all the ingredients, saving a slice or two of banana, together in a blender until smooth.
2 Pour into a large chilled cocktail glass and dress with reserved banana slices and a straw.

Coco Roco

To set the scene – serve this coconut cocktail in a real coconut shell.

Serves : 1

2 measures fresh coconut juice
½ measure white rum
½ measure apricot brandy
½ measure coconut milk
crushed ice

1 Whizz the first four ingredients with ice in a blender for about 5 seconds.
2 Serve in a coconut shell, or chilled tumbler and drink through a straw.

Bolo

A popular eighteenth-century cocktail celebrating the new abundance of citrus fruits.

Serves : 1

1 egg white
1-2 tsp powdered sugar
pinch mixed spice
juice of $\frac{1}{4}$ lemon or lime
juice of $\frac{1}{2}$ orange
1 measure white rum

1 Dip the rim of the glass into egg white and then into a mixture of spice and sugar.
2 Leave to dry before filling the glass.
3 Shake the juices and rum thoroughly together with the sugar until sugar has dissolved.
4 Pour over ice in a cocktail glass and sprinkle with spice.

Hurricane

This flamboyant cocktail is synonymous with Pat O'Brian's Bar in the New Orleans French Quarter. A popular drink with the tourists because if you managed to drink it all you could take your glass home.

Serves : 1

1 measure lemon juice
4 measures dark rum
2 measures sweet fruit cocktail or juice (passion fruit and orange are the usual)
ice
soda water
slices of orange and cherries

1 Fill a tall cocktail glass or highball glass with ice.
2 Pour on the ingredients, stir well then top up with soda and dress with the orange and cherries.

Rum Cooler

(715)

The characteristic sweetness and perfume of rum blends with so many exotic fruits – try this with mango and lychee, for instance.

Serves : 1

2 ice cubes
juice of 1 lime
1¹/₂ measures rum
1¹/₂ measures pineapple juice
1 medium-ripe banana, cut into chunks
lime peel

1 Whizz all the ingredients in a blender for about 1 minute or until smooth.
2 Pour over ice into a chilled glass and finish with a twist of peel.

Kiwi Krush

(716)

Crushed with plenty of ice, this fruity combination quickly makes an adult slush. Enjoy before it goes past its best.

Serves : 1

2 measures light rum
¹/₂ measure melon liqueur
2 measures grapefruit juice
2 kiwi fruit, peeled
2 scoops crushed ice

1 Reserve a slice of kiwi.
2 Whizz all the remaining ingredients in a blender on a slow speed until slushy.
3 Pour into a large glass, finish with the slice of kiwi and drink through a straw.

Brazilian Batida

(717)

Cachaca is also known as Brazilian firewater and is a local white rum, somewhat stronger than the norm.

Serves : 1

2 measures Cachaca or white rum
¹/₂ measure strawberry syrup
few strawberries
crushed ice

1 Whizz all the ingredients in a blender for a few seconds until frothy.
2 Pour into a glass with the crushed ice and serve with a stirrer or straw.

 718

Big City Mist

Served over lots of ice, this becomes quite a long refreshing concoction.

Serves : 1

1 measure Irish Mist

1 measure dark rum

2 measures passion fruit juice

1 measure pink grapefruit juice

dash of grenadine

ice

1 Shake all the ingredients together over ice.

2 Pour into a long glass filled with ice and dress with a stirrer.

Taipan Nectar

A luxurious combination that has no dangerous bite, just super-cool smoothness.

Serves : 1

2 measures brandy

1 measure apricot brandy

1 measure mango nectar

4 cubes ripe mango

1 scoop crushed ice

1 Whizz all the ingredients in a blender for about 20 seconds until thick and frothy.

2 Pour into a large cocktail glass and finish with a piece of mango and a fresh cherry on a stick.

Hawksbill Special

A smooth banana concoction with plenty of West Indian character.

Serves : 1

1 small ripe banana

1 measure white rum

$^1/_2$ measure Galliano

$^1/_2$ measure crème de banane

freshly squeezed juice of $^1/_2$ lime

crushed ice

1 Whizz all the ingredients quickly in a blender until smooth.

2 Pour into a chilled glass with extra ice.

3 Drink with straws.

Beautiful Dreamer

Coconut cream is used in many cocktails, but, as it separates in the can or carton, it will often need a good beat or blend before using.

Serves : 1

2 measures white rum

1 measure coconut cream, beaten until creamy

1 measure guava juice

1 measure pineapple juice

ice

slices of melon or guava to finish

1 Shake all the ingredients except the mint well over ice.

2 Pour into a large cocktail glass and finish with a slice of fruit.

Tropical Fruit Punch

This exotic-looking cocktail is simplicity itself and can be varied with different fruit juices. Top with lavish amounts of fruit for a really festive effect and add ginger ale to make a great long drink.

Serves : 6

1 small ripe mango
4 tbsp lime juice
1 tsp finely grated fresh ginger
1 tbsp light brown sugar
$1^1/_4$ orange juice
$1^1/_4$l pineapple juice
generous $^1/_3$ cup rum
crushed ice
orange, lime, pineapple and star fruit slices

1 Blend or process the mango with the lime juice, ginger and sugar until smooth.
2 Add the orange and pineapple juice and the rum and process again for a few seconds until smooth.
3 Divide the crushed ice between 6 glasses and pour the punch over. Dress with fruit slices and serve at once.

(723) Strawberries and Cream

This becomes thick and icy, almost like a sherbet or slush, so don't leave it sitting around to melt.

Serves : 1

1 measure light rum, iced
1 measure grapefruit juice, chilled
1 measure heavy cream
5-6 large strawberries, hulled (save one to serve)
$^1/_2$ cup crushed ice

1 Whizz all the ingredients together in a blender for 10-15 seconds.
2 Pour into a chilled cocktail glass and finish with the remaining strawberry.

One Enchanted Evening

A long refreshing drink for any occasion when you need cheering up a little.

Serves : 1

2 measures pineapple juice
1 measure crème de banane
1 measure Mount Gay rum
ice
few drops grenadine

1 Shake all the ingredients except grenadine well over ice and pour into an ice-filled highball glass.
2 Top with a few drops of grenadine.

725

Yellow Bird

This really is best made with fresh sweet ripe pineapple, so you will just have to make a jugfull and invite round some friends.

Serves : 6

1 medium-size ripe pineapple
3 measures dark rum
2 measures Triple Sec
2 measures Galliano
1 measure lime juice
ice cubes
pineapple leaves to finish

1 Blend the pineapple for 30 seconds in a processor, then add the next four ingredients and blend for another 10-20 seconds until smooth.
2 Pour into large cocktail glasses or tumblers filled with ice and finish with pineapple leaves or a flower.

Zombie

The individual ingredients of this cocktail, including liqueurs and fruit juices, vary considerably from one recipe to another, but all Zombies contain a mixture of white, golden and dark rum in a range of proportions.

Serves : 1

crushed ice cubes

2 measures dark rum

2 measures white rum

1 measure golden rum

1 measure Triple Sec

1 measure lime juice

1 measure orange juice

1 measure pineapple juice

1 measure guava juice

1 tbsp grenadine

1 tbsp orgeat

1 tsp Pernod

sprigs of fresh mint and pineapple wedges

1 Put crushed ice in a blender with all but the mint and pineapple.

2 Blend until smooth.

3 Pour, without straining, into a chilled Collins glass and dress with mint and a wedge of pineapple.

727. Walking Zombie: Pour 1 measure white rum, 1 measure golden rum, 1 measure dark rum, 1 measure apricot brandy, 1 measure lime juice, 1 measure pineapple juice, and 1 tsp sugar syrup over ice. Shake vigorously until frosted. Half fill a chilled tumbler with cracked ice cubes and strain the cocktail over them. Dress with orange and lemon slices. **Serves : 1**

728. Zombie Prince: Splash Angostura bitters over ice in a mixing glass, pour in 1 measure white rum, 1 measure golden rum, 1 measure dark rum, 1/2 measure lemon juice, 1/2 measure orange juice, and 1/2 measure grapefruit juice and add 1 tsp brown sugar. Stir to mix well, then strain into a tall chilled tumbler. **Serves : 1**

Juicy Lucy

Harvey Wallbanger without the vodka – very nice, very simple and it could be a long drink too.

Serves : 1

2 measures Galliano

4 measures fresh orange juice

ice

stirrer or straw

1 Mix the Galliano and orange juice straight into a tumbler filled with ice.

2 Serve with a straw or stirrer.

730 Coconut Breeze

This cocktail uses clear or white coconut liqueur, but if you can't find it, a creamy coconut liqueur will make a good replacement.

Serves : 1

1 measure coconut liqueur
1/2 measure Drambuie
2 measures papaya juice
few ice cubes
slice of lime

1 Shake the ingredients well over ice until well frosted.
2 Pour into a chilled cocktail glass and finish with a slice of lime.

731 Caribbean Chill

A long and refreshing party punch that you could easily prepare well in advance ready to mix in the glass at the last minute.

Serves : 6

5 measures Malibu
3 measures crème de banane
10 measures fresh orange or pineapple juice
ice
soda water

1 Mix the first three ingredients well together and chill.
2 When required, pour over ice in highball glasses and top up with soda.
3 Serve with a stirrer.

732 Banana Cocktail

This can be quite sweet and rich so enough ice and the right touch of soda water are important.

Serves : 1

1 measure advocaat
1 measure crème de banane
1 ripe banana
1/2 cup crushed ice
soda water

1 Whizz all except the soda in a blender until smooth and well frosted.
2 Pour into a chilled highball glass and top up with soda water to taste.

(733)

Fuzzy Navel

This is another one of those cocktails with a name that plays on the ingredients – fuzzy to remind you that it contains peach schnapps and navel because it is mixed with orange juice.

Serves : 1
2 measures vodka
1 measure peach schnapps
1 cup orange juice
cracked ice cubes
physalis (cape gooseberry)

1 Shake the vodka, peach schnapps and orange juice vigorously over cracked ice until well frosted.
2 Strain into a chilled cocktail glass and dress with a physalis.

734. Halley's Comfort: Half fill a tall chilled tumbler with cracked ice cubes. Pour 2 measures Southern Comfort and 2 measures peach schnapps over the ice and top up with sparkling water. Stir gently and dress with a slice of lemon. **Serves : 1**

735. Woo-woo: Half fill a chilled tumbler with cracked ice. Pour 2 measures vodka, 2 measures peach schnapps and 4 measures cranberry juice over the ice. Stir well to mix. **Serves : 1**

736. Royal Wedding: Shake 1 measure kirsch, 1 measure peach brandy and 1 measure orange juice vigorously over ice until well frosted. Strain into a chilled cocktail glass. **Serves : 1**

737. Southern Peach: Shake 1 measure Southern Comfort, 1 measure peach brandy and 1 measure half and half cream with a dash Angostura bitters vigorously over cracked ice until well frosted. Strain the mixture into a chilled cocktail glass. Dress with a slice of peach. **Serves : 1**

(738)

Japanese Jewel

Sugared fruits always look spectacular as a finishing touch. Prepared them in advance if you are making several drinks.

Serves : 1
4-5 green grapes
1-2 tsp egg white, slightly beaten
powdered sugar
1 measure melon liqueur
1 measure gin
2 measures kiwi juice
crushed ice

1 Pick out the best two grapes to dip in egg white and then sugar. Set aside to dry.
2 Whizz all the rest of the ingredients in a blender with a little crushed ice for about 10 seconds until slushy.
3 Pour into a medium-size cocktail glass with more ice and dress with the two sugared grapes on a cocktail stick.

Watermelon Man

Watermelon is such a colorful and tasty fruit that it makes a great mixer. Don't be tempted to add more though, unless you want to dilute the strength of your cocktail.

Serves : 1

4 measures dry white wine
1 dash grenadine
4 cubes or chunks of watermelon
scoop crushed ice

1 Whizz all the ingredients together in a blender for 5-10 seconds until well frosted.
2 Pour into a tall glass and dress with a piece of melon on a cocktail stick.

Adam'n'Eve

Don't expect this cocktail to be full of apples! The base is sharp and astringent, whilst the top is sweet and frothy – no discrimination here, of course!

Serves : 1

2 measures Triple Sec
1 measure vodka
1 measure grapefruit juice
1 measure cranberry juice
ice
5-6 cubes pineapple
2 tsp powdered sugar
crushed ice
strawberry

1 Shake the first four ingredients over ice until well frosted.
2 Strain into a chilled long glass.
3 In a blender whizz the pineapple with sugar and 1-2 tbsp of crushed ice to a frothy slush.
4 Float gently on the top of the cocktail.
5 Dress with a slice of strawberry.

Strawberry Fayre

Poured over crushed ice, this becomes a delicious long cocktail, but you could top up with soda water too.

Serves : 1

1 measure tequila
3 strawberries
1 tbsp cranberry juice
1/2 measure half and half cream
2 grinds black pepper
crushed ice

1 Whizz all the ingredients in a blender for 10-15 seconds until smooth.
2 Pour into a long glass full of crushed ice.

CLASSIC

Jarana

(742)

Tequila has the reputation of being fiery, but it can be tempered and it is great mixed with pineapple.

Serves : 1

2 measures tequila
2 tsp sugar
ice
pineapple juice
lime wedges

1 MIx the tequila and sugar over ice in a tall glass.
2 Top up with pineapple juice and dress with lime.

Peach Comfort

(743)

Peach flavors are not easy to find for cocktail mixing, so you could use nectarine or even apricot instead.

Serves : 1

2 measures bourbon
1 measure Southern Comfort
2 measures peach juice
juice ¹/₂ lemon
2 dashes dry vermouth
¹/₂ small fresh ripe peach, peeled (keep a slice for later)
small scoop crushed ice

1 Whizz together all the ingredients in a blender until smooth.
2 Strain into an ice-filled highball glass, add a stirrer and dress with a slice of fresh peach.

Strawberry Kiss

(744)

Whiskey and strawberries make a great partnership, well worth remembering next time you need to add a lift to your bowl of summer berries.

Serves : 1

1 measure Jack Daniels
1 measure strawberry syrup
3 strawberries
crushed ice
half and half cream

1 Whizz all the ingredients, except the cream, in a blender on slow speed for about 10 seconds.
2 Pour into a chilled fluted glass and gently float or spoon the cream on top

On the Vine

The wine you use in this mix can change its character totally. If you like a sweet drink, use a medium sweet or sweet wine, otherwise choose a dry or drier wine.

Serves : 1

$^1/_2$ measure apricot brandy

ice

dash grenadine

$^1/_2$ cup white wine or to taste

soda water

small bunch grapes

1 Stir the brandy and ice in a large cocktail glass or wine goblet.

2 Add the grenadine and then pour on the wine.

3 Top up with soda for a longer more refreshing drink.

4 Dress the glass with grapes.

(746) # Pineapple Julep

In place of the traditional mint this Julep has fresh pineapple, which needs finely chopping or well mashing in the glass with the ice.

Serves : 6-8

juice of 2 oranges

2 measures raspberry vinegar

3 measures maraschino

3 measures gin

1 bottle sparkling medium sweet white wine

1 small ripe pineapple, cut into small pieces

crushed ice

1 Muddle or mash the orange, vinegar, maraschino, gin, wine, and pineapple well together.

2 Pour into iced tumblers filled with crushed ice and drink through straws before the ice begins to melt.

Peacemaker

A delightful sparkling fruit cup for summer entertaining al fresco.

Serves : 8

1/2 small fresh pineapple, peeled and crushed

30 strawberries, hulled

1-2 tbsp powdered sugar

1 bottle dry champagne or sparkling white wine

1 measure maraschino

1 bottle sparkling water

few fresh mint leaves

1 Set aside 4-5 of the largest best strawberries to slice and add later.

2 Crush the fruit and sugar with a little water in a large punch bowl.

3 Add the remaining ingredients, a few cubes of ice and some mint.

4 Mix well and serve.

Tonga

This is fruity, fun and a great drink to offer drivers instead of the ubiquitous orange juice or cola!

Serves : 1

juice 1/2 lemon

2 measures pineapple juice

1-2 measures grapefruit juice

dash grenadine

1 egg white

lemonade

slice of kiwi fruit

1 Shake the lemon juice, pineapple juice, grapefruit juice, grenadine, and egg white vigorously over ice.

2 Strain into a tall glass with a couple of ice cubes and top up with lemonade.

3 Dress with a slice of kiwi fruit.

Tropicana

Coconut milk and coconut cream are very similar products but both need well mixing up and shaking before they can be used easily.

Serves : 1

1 measure crème de banane

4 measures grapefruit juice

2 measures coconut milk

ice

soda water or lemonade

fine twists of lemon peel

1 Shake the first three ingredients well over ice.

2 Strain into a chilled tall glass, add more ice and soda or lemonade to top up.

3 Finish with fine twists of lemon peel and serve with straws.

(750) Melon and Ginger Crush

A really refreshing summer drink, this melon crush is quick and simple to make. If you can't buy kaffir limes, ordinary limes are fine.

Serves : 4

1 melon, about 1¹⁄₂ lb
6 tbsp ginger wine
3 tbsp kaffir lime juice
crushed ice
1 lime

1 Peel, deseed, and coarsely chop the melon flesh.
2 Place in a blender or food processor with the ginger wine and lime juice and blend on high speed until the mixture is smooth.
3 Place plenty of crushed ice in 4 medium straight-sided glasses and pour the melon and ginger crush over the ice.
4 Cut the lime into thin slices, cut a slit in four of them, and slip one on to the side of each glass. Add the remaining slices of lime to each glass.

(751) Cranberry Energis

Packed with vitamin C and many other vitamins, this will really wake you up and leave you bursting with energy.

Serves : 2

1¹⁄₄ cups cranberry juice
¹⁄₂ cup orange juice
5oz fresh raspberries
1 tbsp lemon juice
slices of lemon or orange and twists of peel

1 Pour the cranberry juice and orange juice into a food processor and process gently until combined.
2 Add the raspberries and lemon juice and process until smooth.
3 Pour the mixture into glasses and decorate with slices or twists of fresh lemon or orange. Serve immediately.

Faux Kir

A non-alcoholic version of a classic wine cocktail, this drink is just as colorful and tasty. French and Italian fruit syrups are often the best quality and have the most flavor.

Serves : 1

1 measure chilled raspberry syrup
chilled white grape juice

1 Pour the raspberry syrup into a chilled wine glass.
2 Top up with the grape juice.
3 Stir well to mix.

753. Faux Kir Royale: Put 4-6 cracked ice cubes into a mixing glass. Pour 1 1/2 measures raspberry syrup over the ice. Stir well to mix then strain into a wine glass. Top up with chilled sparkling apple juice and stir. **Serves : 1**

754. Knicks Victory Cooler: Half fill a tall chilled tumbler with cracked ice cubes. Pour 2 measures apricot juice over the ice and top up with raspberry soda and stir gently. Decorate with a spiral of orange peel and fresh raspberries. **Serves : 1**

755. Cocoberry: Rub 3 1/2 oz raspberries through a metal strainer with the back of a spoon and transfer the purée to a blender. Add a few crushed ice cubes, 1 measure coconut cream and 2/3 cup pineapple juice. Blend until smooth, then pour the mixture, without straining, into a chilled tumbler. Dress with pineapple and fresh raspberries. **Serves : 1**

(756) Orchard Pickings

Long, cool and refreshing for any hot summer day. Make plenty as it will soon go, especially if you make your own elderflower cordial.

Serves : 1

1 measure elderflower cordial
2 measures apple juice
1/2 measure blackberry syrup or cordial
ice
apple-flavored sparkling water
slices of apple

1 Shake the first three ingredients over ice until frosted.
2 Strain into a chilled highball glass and top up with sparkling water.
3 Dress with slices of apple and serve with straws.

(757) Berry Cream

Pure fruit blended to a perfectly smooth cream but with no wicked cream added! So enjoy some luxury, knowing it is also very healthy.

Serves : 2

1 1/2 cups orange juice
1 banana, sliced and frozen
1lb frozen forest fruits
(such as blueberries, raspberries and blackberries)
slices of fresh strawberry

1 Pour the orange juice into a food processor.
2 Add the banana and half of the forest fruits and process until smooth.
3 Add the remaining forest fruits and process until smooth.
4 Pour the mixture into tall glasses and decorate the rims with slices of fresh strawberry.
5 Add straws and serve.

(758) Memory Lane

Hedgerow pickers will have many happy memories of freshly crushed blackberry or elderberry drinks. This version needs no trips to the hedge, just a few berries from the shops and some fresh citrus. Very healthy and refreshing.

Serves : 1

a few blackberries or blackcurrants
1 tbsp powdered sugar or to taste
juice 1/2 lemon
juice 1/2 lime
crushed ice
lemonade or fruit sparkling water

1 Reserve a few berries for garnish. Place the remaining fruit in a chilled tumbler with sugar and crush or muddle until well mashed.
2 Add crushed ice and the fruit juice and top up with lemonade to taste.
3 Top with the reserved whole berries.

Pink Pussyfoot

759

This is just as delicious made with raspberries and framboise liqueur.

Serves : 1

1 measure lemon juice
1 measure orange juice
2-3 strawberries, mashed
1 measure fraise
1/2 egg yolk
dash grenadine
ice
slice of strawberry

1 Shake all the ingredients really well together.
2 Pour into a cocktail glass and finish with a slice of strawberry.

Cherry Orchard

760

Any orchard fruit could be used in this fruity mix. Experiment with your own favorite flavors or fresh juices in season.

Serves : 1

1 measure apple juice
1 measure pear juice
2 measures cranberry juice
ice
pink lemonade or cherryade
fresh or glacé cherries and wedge of pineapple

1 Mix the fruit juices together over ice in a chilled glass.
2 Top up with lemonade to taste and dress with fruit.

Parson's Particular

761

You can get more juice out of oranges and lemons if you soak them in hot water for a few minutes before squeezing them. Then let grenadine perform its pastel magic on the juice!

Serves : 1

2 measures fresh orange juice
1 measure fresh lemon juice
1 egg yolk
4 dashes grenadine
cracked ice
cherry to garnish

1 Shake all the ingredients together over ice until well frosted and strain into a long glass.
2 Dress with a cherry.

1001 Cocktails

(762) Berry Berry Red

This combination is delicious with fresh or frozen raspberries, so you can make it all year round. Cut down on the meringue if you find it too sweet a finish.

Serves : 1
2oz raspberries
4 measures cranberry and raspberry juice
crushed ice
1 small meringue, crumbled
blackberry-flavored sparkling water

1 Set aside a couple of nice berries for later.
2 In a blender whizz the rest of the fruit with the juice and crushed ice.
3 Put half the meringue in the base of a chilled tall glass, pour on the fruit slush and top up with the water.
4 Dress with raspberries and remaining crumbled meringue.

(763) Summer Strawberry Fizz

Young members of the family will love this summer treat any day, especially if you grow your own strawberries or have picked loads.

Serves : 1
juice of 1/2 lime
4 or more mashed strawberries
1-2 tsp powdered sugar, sifted
1 tbsp cream or ice cream
ice
soda water or lemonade
strawberry syrup to taste

1 Shake all the ingredients, except the soda water or lemonade and syrup, over ice until well frosted.
2 Pour into a long summer glass and fill up with soda water or lemonade.
3 Add a few drops of strawberry syrup to taste. You may need a spoon for the last of the crushed berries.

(764) Raspberry Lemonade

If you like real old-fashioned lemonade – you will love this version.

Serves : 4
2 lemons
4oz powdered sugar
4oz fresh raspberries
few drops vanilla essence
crushed ice
sparkling water, iced
sprigs of lemon balm

1 Trim the ends off the lemons, scoop out and chop the flesh and place in a blender with the sugar, raspberries, vanilla and ice.
2 Blend for 2-3 minutes or until there are no lumps.
3 Strain into tall glasses and top up with ice cubes and water. Finish with sprigs of lemon balm.

765 Eye of the Hurricane

A vast range of fruit juices and syrups are now widely available, perfect for non-alcoholic mixed drinks, once heavily dependent on old favorites of orange, lemon and lime juice.

Serves : 1

2 measures passion fruit syrup
1 measure lime juice
cracked ice cubes
bitter lemon
slice of lemon

1 Pour the syrup and lime juice over cracked ice in a mixing glass.
2 Stir well to mix and strain into a chilled tumbler.
3 Top up with bitter lemon and dress with a lemon slice.

766

Kiwi Cooler

You can only make this at the last minute and serve it almost frozen. Strain to remove the black seeds if they worry you!

Serves : 1

1 ripe kiwi, peeled and crushed
crushed ice
juice of 1 passion fruit
splash of lime juice
lemonade
kiwi-filled ice cubes

1 In a blender quickly whizz the kiwi, ice and passion fruit.
2 Pour into a long chilled glass, add a splash of lime juice and top up with lemonade to taste.
3 Finish with an ice cube with a piece of frozen kiwi frozen inside it.

Grapefruit Cooler

This is a wonderfully refreshing drink that is ideal for serving at a family barbecue. Start making this at least two hours before you want to serve it to allow plenty of time for the mint to infuse in the syrup.

Serves : 6

2oz fresh mint

2 measures sugar syrup

2 cups grapefruit juice

4 measures lemon juice

cracked ice cubes

sparkling mineral water

sprigs of fresh mint

1 Muddle fresh mint leaves in a small bowl with the sugar syrup.

2 Set aside for at least 2 hours to infuse, mashing again from time to time.

3 Strain into a jug and add the grapefruit juice and lemon juice.

4 Cover with film and chill for at least 2 hours until required.

5 To serve, fill six chilled Collins glasses with cracked ice.

6 Divide the cocktail between the glasses and top up with sparkling water.

7 Dress with fresh mint.

768. Bright Green Cooler: Shake 3 measures pineapple juice, 2 measures lime juice and 1 measure green peppermint syrup vigorously over ice until well frosted. Half fill a tall chilled tumbler with cracked ice cubes and strain the cocktail over them. Top up with ginger ale and dress with cucumber and lime. **Serves : 1**

Pineapple Crush

The more iced these ingredients are, the nicer the result will be, so plan ahead to give yourself are least 1 hour to chill everything first.

Serves : 2

1/2 cup pineapple juice

4 tbsp orange juice

4oz galia melon, cut into chunks

5oz frozen pineapple chunks

4 ice cubes

thin slices of fresh galia melon and orange peel

1 Pour the ingredients into a food processor and process quickly until slushy.

2 Pour straight into well-chilled tumblers and top with the fruit.

Juicy Julep

Taken from the Arabic word – meaning a rose syrup – it seems likely that this was always intended to be a non-alcoholic drink and that it was bourbon drinkers who hijacked the term, not the other way round.

Serves : 1

1 measure orange juice
1 measure pineapple juice
1 measure lime juice
¹/₂ measure raspberry syrup
4 crushed fresh mint leaves
cracked ice cubes
ginger ale
fresh sprig of mint

1 Shake the orange juice, pineapple juice, lime juice and raspberry syrup with the mint leaves vigorously over ice until well frosted.
2 Strain into a chilled Collins glass, top up with ginger ale and stir gently.
3 Dress with a fresh mint sprig.

771. Salty Puppy: Mix equal quantities of granulated sugar and coarse salt on a saucer. Rub the rim of a small, chilled tumbler with a wedge of lime and dip in the sugar/salt mixture to frost. Fill the glass with cracked ice cubes and pour ¹/₂ measure lime juice over them. Top up with grapefruit juice. **Serves : 1**

772. Baby Bellini: Pour 2 measures peach juice and 1 measure lemon juice into a chilled champagne flute and stir well. Top up with sparkling apple juice and stir. **Serves : 1**

773. Cool Collins: Put 6 fresh mint leaves into a tall chilled tumbler and add 1 tsp powdered sugar and 2 measures lemon juice. Crush the leaves with a spoon until the sugar has dissolved. Fill the glass with cracked ice cubes and top up with sparkling water. Stir gently and decorate with a fresh mint sprig and a slice of lemon. **Serves : 1**

774. Sunrise: Put cracked ice cubes into a chilled tumbler. Pour 2 measures orange juice, 1 measure lemon juice, and 1 measure grenadine over the ice. Stir together well and top up with sparkling mineral water. **Serves : 1**

Little Prince

Sparkling apple juice is a great mixer, adding flavor and color, as well as fizz. Try using it as a substitute for champagne in non-alcoholic versions of such cocktails as Buck's Fizz.

Serves : 1

cracked ice cubes
1 measure apricot juice
1 measure lemon juice
2 measures sparkling apple juice
twist of lemon peel

1 Put the cracked ice cubes into a mixing glass.
2 Pour the apricot juice, lemon juice and apple juice over the ice and stir well.
3 Strain into a chilled highball glass and dress with a lemon twist.

776. Apple Frazzle: Shake 4 measures apple juice, 1 tsp sugar syrup, and $\frac{1}{2}$ tsp lemon juice vigorously over ice until well frosted. Strain into a chilled tumbler and top up with sparkling mineral water. **Serves : 1**

777. Bite of the Apple: Whizz crushed ice cubes in a blender with 5 measures apple juice, 1 measure lime juice, $\frac{1}{2}$ tsp orgeat and 1 tbsp apple sauce or apple purée until smooth. Pour into a chilled tumbler and sprinkle with cinnamon. **Serves : 1**

778. Red Apple Sunset: Shake 2 measures apple juice, 2 measures grapefruit juice and a dash grenadine over ice until well frosted. Strain into a chilled cocktail glass. **Serves : 1**

779. Prohibition Punch: Pour $3\frac{1}{2}$ cups apple juice, $1\frac{1}{2}$ cups lemon juice and $\frac{1}{2}$ cup sugar syrup into a large jug. Add cracked ice cubes and 9 cups ginger ale. Stir gently to mix. Serve in chilled tumblers with slices of orange and straws. **Serves : 25**

Lemon Fizz

A refreshing summer fizz to enjoy with no effort – keep some in the refrigerator ready to fizz up at the last minute.

Serves : 1

2 fresh lemons
peel of $\frac{1}{2}$ lemon
1 tbsp sugar
lemonade, iced
crushed ice

1 Squeeze the fresh lemons and pour the juice into a chilled highball glass filled with crushed ice.
2 Add the piece of peel and sugar to taste and stir briefly. Add lemonade to taste.

 781

Raspberry Cooler

You can't beat this glass of apple and raspberry, really well iced, on a hot summer day. It is great with other fruit syrups too, like passion fruit and apricot.

Serves : 2
8 ice cubes, crushed
2 tsp raspberry syrup
2 cups chilled apple juice
fresh raspberries and pieces of apple

1 Divide the crushed ice between two glasses and pour over the raspberry syrup.
2 Top up each glass with chilled apple juice and stir well.
3 Dress with the raspberries and pieces of apple on cocktail sticks.

 782

Sparkling Peach Melba

This simple but perfect partnership of peaches and raspberries, originating from the dessert invented by the Savoy Hotel chef Georges-Auguste Escoffier – in honor of Australian opera singer Dame Nellie Melba – has become a classic combination and makes a wonderful cocktail.

Serves : 1
2$^{1}/_{2}$oz raspberries, puréed
4 measures peach juice
crushed ice
sparkling water

1 Shake the sieved raspberry purée and peach juice over crushed ice vigorously until well frosted.
2 Strain into a tall chilled tumbler and top up with sparkling water.
3 Stir gently.

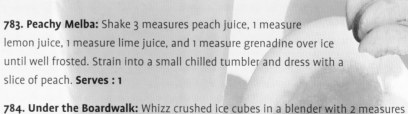

783. Peachy Melba: Shake 3 measures peach juice, 1 measure lemon juice, 1 measure lime juice, and 1 measure grenadine over ice until well frosted. Strain into a small chilled tumbler and dress with a slice of peach. **Serves : 1**

784. Under the Boardwalk: Whizz crushed ice cubes in a blender with 2 measures lemon juice, $^{1}/_{2}$ tsp sugar syrup, and $^{1}/_{2}$ peeled, stoned and chopped peach until slushy. Pour into a chilled tumbler. Top up with sparkling water and stir gently. Dress with raspberries. **Serves : 1**

785. Peachy Cream: Shake 2 measures chilled peach juice and 2 measures half and half cream vigorously until well frosted. Half fill a small chilled tumbler with cracked ice cubes and strain the cocktail over them. **Serves : 1**

Tropical Cooler

Cool, fruity and reviving, this cooler is a taste of the Tropics with a hint of summer.

Serves : 1

2 measures passion fruit juice
2 measures guava juice
2 measures orange juice
1 measure coconut milk
1-2 tsp ginger syrup
ice
slice of star fruit and physalis (cape gooseberry)

1 Shake all the fruit juices with the coconut milk and ginger syrup vigorously over ice until well frosted.
2 Strain into a chilled highball glass or tall wine glass and dress the rim with a thin slice of star fruit and a single physalis.

Lemon Soda

You certainly get the very best and freshest lemony flavor by squeezing your own fresh lemon juice. This can be bottled and kept in the refrigerator for a few days.

Serves : 6

8 large lemons
7oz powdered sugar, plus extra to taste
3/4 cup boiling water
ice
soda water

1 Finely grate the peel and squeeze the juice of 7 lemons into a large heatproof bowl.

2 Thinly slice the remaining lemon and reserve for serving.
3 Stir sugar and boiling water into the lemon juice and chill until required.
4 To serve, strain into serving jug with ice and dilute with soda water to taste.
5 Add extra sugar, if desired.
6 Serve in chilled glasses, dressed with lemon slices.

Strawberry Crush

This is almost a bowl of strawberries, so add cream to it as well if you like...

Serves : 1:

1 egg white
powdered sugar to frost
4oz ripe strawberries
juice 1/2 lemon
2/3 cup lemonade, chilled
crushed ice
sugar to taste
sprig of mint

1 Lightly whisk the egg white, dip the rim of the glass into it, then into the sugar and leave to dry.
2 Put aside 1 strawberry, hull the rest and blend with lemon, lemonade, crushed ice and sugar for 2-3 minutes until smooth but frothy.
3 Pour into frosted glass and finish with a sprig of mint.

Cinders

 (789)

Yes, it's non-alcoholic but no-one needs to know if you dress it up well.

Serves : 1

juice 1/2 orange

juice 1 lime

2/3 cup pineapple juice

several drops Angostura bitters

ice

soda water or dry ginger to taste

slices of orange and pineapple to finish

1 Shake the first four ingredients well together with ice.

2 Strain into a chilled glass and top up with soda water to taste.

3 Finish with a few more drops Angostura bitters and sliced fruit.

Babylove

(790)

Avocado is so luxuriously smooth when blended that this cocktail risks needing a spoon, especially if you like it too much.

Serves : 2

1 1/4 cup cup cold milk

12-14 strawberries, washed and hulled

1/2 ripe avocado

1 measure lemon juice

1 Place all the ingredients (save 2 strawberries) in a blender and whizz for 15-20 seconds until smooth.

2 Pour into iced tall glasses and top with a whole strawberry.

Carrot Cream

 (791)

Carrots have a strong hint of sweetness that makes them and their juice an excellent and delicious base for mixed drinks. Since raw carrots are packed with vitamins and minerals, this is also a healthy option.

Serves : 1

2 measures carrot juice

2 1/2 measures half and half cream

1 measure orange juice

1 egg yolk

cracked ice cubes

slice of orange

1 Pour the carrot juice, cream, and orange juice over ice in a shaker and add the egg yolk.

2 Shake vigorously until well mixed.

3 Strain into a chilled glass and decorate with the orange slice.

Apple Sour

There is a hint of sharpness to this cocktail from the lemon and lime juice, but it is soon masked by the sweet honey and apple flavors.

Serves : 1
4 measures pure apple juice
juice of 1 lemon and 1 lime
1 measure sugar syrup or clear honey
1 small egg white
crushed ice
4-5 raspberries
long strip apple peel

1 Whizz all ingredients except the fruit and peel in a blender until very frothy and partly frozen.
2 Put three raspberries in the base of an iced tall glass, crush with a wooden spoon and pour in the fruit slush.
3 Dress with a strip of peel and the raspberries.

Angelina

Use canned pineapple in this recipe and you are bound to be tempted to make some of this delicious concoction for all the family, too.

Serves : 1
2 measures orange juice
10 pineapple cubes
a few ice cubes
splash of raspberry or strawberry cordial or syrup

1 Whizz the first three ingredients in a blender for about 10 seconds until frothy and well mixed.
2 Put a good splash of cordial in the base of a chilled long glass and slowly pour in the cocktail.
3 Splash with a little more cordial and drink with a straw.

Summer Citrus Slush

Great for a group of friends spending an afternoon in the garden with the kids.

Serves : 2

4 tbsp orange juice

1 tbsp lime juice

$^1/_2$ cup sparkling water

12oz frozen summer fruits such as blueberries, raspberries, blackberries, and strawberries

4 ice cubes

selection of fresh berries and currants

1 Pour the orange juice, lime juice and sparkling water into a food processor and process gently until combined.

2 Add the summer fruits and ice cubes and process until slushy.

3 Pour the mixture into chilled glasses and dress with fresh fruit.

Sweet Dreamer

Wonderfully creamy and thick with fruit and goodness, the perfect wake up package or early evening settler.

Serves : 2

1 measure orange juice

2 measures passion fruit nectar or juice

1 small banana

$^1/_4$ ripe mango or paw paw (papaya)

few drops vanilla essence

crushed ice

1 Whizz all the ingredients together in a blender or processor until smooth and yet slushy.

2 Pour into large cocktail glasses or goblets.

Island Cooler

Nothing could be more refreshing on a hot summer's day than this colorful combination of tropical fruit juices. To get into a party mood, go to town with the decoration and lots of fresh fruit.

Serves : 1

2 measures orange juice

1 measure lemon juice

1 measure pineapple juice

1 measure papaya juice

$^{1}/_{2}$ tsp grenadine

cracked ice cubes

sparkling water

pineapple and maraschino cherries

1 Shake the orange juice, lemon juice, pineapple juice, papaya juice, and grenadine vigorously over ice until well frosted.

2 Half fill a chilled Collins glass with cracked ice cubes and pour the cocktail over them.

3 Top up with sparkling water and stir gently.

4 Dress with pineapple and maraschino cherries.

 797

Pineapple Tang

Plan ahead to ensure you have the frozen pineapple and peach chunks ready.

Serves : 2

$^{1}/_{2}$ cup pineapple juice

juice of 1 lemon

scant $^{1}/_{2}$ cup water

3 tbsp brown sugar

$^{3}/_{4}$ cup plain yogurt

1 peach, cut into chunks and frozen

7oz frozen pineapple chunks

wedges of fresh pineapple

1 Pour the pineapple juice, lemon juice, and water into a food processor.

2 Add the sugar and yogurt and process until blended.

3 Add the frozen peach and pineapple chunks and process until smooth.

4 Pour the mixture into glasses and decorate the rims with wedges of fresh pineapple.

Cranberry and Orange Crush

Long and refreshing but can be quite sharp, so taste first then sweeten to if necessary.

Serves : 1
juice of 2 blood oranges
²/₃ cup cranberry juice
2 tbsp raspberry or other fruit syrup
sugar to taste (optional)
crushed ice
raspberries to finish

1 Shake the first four ingredients well together until really frothy.
2 Pour straight into a tall ice filled glass.
3 Serve dressed with raspberries.

Muddy Puddle

Reminiscent of the mess ones children make when mixing drinks! Well, in fact that's just how this murky-looking but surprisingly refreshing drink was created.

Serves : 1
juice ¹/₂ lemon
juice ¹/₂ orange
crushed ice
cola
slice of orange

1 Pour the fruit juice over crushed ice in a chilled long glass and top up with the well-iced cola.
2 Finish with a slice of orange and a serve with a straw.

Cranberry Punch

A sophisticated, non-alcoholic punch, this can also be served hot for a winter party – it is especially good for celebrating the New Year – as well as chilled in the summer.

Serves : 10

2¹/₂ cups cranberry juice

2¹/₂ cups orange juice

²/₃ cup water

¹/₂ tsp ground ginger

¹/₄ tsp cinnamon

¹/₄ tsp freshly grated nutmeg

cracked ice cubes or block of ice if serving cold

To dress cold punch:

fresh cranberries

1 egg white, lightly beaten

powdered sugar

sprigs of fresh mint

To dress hot punch:

slices of lemon

slices of orange

To make the punch:

1 Put the cranberry juice, orange juice, water, ginger, cinnamon and nutmeg in a saucepan and bring to the boil.

2 Lower the heat and simmer for 5 minutes.

3 Remove the pan from the heat.

If serving hot:

1 Ladle into warmed individual punch glasses or pour into a warmed punch bowl.

2 Decorate with slices of lemon and orange.

If serving cold:

1 Set aside to cool, then pour into a jug, cover with film and chill in the refrigerator for at least 2 hours, until required.

2 Place cracked ice or a block of ice in a chilled punch bowl and pour in the punch. Alternatively, fill tumblers with cracked ice and pour the punch over them.

3 Decorate with the frosted cranberries and mint leaves.

For a party, prepare the decoration in advance:

1 Dip the cranberries, one by one, in the egg white and let the excess drip off, then roll them in the sugar to frost, shaking off any excess.

2 Set aside on baking paper to dry.

3 Brush the mint leaves with egg white and then dip in the sugar to frost, shaking off any excess.

4 Set aside on baking paper to dry.

Forest Fruit Smoothie

801

Not only is this a wonderful color, the flavor is intensely fruity.

Serves : 2

1 cup orange juice

1 banana, sliced and frozen

1 lb frozen forest fruits (such as blueberries, blackberries, raspberries)

fresh strawberry slices

1 Pour the orange juice into a food processor with the banana and half of the forest fruits.

2 Process until smooth. add the remaining forest fruits and continue until smooth.

3 Pour the mixture into chilled glasses and dress the rims with strawberry slices. Drink with straws.

Melon Medley

802

Choose a very ripe, sweet-fleshed melon, such as a cantaloupe, for this lovely fresh-tasting cocktail, perfect for sipping on a hot summer evening.

Serves : 1

crushed ice cubes

2oz/60g diced melon flesh

4 measures orange juice

1/2 measure lemon juice

1 Whizz crushed ice in a blender with the diced melon, orange juice and lemon juice and blend until slushy.

2 Pour into a chilled Collins glass.

Summer Smoothie

803

Whatever the season or state of the weather, you can cheer yourself up with a healthy and refreshing smoothie, even if the only fruit you have got left is in a can of juice.

Serves : 2

3/4 cupl milk

7oz canned peach slices, drained

2 fresh apricots, chopped

14oz fresh strawberries, hulled and sliced

2 bananas, sliced and frozen

slices of fresh strawberries

1 Pour the milk into a food processor.

2 Add the remaining ingredients, reserving a few slices of strawberry and process gently until combined and smooth.

3 Pour into chilled glasses and dress the rims with fresh strawberries.

Fruit Rapture

A silky smooth mix for fruit drink sophistocates. Perfect for any time of the day, unless, of course, you do not wish to share...

Serves : 2

¹/₂ cup milk

¹/₂ cup peach yogurt

¹/₃ cup orange juice

8oz canned peach slices, drained

6 ice cubes

strips of fresh orange peel

1 Pour the milk, yogurt and orange juice into a food processor and process gently until combined.

2 Add the peach slices and ice cubes and process until smooth.

3 Pour the mixture into glasses and decorate with strips of fresh orange peel.

4 Add straws and serve.

Junior Dancer

Smooth, sweet and healthy too, full of energy to dance the night away.

Serves : 1

¹/₂ banana

2 large strawberries

2 tbsp cream or natural yogurt

1 tbsp sugar syrup

dash grenadine

crushed ice

tonic water or lemonade

1 Whizz the first five ingredients with the ice in a blender until almost frozen.

2 Pour into a tall glass and top up with tonic water.

(806)

Raspberry Crusher

This might be one way of persuading children to take an extra portion of fruit or milk without a big battle...

Serves : 1

4 measures cold milk

1 measure grenadine

12 raspberries

1 ripe banana

3-4 ice cubes

1 tsp raspberry syrup or cordial to finish

1 Whizz all the ingredients except the syrup or cordial slowly in a blender for 5-10 seconds.

2 Pour into a chilled tall glass and splash with raspberry cordial.

Nectarine Melt

This golden yellow smoothie is packed with fruit flavor, icy cold, very nourishing and packed with vitamins, so you don't need to feel too guilty!

Serves : 2
1 cup milk
12oz lemon sorbet
1 ripe mango, peeled, stoned and diced
2 ripe nectarines, peeled, stoned and diced

1 Blend the milk with half the lemon sorbet gently until combined.
2 Add the remaining sorbet and process until smooth.
3 When the mixture is well blended, add the fruit and process until smooth.
4 Pour into chilled glasses and drink with straws.

Banana Coffee Break

Thanks to the coffee, this a very adult-tasting smoothie-style cocktail. In warm weather it makes an excellent mid-morning pick-me-up.

Serves : 2
1¼ cups milk
4 tbsp instant coffee powder
5oz vanilla ice cream
2 bananas, sliced and frozen
brown sugar to taste

1 Pour the milk into a food processor, add the coffee powder and process gently until combined.
2 Add half of the vanilla ice cream and process gently, then add the remaining ice cream and process until well combined.
3 When the mixture is thoroughly blended, add the bananas, and sugar to taste, and process until smooth.
4 Pour the mixture into glasses and serve dressed with a few slices of banana.

Quirky
Cocktails

 # My Fair Lady

A very light and airy cocktail perfect to enjoy for a long evening of light entertainment.

Serves : 1

1 measure gin
1/2 measure lemon juice
1/2 measure orange juice
1/2 measure fraise liqueur
1 egg white
ice

1 Shake all the ingredients well over ice and strain into a cocktail glass.

 # Snowball Cocktail

Almost as white as snow but certainly not as pure!

Serves : 1

2/3 measure gin
1/3 measure anisette
1/3 measure crème de violette
1/3 measure white crème de menthe
1/3 measure half and half cream, slightly sweetened
ice

1 Mix well in a glass over ice and strain into a cocktail glass.

 # Freedom Fighter

Crème Yvette is an American liqueur flavored with Parma violets. As it has such a distinctive taste, you either love it or hate it – but it certainly makes pretty colored cocktails. You could also use crème de violette, or Parfait Amour.

Serves : 1

3 measures sloe gin
1 measure Crème Yvette
1 measure lemon juice
1 egg white
cracked ice cubes

1 Shake the gin, Crème Yvette, lemon juice and the egg white over ice vigorously until well frosted.
2 Strain into a chilled wine glass.

812 Lemon Sherbet

This turns into a delicious fluffy thick drink that you may well need a spoon for.

Serves : 1
2 measures gin
1 measure lemon juice
1 measure cream
1/2 measure orange curaçao
1 tsp powdered sugar
1 dash orange flower water
little crushed ice

1 Whizz all the ingredients together in a blender for 10-15 seconds.
2 Pour into a chilled small tumbler. Serve with straws.

813 White Charger

Definitely a summertime drink. You could try it with other freezes like a lemon sorbet for instance, especially good for a fun barbecue cocktail.

Serves : 1
1/2 scoop vanilla ice cream
1 measure gin
2 measures white wine, chilled, or soda water

1 Shake together ice cream and gin (no ice is necessary) until well mixed.
2 Pour into a medium-size chilled glass and stir in wine or water to taste.

Tony Bennett

The old crooner enjoyed his favorite drink before any show but especially when there was cold and damp in the air.

Serves : 1

1 measure gin

1 measure crème de cassis

1 measure triple sec

1/2 measure lemon juice

cracked ice

soda water

1 Stir all the ingredients except soda water over ice until well chilled.

2 Strain into a long glass filled with ice and add a touch of soda, or to taste.

Bullshot

This is not unlike drinking chilled consommé but with a kick. It is best really cold.

Serves : 1

1 measure vodka

2 measures beef consommé or good stock

dash fresh lemon juice

2 dashes Worcestershire sauce

ice

celery salt

strip of lemon peel

1 Shake all the ingredients, except the celery salt, well with ice and strain into a medium cocktail glass with extra ice.

2 Sprinkle with celery salt and dress with a strip of lemon peel.

Grimace and Grin

Cocktails flavored with sweets are in fashion at the moment, probably an indicator of how enthusiastically a new, young generation is rediscovering the joys of unusual mixed drinks.

Serves : 15

3¹/₂ oz sharp-flavored jellybeans, such as sour cherry, lemon and apple

2 cups or about ³/₄ bottle vodka

1 Set aside 1oz of the jellybeans and place the remainder in a microwave-proof or heatproof bowl. Add about 4 tablespoons of the vodka. Either microwave until the jellybeans have melted or set the bowl over a pan of barely simmering water and heat until the beans have melted.

2 Pour the mixture through a funnel into the bottle with the remaining vodka, and add the reserved jellybeans. Replace the cap and chill in the refrigerator for at least 2 hours.

3 To serve, shake the bottle vigorously, then pour into chilled cocktail glasses.

817. Gumdrop Martini: Rub the rim of a chilled cocktail glass with a wedge of lemon, then dip in a saucer of powdered sugar to frost. Shake 2 measures lemon rum, 1 measure vodka, ¹/₂ measure Southern Comfort, ¹/₂ measure lemon juice, and ¹/₂ tsp dry vermouth over ice vigorously until well frosted. Strain into the prepared glass. Dress with gumdrops. **Serves : 1**

Sputnik

If you are making several of these they can be prepared in advance ready with different colored cherries on top in orbit.

Serves : 1

1 measure vodka

1 measure half and half cream

1 tsp maraschino

ice

maraschino cherry

1 Shake all the ingredients well over ice and strain into a tall thin cocktail glass.

2 Finish with a cherry supported on 2 or more diagonal cocktail sticks.

Berry Blush

If you can't find and any framboise use fraise instead, or try it with cassis for a complete change.

Serves : 1

2 measures vodka

1 measure framboise liqueur

1 scoop vanilla ice cream

$1/2$ measure strawberry syrup

3-4 strawberries

1 Whizz all the ingredients except the strawberries in a blender for about 10 seconds until smooth and frothy.

2 Pour into a medium-size cocktail glass, finish off with strawberries.

Russian Double

820

Vodka and schnapps are both very strong drinks, so handle with care!

Serves : 1

1 measure red vodka, iced
strips of lemon or orange peel
1 measure lemon vodka or schnapps, iced

1 Layer the drinks carefully, putting a piece of peel in the first layer, in a chilled shot glass and drink immediately.

Iced Lemon Cream

821

This really is like drinking a very adult and alcoholic slush – perfect for a hot day.

Serves : 1

1¹/₂ measures lemon vodka or Citroen
³/₄ measure Galliano
³/₄ measure half and half cream
small scoop lemon sorbet
mint leaf

1 Blend all the ingredients together to a smooth slush.
2 Pour into a chilled shallow cocktail glass and dress with a mint leaf.
3 Drink with a straw.

Tip: To flavor vodka add 1-2 strips of lemon peel to a bottle of good vodka and steep for 24 hours, iced. Remove peel.

Rompope

822

This is Mexico's version of the better-known Dutch advocaat, a thick, yellow, custardy treat for the sweet-toothed.

Serves : 7-8

1¹/₂ cups sweetened condensed milk
1¹/₄ cups chilled milk
4 egg yolks
¹/₄ tsp vanilla essence
²/₃ cup vodka
¹/₄ tsp cinnamon

1 Reserve the cinnamon and blend all the other ingredients in a liquidizer at top speed for 45 seconds.
2 Strain and chill.
3 Pour into glasses and dust with cinnamon.
4 For a finishing touch, add a cinnamon stick for a stirrer.

Vodga

(823)

As a rule, classic vodka cocktails were intended to provide an alcoholic drink with no tell-tale signs on the breath and were usually fairly simple mixes of non-alcoholic flavors. Contemporary vodka cocktails often include other spirits.

Serves : 1

2 measures vodka

1 measure Strega

1/2 measure orange juice

cracked ice cubes

1 Shake the vodka, Strega and orange juice vigorously over ice until well frosted.

2 Strain into a chilled cocktail glass.

824. Golden Frog: Whizz 4-6 ice cubes in a blender with 1 measure vodka, 1 measure Strega, 1 measure Galliano and 1 measure lemon juice. Blend until slushy and pour into a chilled cocktail glass. **Serves : 1**

825. Genoese: Shake 1 measure vodka, 1 measure grappa, 1/2 measure Sambuca and 1/2 measure dry vermouth over ice vigorously until well frosted. Strain into a chilled cocktail glass. **Serves : 1**

826. White Spider: Put 4-6 cracked ice cubes into a mixing glass. Pour 1 measure vodka and 1 measure white crème de menthe over the ice. Stir well and strain into a chilled cocktail glass. **Serves : 1**

827. Tailgate: Put 4-6 cracked ice cubes into a mixing glass. Dash orange bitters over the ice and pour in 2 measures vodka, 1 measure green Chartreuse and 1 measure sweet vermouth. Stir well to mix, then strain into a chilled cocktail glass. **Serves : 1**

Serenade

(828)

Nuts and fruit mixed with vodka need little but thorough icing to produce a great tasting cocktail.

Serves : 1

1 measure vodka

1 measure Amaretto

1/4 measure coconut cream

1 measure pineapple juice

crushed ice

1 Whizz all the ingredients together in a blender on slow speed for 5-10 seconds until frozen and slushy.

2 Pour into a chilled cocktail glass and serve with a straw.

1001 Cocktails

Cream Dream

Smooth and creamy this certainly is, and the Grand Marnier adds a special hint of orange sweetness.

Serves : 1

1 measure Grand Marnier

1 measure vodka

ice

1 measure whipped cream

piece orange peel

1 Shake the first two ingredients over ice until frosted.

2 Strain into an iced martini glass and gently spoon on the whipped cream.

3 Finish with a piece of peel.

Golden Flip

Sherry and almond liqueur are the bases for this flip, with an added kick of vodka.

Serves : 1

1 measure vodka

1 measure sweet sherry

1 measure Amaretto

1 egg yolk

1 tbsp powdered sugar

ice

grated nutmeg

1 Shake all the ingredients except the nutmeg well over ice until frosted.

2 Strain into a chilled small wine glass and sprinkle with freshly grated nutmeg.

Chilly Willy

Truly a cocktail for the brave-hearted – the heat depends on the type of chilli (some are much more fiery than others) as well as the quantity you add and whether the chilli was deseeded first. For an even spicier cocktail, use chilli vodka as well!

Serves : 1

2 measures vodka

1 tsp chopped fresh chilli

cracked ice cubes

1 Shake the vodka over ice with the chilli until a frost forms.

2 Strain into a small chilled tumbler.

832. Hot and Dirty Martini: Shake 3 measures chilli vodka, ¹/₂ measure dry vermouth and 1 tsp olive brine over ice until well frosted. Strain into a chilled cocktail glass and dress with a stuffed olive. **Serves : 1**

833. Fuzzy Martini: Shake 2 measures vanilla vodka, ¹/₂ measure coffee vodka and 1 tsp peach schnapps over ice until well frosted. Strain into a chilled cocktail glass and dress with a peach slice. **Serves : 1**

834. Stockholm: Put a sugar cube in a goblet with 2 measures lemon vodka, and 1 measure lemon juice. Stir to dissolve sugar. Top up with chilled sparkling wine. **Serves : 1**

Apple Toddy

A toddy is traditionally served warm, but in fact this one is just as good served cold in the fall, or during not-so-cold weather.

Serves : 1

1 measure whiskey, rum or brandy

3 measures cider or apple juice

1 slice lemon

1 Warm the whiskey and apple juice gently together and pour into a medium tumbler with a slice of lemon.

Jagger Tae

Take this in a flask when walking in the mountains and you will never be alone.

Serves : 1

hot fresh tea without milk
sugar to taste
2-3 measures schnapps or brandy
slice of lemon

1 Pour the hot tea into a heated glass or mug, add sugar to taste and stir until it is dissolved.

2 Add the schnapps and finish with a slice of lemon. Serve very hot.

Irish Coffee

This is thought to have been created by Joe Sheridan in the 1940s when he was head chef at Shannon Airport, Ireland.

Serves : 1

2 measures Irish whiskey
sugar to taste
freshly made strong black coffee
2 measures heavy cream

1 Put the whiskey into a warmed heatproof glass with sugar to taste.

2 Pour in the coffee and stir.

3 When the sugar has completely dissolved, pour the cream very slowly over the back of a spoon, which is just touching the top of the coffee and the edge of the glass.

4 Keep pouring until all the cream is added and has settled on the top.

5 Do not stir but drink the coffee through the cream.

838. Hungarian Coffee: Instead of whiskey use brandy, stir in 1 tbsp grated chocolate, top with whipped cream and serve with a stick of cinnamon. **Serves : 1**

839. Mexican Coffee: Replace whiskey with Kahlua, top with whipped cream and grated chocolate. **Serves : 1**

840. Espresso Galliano: Replace the whiskey with Galliano, add lemon or orange juice and sugar to taste. This is best without cream. **Serves : 1**

Bourbon Fog

(841)

If you like iced coffee, you will love this drink. Serve it at a summer party or barbecue and have everything ready in advance to add the ice cream at the last minute.

Serves : 20

4 cups strong black coffee, ice cold

4 cups vanilla ice cream

4 cups bourbon

1 Gently blend all the ingredients together in a large punch bowl.

2 When smooth and frothy, serve in little mugs or small chilled glasses.

(842)

After Nine

There is certainly no need to serve chocolate after dinner to anyone who is enjoying this rich cocktail.

Serves : 1

1 measure whiskey

1 measure mint chocolate liqueur

1 measure cream

ice

grated chocolate

1 Stir or whisk all the ingredients except the chocolate together briefly with a little ice.

2 Strain into a cocktail glass and sprinkle with grated chocolate.

A Scotch Cocktail

Just the drink to warm a lady's heart, especially after a day out on the grouse moors.

Serves : 1
2 measures Scotch whiskey
1 measure cream
1 measure honey

1 Mix all the ingredients well in a warmed glass and allow to cool.
2 Add a spoon or stirrer to mix on cooling.

844

Hair of the Dog

This well-known expression – a tot of whatever gave you the hangover – is in fact a popular Scottish "morning after" tipple!

Serves : 1
1 measure Scotch whiskey
1 1/2 measures half and half cream
1/2 measure clear honey
ice

1 Gently mix the whiskey, cream and honey together.
2 Pour into a cocktail glass over ice and serve with a straw.

The Green Man

845

The color of this drink is most unusual and doesn't look as though it might contain whiskey but it makes an excellent drink.

Serves : 1

1 measure Irish whiskey

1/2 measure blue Curaçao

1 measure fresh lemon juice

dash egg white

ice cubes

1 Shake all the ingredients with a little ice until well frosted.

2 Pour into a medium-size tumbler or glass and fill up with more ice.

Boilermaker

846

Originally, boilermaker was American slang for a shot of whiskey, followed by a beer chaser. This version is marginally more sophisticated, but every bit as lethal.

Serves : 1

1 cup English pale ale

1¹/2 measures bourbon or rye whiskey

1 Pour the beer into a chilled beer glass or tankard.

2 Pour the bourbon or rye whiskey into a chilled shot glass.

3 Gently submerge the shot glass into the beer.

847. Depth Charge: Pour 2 measures of schnapps – choose your favorite flavor – into a chilled beer glass or tankard, then pour in 2 cups English pale ale. **Serves : 1**

848. Submarino: Pour 1 cup Mexican beer into a chilled beer glass or tankard. Pour 2 measures white tequila into a chilled shot glass, then gently submerge the shot glass in the beer. **Serves : 1**

849. Yorsh: Pour 1 cup English pale ale into a chilled beer glass or tankard, then pour in 2 measures vodka. **Serves : 1**

850. Ginger Beer: Pour 1 cup bitter into a chilled beer glass or tankard, then pour in 2 measures ginger brandy. **Serves : 1**

851. Dog's Nose: Pour 1 cup English pale ale into a chilled beer glass or tankard, then pour in 1 measure gin. **Serves : 1**

1001 Cocktails

Scottish Nightcap

You should certainly sleep well after a glass or two of this surprisingly good concoction.

Serves : 2

1¼ cups light ale

1 tsp cocoa powder

4 tbsp Scotch whiskey

2 small egg yolks

2 tsp sugar

sugar swizzle sticks

1 Heat the light ale with the cocoa powder and the Scotch whiskey until nearly boiling.

2 Whisk the egg yolks with the sugar and the gradually whisk into the hot ale.

3 Serve in heatproof glasses with sugar swizzle sticks .

(853)

Gold Coffee

Far richer than iced coffee with cream and topped with sweet passion fruit.

Serves : 1

1 measure dark rum

1 measure Curaçao

3 measures strong cold black coffee

ice cubes

1 scoop vanilla ice cream

2 tsp strained passion fruit flesh or sauce

1 Whizz the first three ingredients in a blender with a few cubes of ice until slushy.

2 Pour into a chilled sundae glass, add the scoop of ice cream and spoon over the passion fruit sauce.

(854)

Mysterious

Dark rum and coffee could hide many a mysterious combination. This combination is sweet and slightly orangey, perfect for after dinner.

Serves : 1

1 measure dark rum

1 measure orange Curaçao

½ measure coffee liqueur

½ measure fresh orange juice

ice

1 tbsp heavy or whipped cream

1 Shake all the ingredients, except cream, over ice until well frosted.

2 Strain into a chilled cocktail glass and top with curl of cream.

Gretna Green

Light and frothy and wonderfully iced, this is a great drink for a warm summer afternoon.

Serves : 1

1 measure light rum
½ measure crème de menthe
1 measure pineapple juice
1 measure coconut ice cream or sorbet
mint chocolate stick

1 Whizz all the ingredients except the ming in a blender for 10-20 seconds or until partly frozen.
2 Pour into a chilled cocktail glass and finish with a mint chocolate stick.

Wedding Bowl

For a summer wedding, this stunning punch is bound to get everyone talking and guessing as to what is in it! This can be made well in advance.

Serves : 24

1lb canned pineapple chunks
1 cup pineapple juice
1 cup fresh lemon juice
2 measures syrup de gomme
freshly grated nutmeg
1 bottle light rum
2-3 bottles soda water
1lb sliced strawberries

1 Whizz the first five ingredients, plus half the rum, in a blender on slow speed until smooth.
2 Chill 24 hours or overnight.
3 When ready to serve, pour into a punch bowl filled with ice and add the rest of the rum, the fruit, and soda water.
4 Decorate each glas with a piece of strawberry.

Sensations

This certainly has something for all the senses – huge taste, rich creamy texture, the zingy aroma of limes and, of course, it should be ice cold.

Serves : 1

1 measure Sambuca
1 measure light rum
1 measure lime juice
1 measure cream
crushed ice
flowers or petals

1 Whizz all the ingredients slowly in a blender for about 10 seconds until thick and slushy.
2 Pour into a chilled glass and finish with flowers or petals.

858

Mango Freeze

These can be made in advance and would be great served in carefully hollowed out orange shells or a whole pineapple.

Serves : 4

6 measures golden rum

4 measures mango or pineapple juice

4 measures fresh orange juice

1 measure sugar syrup

good squeeze lemon juice

1 egg white

ice

lemonade

1 Whizz the first six ingredients together in a blender with ice until frothy and frozen.

2 Pour into frozen glasses or containers and top up with a little lemonade to taste.

859

Polar Bear

Although you can use prepared passion fruit juice in this recipe, you only need a little so hunt down the fresh fruit and enjoy the fun of these striking black seeds.

Serves : 1

2 measures light rum

2 measures advocaat

juice of 1 passion fruit, sieved

crushed ice

lemonade

1 passion fruit

1 Whizz all the ingredients except the lemonade in a blender for about 10 seconds until thick and frothy.

2 Pour into a glass filled with ice and top up with lemonade to taste.

3 Finally, swirl more passion fruit juice, with pips, on top of the ice before serving.

Hayden's Milk Float

860

An irresistible melding of perfect partners – rum, cherry, chocolate and cream – this cocktail is almost too good to be true.

Serves : 1

2 measures white rum
1 measure kirsch
1 measure white crème de cacao
1 measure half and half cream
cracked ice cubes
grated chocolate
cocktail cherry

1 Shake the rum, kirsch, crème de cacao and cream vigorously over ice until well frosted.
2 Strain into a chilled highball glass.
3 Sprinkle with grated chocolate and decorate with a cocktail cherry.

861. Bourbon Milk Punch: Shake 2 measures bourbon, 3 measures milk, 1 tsp clear honey and a dash vanilla essence until well frosted. Strain into a chilled tumbler and sprinkle with freshly grated nutmeg. **Serves : 1**

862. Irish Cow: Heat 1 cup milk in a small saucepan to just below boiling point. Remove from the heat and pour into a warmed punch glass or mug. Pour in 2 measures Irish whiskey and 1 tsp powdered sugar. Stir until the sugar has dissolved. **Serves : 1**

863. Brown Cow: Shake 1 measure Kahlua and 3 measures chilled milk vigorously over ice until well frosted. Half fill a small chilled tumbler with cracked ice cubes and strain the cocktail over them. **Serves : 1**

Chocolate Orange Toddy

864

Rich and soothing – just what you need to help ease away the stresses of the day.

Serves : 4

3oz orange-flavored dark chocolate
2$\frac{1}{2}$ cups milk
3 tbsp rum
2 tbsp heavy cream
grated nutmeg

1 Break the chocolate into squares and place in a small saucepan with the milk.

2 Heat the mixture over a low heat until just boiling, stirring constantly.
3 Remove the pan from the heat and stir in the rum.
4 Pour into cups. Pour the cream over the back of a spoon or swirl over the top so that it sits on top of the hot chocolate.
5 Sprinkle with grated nutmeg and serve immediately.

1001 Cocktails

Chocolate Egg Nog

The perfect pick-me-up on a cold winter's night, this delicious drink will get the taste buds tingling.

Serves : 8

8 egg yolks

7oz sugar

4 cups milk

8oz dark chocolate, grated

$^2/_3$ cup dark rum

1 Beat the egg yolks with the sugar until thickened.

2 Pour the milk into a large pan, add the grated chocolate and bring just to the boil.

3 Remove from the heat and gradually beat in the egg yolk mixture.

4 Stir in the rum and pour into heatproof glasses.

Chocolate Cream Fizz

This is a seriously rich version of a fizz with ice cream added – it's certainly not for dieters!

Serves : 1

1 measure white rum

$^1/_2$ measure chocolate mint liqueur

generous dash of crème de menthe

dash lemon juice

scoop chocolate mint ice cream

soda water

flaked white chocolate

1 In a blender on slow speed, whizz all the ingredients except the soda water.

2 Pour into an iced glass, top up with soda water to fizz and serve with flaked white chocolate.

 # Rum Noggin

Noggin is the old-fashioned word for a small mug and also for sharing a drink. What better way to send winter guests off into the night?

Serves : 8
6 eggs
4-5 tsp powdered sugar
2 cups dark rum
4$^{1}/_{4}$ cups milk, warmed
freshly grated nutmeg

1 Whizz the eggs in a punch bowl with the sugar and a little nutmeg.
2 Whisk in the rum and gradually stir in the milk.
3 Warm through gently if you wish and serve in small heatproof mugs, sprinkled with more nutmeg.

 # The Real Thing

This is one way to make your own cream liqueur at home. If you can find the really strong rum, bottle it and keep in the refrigerator.

Serves : 4
1$^{1}/_{4}$ cups sweetened condensed milk
$^{2}/_{3}$ cup rum
3 eggs
$^{1}/_{2}$ tsp vanilla essence
few drops lime juice
Angostura bitters
crushed ice

1 Blend all the ingredients except the Angostura bitters together in a blender until smooth and creamy.
2 Serve poured over crushed ice with a few drops of Angostura bitters as a delicious after dinner treat.

 # Tom and Jerry

You really should have a Tom and Jerry mug to serve this in, but your favorite will probably do just as well.

Serves : 1
1 measure Jamaican rum
1 measure brandy
1 egg, lightly beaten into
$^{1}/_{3}$ cup milk
sugar to taste

1 Gently stir all the ingredients together while warming the milk through (do not heat too much or the egg will separate).
2 Serve immediately.

Rum Toddy

Be prepared that warming alcohol always makes it seem stronger.

Serves : 1

1 measure rum or brandy
water and sugar to taste
twist of orange peel

1 Warm the rum with equal quantity of water and sugar to taste.
2 Add the peel and serve in a heatproof mug or glass.

Eye-Opener

Living up to its name, this cocktail has a serious kick and will make a worthwhile breakfast on certain occasions.

Serves : 1

1 measure rum
2 dashes crème de noyeau
2 dashes absinthe
2 dashes Curaçao
1 egg yolk
1 tsp powdered sugar
ice

1 Shake all the ingredients well over ice and strain into a cocktail glass.

Orange Rum Shrub

If you ever find yourself in possession of extra strong rum, this is the time to use it to good advantage. It will keep really well and makes a superb long drink.

Serves : 24

8 cups fresh orange juice
1lb sugar
20 cups dark rum
ice
soda water

1 Mix the ingredients together thoroughly in a large jug or container.
2 Store in a demijohn or bottles in a cool dark place for about 6 weeks.
3 To serve, strain into chilled long glasses filled with ice and top up with soda water to taste.

Haiti

This is really a party cocktail but only for a small crowd, as you all drink through straws. If you prefer, ladle it out into small glasses from the melon shell.

Serves : 4

1 large ripe honeydew melon
ice cubes
2 measures rum
2 measures cream sherry
2 measures Galliano
dry ginger or bitter lemon

1 Cut the top off the melon, scoop out and discard all the seeds.
2 Remove the melon flesh (use in a fruit salad).
3 Shake all but the dry ginger together over ice until well frosted and pour the cocktail into the melon with some of the ice.
4 Add dry ginger to taste, dress with slices of melon or mint and drink with straws.

Parisian Blonde

There are a surprising number of cocktails that include cream. This dreamy mixture is creamy, smooth and very sophisticated.

Serves : 1

1 measure dark rum
1 measure Curaçao
1 measure cream
ice
orange peel

1 Shake ingredients well over ice and strain into a chilled cocktail glass.
2 Dress with a long shred of orange peel.

Egg Nog

The perfect lift when recovering and a marvellous energy boost when you are feeling a little bit under the weather.

Serves : 1

1 egg
1 tbsp powdered sugar
2 measures brandy or your favorite spirit
milk, warm or cooling
grated nutmeg

1 Whisk the first three ingredients together, strain into a tall glass and top up with milk.
2 Sprinkle with freshly grated nutmeg.

Banana Smooth

For an after-dinner drink, this is a delicious mix. Crème de banane has very rich overtones but it is balanced by the cognac.

Serves : 1

$1^1/4$ measures cognac
$1^1/4$ measures crème de banane
1-2 tbsp cream, chilled
mint leaves

1 Mix the first two ingredients with ice in a mixing glass.
2 Strain into a chilled cocktail glass. Then carefully pour the cream in over the back of a spoon to form a layer.
3 Dress with mint leaves.

 877

Glacier

A dark and rich combination of liqueurs like this needs to be well iced before being topped with a whirl of soft cream.

Serves : 1
2 measures brandy
1 measure crème de cacao
$^1/_2$ measure framboise
roughly crushed ice
whipped cream

1 Mix the first four ingredients together in a mixing glass over ice.
2 Pour into a chilled cocktail glass and top with a little whipped cream.

878 Archipelago

A colorful selection of flavors and fruits from many places is topped with a layer of cream, almost like fruit salad and cream in a bowl.

Serves : 1
1¼ measures cognac
¾ measure kiwi juice or syrup
¼ measure mandarin liqueur
¼ measure chocolate liqueur
ice
1 tbsp half and half cream
piece of kiwi or mint

1 Stir all the ingredients except the cream and fruit in a chilled mixing glass and strain into a cocktail glass.
2 Carefully pour the cream in a layer over the top. Dress with kiwi slices.

879 The Reviver

There are many cocktails designed to revive after a heavy night of drinking. This is the one that most people say really works, but that's up to you...

Serves : 1
⅓ measure brandy
⅓ Fernet Branca
⅓ measure crème de menthe
ice

1 Shake the liquids well over ice until frosted.
2 Strain into a cocktail glass and drink as quickly as possible.

880 Yankee Invigorator

This enriched version of iced coffee would be great for a Sunday morning brunch. Give it plenty of time to chill to be at its best.

Serves : 1
1 egg
1¼ cups strong black coffee (cold)
2 measures brandy
1 measure port
sugar
ice

1 Beat the egg in a cocktail shaker.
2 Add the coffee, brandy, port and sugar to taste.
3 Shake with a little ice until frothy and pour into a large goblet or wine glass with more ice if you wish.

La Bamba

A glorious combination that needs to be well iced as it can be too rich for some.

Serves : 1

1 1/4 measures cognac

1 measure coffee liqueur

1/2 measure Malibu

ice

1 Stir all the ingredients in a mixing glass with a few cubes of ice.

2 Strain into a small chilled liqueur glass.

Black Magic

Drinking your after-dinner cognac with a touch of chocolate and orange sounds a bit like enjoying liqueur chocolates in a glass!

Serves : 1

1 1/4 measures cognac

1/2 measure chocolate liqueur

3/4 measure mandarin liqueur

1 tbsp cream

few flakes or curls of chocolate

1 Stir all the ingredients, except the cream and chocolate, over ice in a mixing glass.

2 Then strain into a chilled cocktail glass and carefully float the cream on top.

3 Dress with a curl of chocolate.

Coffee di Saronno

This could send anyone to sleep after a good dinner, so you had better make the coffee nice and strong.

Serves : 1

1 measure brandy

1/2 measure Amaretto

1 cup espresso coffee

sugar to taste

whipped cream (optional)

1 Warm the brandy and Amaretto in a small cup in a pan of hot water.

2 Pour into a warmed brandy glass and top up with freshly brewed coffee.

3 Sweeten to taste, but you shouldn't need too much sugar.

4 Top with a spoonful of whipped cream if you wish, but don't stir it.

Dark Secrets

The hidden secret is, of course, all the rich liqueurs and brandy wrapped up in thick cream.

Serves : 1
1¼ measures cognac
¾ measure Amaretto
¾ measure coffee liqueur
1-2 tbsp heavy cream
ice
few toasted flaked almonds

1 Stir all the ingredients except the almonds rapidly in a mixing glass full of ice.
2 Strain into an iced liqueur glass and dress with toasted almonds.

885

Midnight Cowboy

You have to be a cola lover to want to do this to your brandy! But perhaps at midnight anything goes...

Serves : 1
1 measure brandy
½ measure coffee liqueur
½ measure cream, chilled
crushed ice
cola

1 Whizz together all except the cola in a blender slowly until frothy.
2 Pour into a chilled long glass.
3 Top up with cola.

Orange Dawn

Not quite a breakfast-time drink, but it would make a very good "morning after" tempter.

Serves : 1
1/2 measure Galliano
1/2 measure brandy
1/2 measure orange juice
1/2 egg white
crushed ice
candied orange peel

1 Whizz all the ingredients except the peel in a blender until well frosted.
2 Pour into a chilled cocktail glass and finish with a twist of candied orange peel.

Stinger

Aptly named, this is a refreshing, clean-tasting cocktail to tantalise the taste buds and make you sit up and take notice. However, bear in mind that it packs a punch and if you have too many, you are likely to keel over.

Serves : 1
2 measures brandy
1 measure white crème de menthe
cracked ice cubes

1 Pour the brandy and crème de menthe over ice and shake vigorously until well frosted.
2 Strain into a chilled highball glass.

888. Amaretto Stinger: Pour 2 measures Amaretto and 1 measure white crème de menthe over ice. Shake vigorously until well frosted and strain into a chilled cocktail glass. **Serves : 1**

889. Chocolate Stinger: Pour 1 measure dark crème de cacao and 1 measure white crème de menthe over ice. Shake vigorously until well frosted. Strain into a chilled cocktail glass. **Serves : 1**

890. Irish Stinger: Pour 1 measure Baileys Irish Cream and 1 measure white crème de menthe over ice. Shake vigorously until well frosted and strain into a chilled shot glass. **Serves : 1**

1001 Cocktails

Swiss Silk

Creamy smooth and icy, laced with brandy and with a hint of cherries, this is a summer special.

Serves : 2

1 measure cherries-suisse (or cherry liqueur)
1 measure brandy
1 scoop vanilla ice cream
crushed ice
2 maraschino cherries

1 Whizz all the ingredients except the cherries in a blender until smooth and then pour into sundae or large cocktail glasses.
2 Finish with maraschino cherries.

(892)

Under Milkwood

This is a punchy mixture made smooth and mellow with the addition of cream and chocolate, definitely for after dinner.

Serves : 1

3/4 measure cognac
3/4 measure white crème de cacao
1/2 measure cream
1 measure Grand Marnier
ice
pinch of cocoa powder or grated chocolate

1 Stir all the ingredients except the cocoa in a mixing glass with ice.
2 Strain into a chilled cocktail glass and sprinkle with cocoa powder.

(893)

Hot Brandy Chocolate

Brandy and chocolate have a natural affinity, as this delicious drink demonstrates.

Serves : 4

4 cups milk
4oz dark chocolate, broken into pieces
2 tbsp sugar
5 tbsp brandy
6 tbsp whipped cream
grated nutmeg or cocoa powder

1 Pour the milk into a pan and bring to the boil, then remove from the heat.
2 Add the chocolate and sugar, stir over a low heat until the chocolate has melted.
3 Pour into 4 heatproof glasses and then pour the brandy over a spoon on the top of each one.
4 Finish with a swirl of cream and a sprinkling of nutmeg or cocoa.

894 Napoleon's Nightcap

Instead of hot chocolate, he favored a chocolate-laced brandy with a hint of banana and mint. Daring and extravagant!

Serves : 1

1¼ measures cognac

1 measure dark crème de cacao

¼ measure crème de banane

1 tbsp cream

1 Stir the first three ingredients in a mixing glass with ice.

2 Strain into a chilled cocktail glass and spoon on a layer of cream.

895 Thunderbolt

If names are anything to go by this should wake you up – and it is designed to make you feel better...

Serves : 1

½ measure cognac

1 egg yolk

½ measure fresh orange juice

ice

1-2 drops Angostura bitters

1 Whisk together the cognac and egg yolk and add the fresh orange juice.

2 Strain into a small cocktail glass with ice and top with a few drops of bitters.

Nocturne

No need to be nocturnal to enjoy this delicious mix, just a little daring.

Serves : 1

1 1/4 measures cognac

pinch cinnamon

little powdered sugar

3/4 measure crème de noyeau

1/4 measure crème de cacao

ice

3 coffee beans

1 Rub the rim of a chilled cocktail glass with a little cognac.

2 Mix the cinnamon and sugar and dip the rim into this.

3 Stir the three liquors in a mixing glass with ice and strain into the chilled glass.

4 Float three coffee beans to decorate.

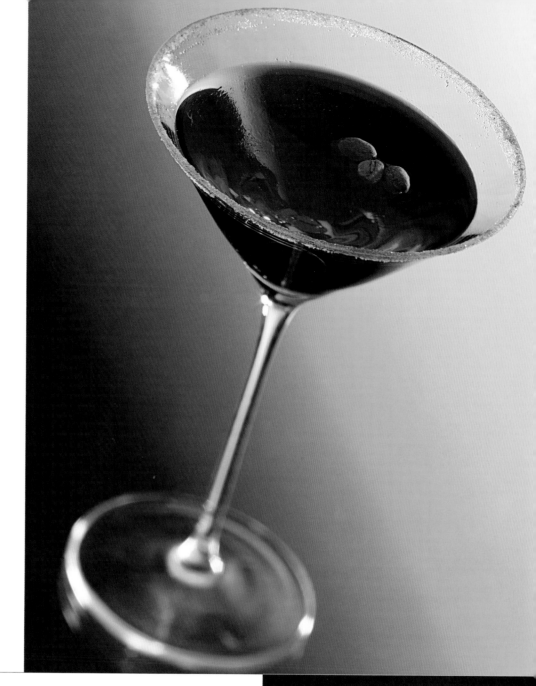

Baltimore Egg Nog

Most nogs are hot or warmed through, this one is cold, but it is still extremely good.

Serves : 1

1 egg

1 tsp sugar

3 measures Madeira

1/2 measure brandy

1/2 measure dark rum

milk

ice

grated nutmeg

1 Shake the first five ingredients together over ice with a little milk.

2 Strain into a large tumbler and top with grated nutmeg.

3 Serve with a straw.

(898)

Albertine

Although originally an after-dinner cocktail, this drink is good any time and it certainly has a soothing and calming effect.

Serves : 1

¹/₃ measure kirsch
¹/₃ measure Cointreau
¹/₃ measure Chartreuse
few drops maraschino
ice
1 maraschino cherry

1 Shake all the ingredients together well over ice and strain into a small chilled cocktail glass.
2 Dress with a maraschino cherry.

(899)

Nuclear Fallout

This is similar to a pousse-café, where the liqueurs are layered, but, in this case, the heaviest liqueur is coldest and added last, to create the slow dropping effect!

Serves : 1

1 tsp raspberry syrup
¼ measure of maraschino
¼ measure of yellow Chartreuse
¼ measure Cointreau
½ measure well-iced blue Curaçao

1 Chill all the liqueurs but specifically putting the blue Curaçao in the coldest part of the freezer. Also chill a shot, pousse-café or elgin glass.
2 Carefully pour the drinks in layers over the back of a teaspoon except the blue Curaçao.
3 Finally, pour in the blue Curaçao and wait for the fallout!

(900)

Aurora Borealis

Like a pousse-café, this spectacular colored drink should not be mixed or stirred. Leave it to swirl around the glass, creating a multi-hued effect and try to guess the various flavors.

Serves : 1

1 measure iced grappa or vodka
1 measure iced green Chartreuse
½ measure iced orange Curaçao
few drops iced cassis

1 Pour the grappa slowly round one side of a well-chilled shot glass.
2 Gently pour the Chartreuse round the other side.
3 Pour the Curaçao gently into the middle and add a few drops of cassis just before serving. Don't stir. Drink slowly!

 (901)

Pousse-Café 81

 CLASSIC

A pousse-café is a layered cocktail of many different colored liqueurs. It is crucial to ice all the liqueurs first.

Serves : 1

1/4 measure grenadine

1/4 measure crème de menthe

1/4 measure Galliano

1/4 measure kümmel

1/4 measure brandy

1 Ice all the liqueurs and a tall shot, elgin or pousse-café glass.

2 Carefully pour the liqueurs over a spoon evenly into the glass.

3 Leave for a few minutes to settle.

 (902)

Capucine

Well-iced liqueurs are often served over finely crushed ice as a frappé, this version is tiered for twice the effect.

Serves : 1

1 measure iced blue Curaçao

1 measure iced Parfait Amour

crushed ice

1 Pack a small cocktail or shot glass with finely crushed ice.

2 Pour in the Curaçao slowly and then carefully top up with the Parfait Amour.

 (903)

Stars and Swirls

You will need a steady hand for this one – preferably two pairs of steady hands.

Serves : 1

1 measure Malibu

1/2 measure strawberry or raspberry liqueur

1 tsp blue Curaçao

ice

1 Chill a small shot glass really well.

2 Pour in the Malibu and add a large ice cube.

3 Carefully pour in the other two liqueurs from opposite sides of the glass very slowly so they fall down the sides and swirl around.

Mint Frappé

This is the classic original frappé. Simply pour your favorite liqueur – in this case crème de menthe – over finely crushed ice to dilute it slightly, and enjoy quickly.

Serves : 1

2 measures crème de menthe
crushed ice

1 Fill a small cocktail glass with crushed ice and pour in the crème de menthe.
2 Drink immediately with straws.

905. Traffic Lights: Pour ¹/₂-1 measure of each of three different colored chilled liqueurs – mint, orange and cherry brandy, for instance – carefully in order in a small elgin or straight-sided cocktail glass filled with crushed ice. **Serves : 1**

White Diamond Frappé

This is a crazy combination of liqueurs, but it works well once you've added the lemon. Extra crushed ice at the last minute brings out all the separate flavors.

Serves : 1
¹/₄ measure peppermint schnapps
¹/₄ measure white crème de cacao
¹/₄ measure anise liqueur
¹/₄ measure lemon juice
ice

1 Shake all the ingredients over ice until frosted.
2 Strain into a chilled cocktail glass and add a small spoonful of crushed ice.

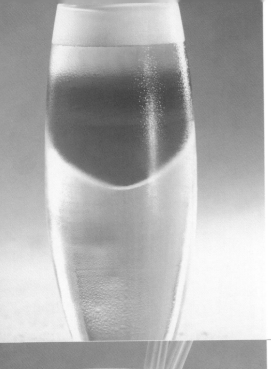

Angel's Delight

This is a modern version of the classic pousse-café, an unmixed, mixed drink, in that the ingredients form separate layers in the glass – providing you have a steady hand – to create a rainbow effect. You can drink it as a slammer or sip it.

Serves : 1

½ measure chilled grenadine
½ measure chilled Triple Sec
½ measure chilled sloe gin
½ measure chilled half and half cream

1 Pour the grenadine into a chilled shot glass, pousse-café glass or champagne flute, then, with a steady hand, pour in the Triple Sec to make a second layer.
2 Add the sloe gin to make a third layer and, finally, add the cream to float on top.

Grasshopper

Experts disagree on this original recipe and there seem to be at least three versions with the same name – as well as numerous variations. The recipe given here is also known as a Grasshopper Surprise.

Serves : 1

2 measures green crème de menthe
2 measures white crème de cacao
2 measures half and half cream
cracked ice cubes

1 Shake the crème de menthe, crème de cacao and half and half cream over ice until a frost forms.
2 Strain into a chilled goblet.

Chocolate-Covered Cherry

The "cherry" is supposedly the striking red grenadine as it sits at the bottom of the glass, then a middle layer of chocolate, topped off with a measure of Baileys.

Serves : 1

1 measure grenadine
1 measure crème de cacao
1 measure Baileys Irish Cream

1 Pour the grenadine into the bottom of a shot glass.
2 Slowly and carefully pour in the crème de cacao over the back of a spoon, so that it floats on the grenadine.
3 Gently pour in the Baileys, using the spoon again, so that each ingredient creates a separate layer. Drink slowly.

Springbok Coffee

910

A fruity but rather rich coffee to serve hot or iced.

Serves : 1

1 cup strong black coffee

1 measure apricot brandy

1 measure Amarula

whipped cream

toasted flaked almonds

1 Pour the coffee into a tall heatproof glass or cup.

2 Pour in the brandy and then carefully pour in the Amarula cream liqueur.

3 Finish with a swirl of whipped cream and a few almonds.

Café Brulot

911

Serve this after a leisurely brunch, when you have time to linger and enjoy. For a really dramatic display, flambé it at the table using the peel of a whole orange removed all in one piece.

Serves : 2

$^1/_2$ stick cinnamon

several cloves

peel of 1 orange, in one strip or thick pieces

peel of 1 lemon, in strips

3 sugar cubes

$^2/_3$ cup brandy

1-2 tbsp Curaçao, warmed

2 cups hot fresh coffee

1 Warm spices, peel, sugar and brandy in a pan until the sugar has dissolved.

2 Remove the orange peel with tongs.

3 Flambé the Curaçao and carefully pour it over the orange peel into the pan.

4 Gradually add the hot coffee and stir until the flames die down.

Strong, Black and Sweet

912

The French have always enjoyed a brandy with their first morning espresso! Try this blend and you will soon understand why...

Serves : 1

1 measure Mandarine Napoleon

$^1/_2$ measure brandy

espresso coffee

sugar swizzle stick

1 Pour the first two ingredients into a small coffee cup.

2 Add the espresso and stir with the swizzle stick.

 Jealousy

This really is an after-dinner cocktail and if you want a change, you could occasionally flavor the cream with a different liqueur.

Serves : 1

1 tsp crème de menthe
1-2 tbsp heavy cream
2 measures coffee or chocolate liqueur
crushed ice
chocolate matchsticks

1 Gently beat the mint liqueur into the cream until thick.

2 Pour the coffee liqueur into a very small iced cocktail glass and carefully spoon on the whipped flavored cream.

3 Serve with chocolate matchsticks.

Amaretto Coffee

This is a lovely variation of Irish coffee. Amaretto is a deliciously sweet, almond-flavored liqueur made from apricot kernels. It is delicious drunk on its own, but it also forms the basis of a number of cocktails.

Serves : 1

2 tbsp Amaretto

1 cup hot black coffee

1-2 tbsp heavy cream

1 Stir the Amaretto into the hot coffee.

2 Carefully pour the cream on top over the back of a spoon to form a layer.

Passion

Almonds, cocoa and the fruity Amarula make a great combination and although it is quite creamy, it is not too rich.

Serves : 1

1 measure Amaretto

1 measure crème de cacao

1 measure Amarula

1 measure half and half cream

ice

chocolate-covered coffee beans

1 Shake the first four ingredients well over ice and strain into a small chilled cocktail glass.

2 Enjoy after dinner with chocolate-covered coffee beans.

(916) Café Crème with Attitude

A delicious way to end a light meal, as it is very rich.

Serves : 1

2 measures Tia Maria
2 measures Kahlua
ice
1 measure Baileys Irish Cream
1/2 measure cream
few chocolate-covered coffee beans

1 Mix the Tia Maria and Kahlua with ice in a mixing glass.
2 Strain into a small cocktail glass or shot glass.
3 Carefully pour on the Baileys over the back of a spoon so it floats, then do the same with the cream.
4 Serve immediately, decorated with chocolate covered coffee beans.

(917) Coffee Time

This is a luxurious coffee for any after-dinner occasion. Have plenty ready, as it will go down very well.

Serves : 1

1 measure coconut liqueur
1 measure coffee liqueur
1 measure brandy
freshly brewed hot coffee
whipped sweetened cream

1 Mix the liqueurs and brandy in a heatproof glass or mug.
2 Pour in the fresh coffee and top with a spoonful of whipped cream.

1001 Cocktails

Snowboat

This is such a good combination, it is perfect for special occasions like Christmas, and could easily be made into an ice cream or creamy dessert.

Serves : 2

1 measure chocolate mint liqueur, iced

1 measure milk, iced

1/2 measure Malibu, iced

small scoop coconut ice cream

crushed ice

coconut or flaked chocolate

1 Whizz the first five ingredients together in a blender until frothy and well-chilled.

2 Pour or spoon into iced cocktail glasses and top with the coconut or chocolate.

The Chocolate Diva

Chocaholics will not be able to resist this wicked alcohol and chocolate combination, but it really needs to be very cold.

Serves : 1

4 cubes good quality milk chocolate, melted

1 measure Grand Marnier

1 measure vodka

1 measure crème de cacao

1 tbsp fresh orange juice

fresh edible flower to finish – pansy, rose petals, nasturtium

1 Mix the melted chocolate gently with the liqueurs and orange juice until well blended.

2 Pour into a chilled cocktail glass and float a flower or petals on the top to finish.

(920) Chocorange Chiller

Rimming the glass with cocoa looks dramatic but it is just one of many variations you could use to give style to a cocktail.

Serves : 2

$^1/_2$ tsp cocoa powder
$^1/_2$ tsp powdered sugar
3 measures Drambuie
juice of one orange
$^2/_3$ cup sparkling water
few drops Angostura bitters
few cubes of ice
2 flakes or curls of chocolate

1 Mix the cocoa and sugar together.
2 Rub the rims of the glasses with a drop or two of Drambuie, then dip into the cocoa mixture. Set aside until dry.
3 Mix the orange juice, Drambuie and sparkling water.
4 Put 2-3 cubes ice and a few drops of bitters in the base of each glass, pour on the orange fizz and top with a flake of chocolate.

(921) The Babysitter

Perhaps the babysitter should just have the ice cream sundae part, and add the liqueurs for those with fewer responsibilities.

Serves : 1

2 measures coconut liqueur
1 measure crème de cacao
$^1/_2$ scoop vanilla ice cream
cola
chocolate flakes or pieces

1 Whizz the first three ingredients in a blender for about 5 seconds until thick and frothy.
2 Pour into a large chilled glass and top up with cola to taste.
3 Dress with flakes of chocolate and drink with a straw.

Mermaid

(922)

Adding egg white gives a tempting frothy topping to any shaken cocktail. It looks so professional too.

Serves : 1

1 measure aquavit
¹/₂ measure cherry brandy
¹/₂ measure dry vermouth
dash lime cordial
1 dash egg white
ice
cherry

1 Shake all the ingredients together well over ice.
2 Pour into a chilled cocktail glass and finish with a cherry.

Yankee Doodle

Serve this delicious concoction after dinner on a warm summer evening.

Serves : 1

1 measure crème de banane
1 measure cognac
1 measure Royal Mint Chocolate
ice

1 Shake all three ingredients together over ice until well frosted and strain into a small cocktail glass.

Tornado

If these liquors are really well iced, you will certainly create a tornado in your glass when you pour one into the other – just sit and watch them swirling for a moment!

Serves : 1

1 measure peach or other favorite schnapps, frozen
1 measure black Sambuca, frozen

1 Pour the schnapps into an iced shot glass.
2 Then gently pour on the Sambuca over the back of a spoon.
3 Leave it for a few minutes to settle and separate before you down it.

Banana Bomber

(925)

This cocktail is as dazzling as it is delicious and gloriously addictive. Try it with white crème de cacao and a layer of cream too – equally irresistible!

Serves : 1

1 measure banana liqueur
1 measure brandy

1 Pour the banana liqueur gently into a shot glass.
2 Gently pour in the brandy over the back of a teaspoon, taking care not to let the layers mix.

(926)

Smart Alec

If you have the glasses and the liqueurs are really well iced, they will stay in layers, but you can't tell until you drink it as they are almost the same color!

Serves : 1

3/4 measure crème de cacao, chilled
1/2 measure orange Curaçao
1/2 measure chilled cream
cocoa powder

1 Pour the crème de cacao slowly into the base of an iced elgin or liqueur glass, then top with the Curaçao.
2 Finally carefully pour the cream in a layer over the top.
3 Finish with a sprinkle of cocoa powder.

(927)

Toffee Split

You should not need a dessert as well, but you could always pour it over some ice cream.

Serves : 1

1 measure toffee liqueur, iced
2 measures Drambuie
crushed ice

1 Fill a small cocktail glass or shot glass with crushed ice.
2 Pour on the Drambuie and pour in the toffee liqueur carefully from the side of the glass so it layers on top.
3 Drink immediately.

 928

Fifth Avenue

After-dinner cocktails often include cream and this one also has the delicate flavors of apricot and cocoa.

Serves : 1

1 measure dark crème de cacao, iced
1 measure apricot brandy, iced
1 measure cream

1 Pour the ingredients, one at a time, into a chilled tall cocktail glass. Pour the layers slowly over the back of a spoon resting against the edge of the glass. Each layer should float on top of the previous one.

Fancy Free

The key to this layered drink is to ice the liqueur and ice the glass. If it does seem to mix on impact, give it a little time to settle and form its layers again.

Serves : 1

$^1/_3$ measure cherry brandy, iced

$^1/_3$ measure Cointreau, iced

$^1/_3$ measure apricot liqueur, iced

1 Into an iced elgin, tall shot glass or liqueur glass pour the three liqueurs in order. Pour them over the back of a spoon so they form colored layers.

Five Fifteen

Don't be fooled by the cream, this is a serious tea-time concoction.

Serves : 1

¹/₃ measure Curaçao
¹/₃ measure dry vermouth
¹/₃ measure sweet cream
ice

1 Shake all the ingredients together well over ice and strain into a small glass.

Toasted Almonds

You can't beat this for a wonderfully rich after-dinner treat. Serve with sugared almonds for a good effect.

Serves : 1

2 ice cubes
2 measures Amaretto
1 measure brandy
1-2 measures heavy cream
toasted flaked almonds

1 Place 2 ice cubes in a chilled cocktail glass.
2 Stir in the Amaretto and brandy to mix well and chill.
3 With the help of a spoon, pour the cream in a layer over the top and finish with a few toasted flaked almonds.

Avalanche

Amaretto is a rich almond-flavored liqueur so this combination would be delicious after dinner, instead of pudding...

Serves : 1

1 measure Amaretto
1/2 measure apricot brandy
1 measure apricot or mango juice
1 scoop vanilla ice cream

1 Whizz all the ingredients in a blender until well frosted and frothy.
2 Pour into an iced cocktail glass and drink through a straw.

Melon Freeze

A very refreshing and cooling cocktail for warm summer days, but don't try to make too many at once, as it needs to be kept well frozen.

Serves : 1

2 measures melon liqueur, iced
1 measure fresh lemon juice
1 small scoop vanilla ice cream
a little crushed ice
slice or cube of green melon to finish
extra melon liqueur, iced

1 Whizz the first four ingredients together in a blender until partly frozen and then pour into a well-chilled cocktail glass.
2 Spoon over a few drops of frozen melon liqueur and finish with a slice of melon.

Down Under

A fruit salad mix of liqueur flavors
that produce a great-tasting cocktail.

Serves : 1
1 measure crème de banane
1 measure strawberry liqueur
1 measure orange Curaçao
1 measure orange juice
small scoop ice cream
fresh strawberry

1 Whizz all the ingredients except the
strawberry in a blender for about 10
seconds until smooth and almost
frozen.
2 Pour into a chilled cocktail glass and
finish with a strawberry.

935

Mexican Dawn

Creamy and richly flavored with a hint of daring, just like Mexico.

Serves : 1
1 measure coconut liqueur
1 measure tequila
1 scoop strawberry ice cream
dash strawberry liqueur
dash tamarind syrup
flake or piece of fresh coconut

1 Whizz all the ingredients except the
coconut in a blender slowly for about
10 seconds.
2 Pour into a chilled cocktail glass and
decorate with a flake of fresh or
candied coconut. Serve with a stirrer.

936

Silver Slipper

The caraway flavor of the kümmel comes through strongest in this creamy combination, but do choose a good pure vanilla ice cream.

Serves : 1

1 measure kümmel
1 measure vodka
1 scoop vanilla ice cream

1 Blend all the ingredients together on slow speed until thick.
2 Pour into a chilled cocktail glass.

937

Vintage Cadillac

Luxury and style all rolled into one sophisticated drink.

Serves : 1

1 measure Galliano
1 measure crème de cacao
1 measure cream
ice

1 Shake all the ingredients together with ice and strain into a small chilled cocktail glass.

938

Snowy Ridge

Cream-topped liqueurs are delicious after-dinner drinks. Any favorite can be used but it works best with a well-chilled liqueur.

Serves : 1

1 measure crème de cacao, chilled
1/2 measure heavy cream

1 Pour the crème de cacao into an iced shot glass or small cocktail glass.
2 Carefully pour the cream over the back of a spoon on top of the liqueur so that it floats.
3 Sip slowly through the cream.

Cold Comfort

Ice-cold drinks are very soothing during really hot weather, especially when mixed with herbal liqueurs like kümmel.

Serves : 1

1 measure cream, chilled
¹/₂ measure kümmel
¹/₂ measure kirsch
few drops orange flower water
1-2 measures pineapple juice
ice
slices of fruit or cherry

1 Shake all the ingredients except the fruit together over ice until well frosted.
2 Strain into a large cocktail glass or wine glass and dress with fruit.

Jack Frost

It looks dramatic and icy cold, but it tastes delicious and has enough kick to warm you up despite the cool blue.

Serves : 1

³/₄ measure blue Curaçao, iced
powdered sugar
1 measure tequila, cold
2 measures cream, cold
¹/₂ cup crushed ice

1 Dip the rim of a medium size cocktail glass in the Curaçao, shake off any excess and dip immediately into castor sugar.
2 Set aside in a cold place to dry and set.
3 Shake the rest of the ingredients and the Curaçao over ice until really frosted.
4 Pour carefully into the glass.

Louisa

Blue cocktails look such fun, so enhance the effect with a few colored ice cubes.

Serves : 1

³/₄ measure blue Curaçao
¹/₂ measure vodka
¹/₄ measure barley water
squeeze lemon juice
ice
soda water

1 Mix the first four ingredients in long glass full of ice.
2 Top up with soda water to taste.
3 Finish with blue ice cubes.

942 Minty Cappuccino

You could also add a good sifting of cocoa powder on top of this cocktail as well, if you like the total effect...

Serves : 1

1 measure white crème de menthe

1 measure chocolate cream liqueur

1 measure coffee liqueur

1 tbsp half and half cream

crushed ice

soda water to taste

1 Stir all the ingredients well over the crushed ice and pour into a chilled cocktail glass.

2 Drink through a straw.

943 Minted Diamonds

Make these stunning ice cubes well in advance and only take out of the freezer at the very last second – they melt almost immediately.

Serves : 1

1 tsp green crème de menthe

1 tbsp iced water

1 measure white crème de menthe

2 measures apple or pear schnapps

ice

1 Mix the green crème de menthe with 1 tbsp iced water and freeze in 1 or 2 small ice cubes for about 2 hours.

2 Stir the other liqueurs over ice until well frosted.

3 Strain into a chilled cocktail glass and float the mint ice cubes on top at the last moment.

4 Don't start drinking until the mint cubes begin to melt!

944 Green Daze

Looks like it should smell of newly mown grass in early summer, but at least you can dream all through the winter.

Serves : 1

1 measure melon liqueur, chilled

1 measure green Chartreuse, chilled

1/2 measure half and half cream, chilled

1/2 measure lime juice

cracked ice

slice of star fruit

1 Stir all the ingredients except the fruit together over ice until well frosted.

2 Strain into a chilled cocktail glass and dress with a slice of star fruit.

Around the World

Flavors from all around the world go into this glorious mix, so serve it on a cosmopolitan occasion.

Serves : 1

1 measure Mandarine Napoleon
1 measure Polish vodka
1/2 measure Campari
1/2 measure crème de banane
1/2 measure coconut liqueur
ice
lemonade

1 Shake all the ingredients except lemonade over ice until frosted.
2 Strain into a glass filled with ice, top up with lemonade and decorate with fruit.

(946)

Nightcap Flip

A flip always contains egg so this makes for a soothing and interesting nightcap, even if it is a strange color...

Serves : 1

1/3 measure brandy
1/3 measure anisette
1/3 measure blue Curaçao
1 egg yolk
ice
maraschino cherry

1 Shake the first four ingredients well over ice and then strain into a cocktail glass.
2 Dress with a cherry.

(947)

Angel's Wings

Drink slowly through a straw to appreciate the minty flavors and the subtle frothy vanilla topping.

Serves : 3

1 egg white
4 measures advocaat
1 measure Cointreau
ice
1 measure crème de menthe

1 Shake the egg white, advocaat and Cointreau over ice until frothy and frosted.
2 Place an ice cube in each chilled glass, slowly pour on the crème de menthe and the frothy egg mixture. The colors will separate to give a layered effect.
3 Serve immediately.

(948)

El Diablo

One or two Diablos and you will certainly feel a bit of a devil, but one or two too many and you will feel like the very devil!

Serves : 1

2-3 strips of lime peel

1 measure lime juice

3 measures white tequila

1 measure cassis

cracked ice cubes

1 Fill a small chilled glass with ice, add lime peel and juice, the tequila and cassis.

2 Stir well to mix.

(949)

Mulled Marsala

Perfect for serving as a stirrup cup if you are not riding, or on an a bitter cold Sunday morning before lunch.

Serves : 8

1 bottle Marsala

2 ¼ cups water

6 cloves

4 measures Amaretto

sugar

1 Heat all the ingredients together except sugar slowly and bring almost to the boil.

2 Remove from the heat, add sugar and stir to dissolve before serving in very small heatproof glasses.

(950)

John Wood

Vermouth is an immensely useful cocktail flavoring as it contains more than 50 herbs and spices and combines well with many spirits. It had fallen in popularity as a base for cocktails over the last decade, but is now enjoying a revival.

Serves : 1

2 measures sweet vermouth

½ measure kümmel

½ measure Irish whiskey

1 measure lemon juice

cracked ice cubes

dash Angostura bitters

1 Shake the vermouth, kümmel, whiskey and lemon juice vigorously over ice with a dash of Angostura bitters until well frosted.

2 Strain into a chilled wine glass.

Dr Johnson's Mull

951

This is definitely a medicinal mulled wine, much stronger than most of us are used to, so drink in small quantities.

Serves : 16

4 cups claret

1 sliced orange

12 cubes sugar

6 cloves

2 1/4 cups water

wine glass of brandy

nutmeg

1 Pour the claret into a medium pan with orange slices, sugar and cloves.

2 Bring almost to the boil.

3 Boil the water and pour into pan.

4 Add the brandy and nutmeg, then pour into warmed cups or glasses.

Port and Lemon Mull

952

This clove-studded lemon is a very successful old-fashioned way of adding a subtle amount of flavor to a pot of wine or port.

Serves : 10

few cloves

2 lemons

1 bottle port

mixed spices

2oz sugar cubes

1 Push the cloves into one lemon and warm in a medium oven for 15 minutes.

2 Pour the port into a medium-large pan, bring just to scalding and turn off. Boil a pint of water and add pinch of mixed spices.

3 Rub sugar cubes over the other lemon and squeeze out half the juice.

4 Add everything to the pan of port and heat to dissolve the sugar.

5 Remove the cloved lemon before serving. Serve really hot in small heatproof mugs or glasses.

The Archbishop

 CLASSIC

 953

If you are feeling brave you can flambé this just before serving, then cool it slightly.

Serves : 4
few cloves
1 small orange
2¼ cups port
10z soft brown sugar

1 Push the cloves into the orange and place in a small pan with the port and brown sugar.
2 Heat through gently and serve when well mulled, in ready-heated mugs or glasses.

954

Glühwein

The skier's favorite "Après" warmer can be enjoyed on most cold winter nights, with no need for the snowy excuse.

Serves : 8
3 bottles red wine
a few pieces of lemon and orange zest
good pinch each of ground ginger, cinnamon and cloves (or use whole spices if you prefer, but remember to remove them before serving)
2oz sugar
cinnamon sticks

1 Heat the wine in a stainless steel or non-stick saucepan with the zest, spices and sugar.
2 When the sugar has dissolved and the wine is hot but not boiling, leave to infuse for 5-10 minutes before serving.
3 Dilute with a little water to taste.
4 Serve with cinnamon stick stirrers.

955

Cider-Berry Punch

This bright and cheery punch can be well spiced and may need sugar, preferably brown, adding to taste, or use a sweet cider. Perfect for a cold Christmas Eve...

Serves : 10
4$\frac{1}{4}$ cups cider
1 cinnamon stick
pinch grated nutmeg
4oz cranberries
2 cups red wine
sugar to taste

1 Heat the cider, spices and cranberries until the fruit bursts.
2 Add the wine and bring almost to the boil.
3 Add sugar to taste and then strain into a serving jug.
4 Serve with swizzle sticks.

956

Glogg

This hot punch will soon get the party going with a swing.

Serves : 20
1 bottle red wine
1 bottle medium sherry
3-4 tbsp sugar
$\frac{1}{2}$ bottle brandy
dashes Angostura bitters
raisins and unsalted almonds

1 Heat all the ingredients except the raisins and almonds together until the sugar is dissolved and it is piping hot.
2 Pour into heatproof cups or mugs with a few nuts and raisins in the base.

Negus

CLASSIC

Named after Colonel Francis Negus, who invented it in the eighteenth century when sherry/wine was more readily available than most other drinks.

Serves : 18

1 bottle cream sherry

1 lemon, sliced and halved

4¼ cups boiling water

nutmeg

sugar

1-2 measures brandy

1 Warm the sherry slowly in a medium-size pan.

2 Add the lemon and boiling water, grated nutmeg, sugar to taste and brandy.

3 Warm through well and serve in small heatproof glasses.

Stirrup Cup

CLASSIC

This should really stir up the winter gathering on a cold morning, as it is strong when well warmed. Small cups are ideal.

Serves : 24

1 bottle red wine

7-8 measures dark rum

3 dashes Angostura bitters

1 tsp ground cinnamon

few cloves

8 measures fresh orange juice

4oz sugar

1 bottle cider

1 Gently heat all but the cider together in a large pan until really warmed through and mulled, but do not allow to boil.

2 Add the cider just before serving it in small heatproof mugs or cups.

Twelfth Night

The longer you leave this mixture to marinate the better the final result will be. You may want to add sugar to taste, but try it first.

Serves : 8

1 apple

cloves

1 bottle red wine

hot water

1 Stick the apple full of cloves, place in a large bowl or saucepan with the heated red wine and boiled water to taste.

2 Leave for 5-15 minutes to mull.

3 Serve in small heatproof mugs or glasses.

1001 Cocktails

Mistletoe Mull

There are numerous ways to make a mulled wine, but this one is by far the simplest and easiest. And you can always add more wine if you prefer a stronger brew!

Serves : 8

2 cups water
sugar to taste
1 stick cinnamon
4 cloves
2 lemons, sliced
1 bottle red Burgundy

1 Boil the water with sugar, cinnamon and cloves for 3-5 minutes.
2 Add the lemon slices and leave to stand for 10 minutes.
3 Add the wine and heat through slowly without boiling.
4 Serve piping hot.

Santa's Sip

Unusually, this hot wine mix is unsweetened, so if you find it too dry when warmed through, add a cube of brown sugar to each glass.

Serves : 20

4 bottles red wine
4 cups water
¼ bottle dark rum
1 lemon
several cloves
½ tsp cinnamon
nutmeg

1 Heat the wine, water to taste (add gradually), and rum together.
2 Stick the cloves into the lemon and add to the pan with the cinnamon.
3 Heat through until almost boiling, reduce heat and leave to mull for 5-10 minutes.
4 Sprinkle with nutmeg and serve in heatproof mugs or cups.

Het Pint

An old-fashioned mix originating in Scotland to keep the cold out on occasions like Hogmanay (Scottish New Year) and help ward off winter colds.

Serves : 6

4 cups light ale
4 egg yolks
4 tbsp soft brown sugar
grated nutmeg
2 egg whites

1 Heat the ale slowly in a large pan.
2 Beat the egg yolks with the sugar and nutmeg, and beat the whites separately.
3 Then whisk the yolk mixture and the beaten whites together gently and slowly pour on the hot ale, whisking all the time.
4 Using two jugs, pour from jug to jug until you have a smooth and frothy mix.

963

Redcurrant Shrub

This cocktail is one for bottling when you have a glut of fruit, ready to enjoy later in the year. You could make it with blackcurrants too.

Serves : 20

2½ lb redcurrants
2½ lb sugar
brandy or rum to taste
soda water or lemonade
fresh redcurrants to serve

1 Crush the redcurrants well and strain the juice through muslin.
2 Stir the juice and sugar in a pan until the sugar has dissolved, then heat to boiling and boil gently for 8-10 minutes, spooning off the scum occasionally.
3 Allow to cool and then add brandy to taste.
4 Bottle and leave to mature for 5-6 weeks.
5 To serve, dilute with iced soda water, or lemonade, and top up with a little brandy if you wish.
6 Dress with fresh redcurrants.

964

Tamagozake

This is a brave drink for some rare tasting occasion, but be careful not to burn away all the sake. You might want to blow it out before all the flavor and spirit has been burnt up.

Serves : 1

6 measures sake
1 egg
1 tsp sugar

1 Boil the sake and ignite it.
2 Remove from the heat and stir in the egg and sugar lightly beaten together.
3 Serve in a mug with a handle.

The Navigator

These look like surprisingly calm waters with a few white horses, but you may find it a bit of a handful!

Serves : 1

1 measure coconut liqueur
splash blue Curaçao
champagne or sparkling white wine

1 Stir the liqueurs over ice in a wine glass and top up with champagne to taste.

Manhattan Cooler

Nothing like the classic Manhattan cocktail, more like a red wine punch.

Serves : 1

2 measures claret or good red wine
3 dashes dark rum
juice ½ lemon
2 tsp powdered sugar
slice of lemon
ice

1 Stir all the ingredients except the lemon slice well with ice until the sugar has dissolved.
2 Strain into chilled wine goblet and dress with lemon before serving.

Avocado Chill

As avocados are packed with vitamins, this can be classed as a healthy cocktail and included in your diet – no pretending any more!

Serves : 1

$^1/_4$ ripe avocado
juice $^1/_2$ lime
1 tsp powdered sugar
$^1/_2$ measure dry vermouth
1 measure gin (optional)
ice
tonic water

1 Blend the avocado, lime and sugar together, until smooth.
2 Then shake well with the vermouth and gin, over ice.
3 Strain into a chilled long cocktail glass and top up with tonic water.
4 Float a lime ice cube in the top.

Tip: To make fruit ice cubes, simply add slices or pieces of citrus peel or whole berries to the ice tray, then freeze as usual. They will add a little tang of flavor.

American Apple Pie

It's so good you will come back for seconds! For a special occasion, try it with a measure of Calvados too!

Serves : 1

1 measure sweet vermouth
3 measures apple juice
1 small scoop vanilla ice cream
crushed ice
soda water
cinnamon sugar
slice of apple

1 Whizz the first three ingredients with crushed ice for 10-15 seconds in a blender until frothy and frosted.
2 Pour into a chilled long glass and top up with soda water.
3 Dress with cinnamon sugar and a slice of apple.

Shepherd's Fizz

A meal in a glass with a difference, perfect to set you up for a day out in the cold.

Serves : 4

3 eggs

the same volume in cream

4 measures schnapps or eau de vie

4 measures fresh lemon juice with

3 tbsp sugar or 4 measures lime juice cordial

1 cup crushed ice

1 Whizz the eggs, cream, and schnapps with the lemon juice or lime cordial and ice in a blender until it turns to a frozen slush.
2 You may need a spoon at first while it's partly frozen.

Cucumber Whizz

Perfect to enjoy after your sauna, swim and work-out, but this cocktail does have some added inner strength!

Serves : 1

¹/4 cucumber, peeled

juice 1 lime

1 measure vodka

crushed ice

soda water

cucumber slice and mint

1 Put the cucumber, lime juice, vodka and ice in a blender and whizz to almost a purée.
2 Serve on the rocks, topped up with soda to taste and decorated with a slice of cucumber and sprig of mint.

Mint and Cucumber Refresher

971

Put this top of the list when you next go on a diet – it's the perfect booster.

Serves : 1

few sprigs mint
1 tsp powdered sugar
juice 1 lime
1in piece cucumber, thinly sliced
your favorite sparkling water, chilled
ice cubes

1 Chop a few mint leaves and mix with sugar.

2 Rub a little lime juice round the rim of a pretty glass and dip in the minted sugar. Leave to dry.

3 Mix the rest of the lime juice, cucumber and mint – some chopped and some whole – in a jug and chill.

4 To serve, pour lime and cucumber into the prepared glass and top up with chilled water to taste.

972 # Hazelnut Coffee Sparkle

A very well-chilled and refreshing glass of sparkling black coffee flavored with a little hazelnut syrup.

Serves : 1

1 cup strong black coffee, chilled
1 tbsp hazelnut syrup
2 tbsp brown sugar
6 ice cubes
1¹/₂ cups sparkling water
slices of fresh lemon and lime

1 Blend all except the sparkling water and fruit slices in a food processor with the ice until smooth and frothy.

2 Pour into a tall chilled glass and top up with iced sparkling water.

3 Dress with slices of fresh lime and lemon.

Cinnamon Tea

If you like herbal or fruit teas you will enjoy this spicy, citrusy tea. It's also good cold.

Serves : 2

1¹/₂ cups water
4 cloves
1 small stick of cinnamon
2 tea bags
3-4 tbsp lemon juice
1-2 tbsp brown sugar
slices of fresh lemon

1 Bring water, cloves, and cinnamon to boil.
2 Remove from heat and add tea bags. Leave to infuse 5 minutes, then remove.
3 Stir in lemon juice, sugar, and extra hot water to taste.
4 Heat through again gently and strain into heatproof glasses.
5 Decorate with slices of fresh lemon and serve. Serve chilled if you prefer.

Orange and Lime Iced Tea

Iced tea is always refreshing and even if you are not a keen tea drinker, this version is especially fresh and fruity. Keep some in the refrigerator if you don't use it all up.

Serves : 2

1¹/₃ cups freshly brewed tea, cooled
¹/₂ cup orange juice
4 tbsp lime juice
1-2 tbsp brown sugar
wedges of lime
granulated sugar
8 ice cubes
slices of fresh orange, lemon or lime

1 When the tea has chilled, add the orange juice, and lime juice and sugar to taste.
2 Take two glasses and rub the rims with a wedge of lime, then dip them in granulated sugar to frost.
3 Fill the glasses with ice cubes and pour on the tea.
4 Dress with slices of fresh orange, lemon or lime.

Pineapple Soda

This looks great when served in pineapple shells and will certainly put you in the holiday mood.

Serves : 2

3/4 cup pineapple juice
¹/₃ cup coconut milk
7oz vanilla ice cream
4¹/₂oz frozen pineapple chunks
3/4 cup sparkling water
2 scooped out pineapple shells (optional)

1 Blend the pineapple juice, coconut milk with the ice cream and pineapple chunks until smooth.
2 Pour the mixture into scooped out pineapple shells or tall glasses, until two-thirds full.
3 Top up with sparkling water, add straws and serve.

Citrus Slush

(976)

Youngsters often don't like bits of greenery in their drinks, so you could use a little essence instead of the mint or strain it well before serving.

Serves : 1

1 grapefruit or 1 orange and 1 lemon

4 measures cold milk

1 scoop vanilla ice cream

1 scoop crushed ice

6 mint leaves (optional)

1 Peel the fruit, removing the pips and as much white pith as possible.

2 Place the fruit in a blender with the rest of the ingredients and whizz for 15-20 seconds, until slushy.

3 Pour into a chilled sundae glass or wide rimmed glass and serve with a sprig of mint and a spoon.

Almondine

(977)

A smooth and velvety cocktail with loads of goodness in it. Enjoy immediately and add more fruit juice to taste.

Serves : 1

2 measures peach or mango juice

4 measures cold milk

few drops almond essence

1-2 tbsp clover honey

1 small egg

ice cubes

1 small ratafia biscuit

1 Shake the first six ingredients together well until frosted.

2 Pour into a large cocktail glass or wine glass and crumble the ratafia on top.

Rose Sunset

(978)

You won't need much of this as it is wonderfully flavored and also delightfully scented with the rose water. It is an unusual and delicious combination.

Serves : 4

½ cup natural yogurt

2 cups milk

1 tbsp rose water

3 tbsp honey

1 ripe mango, peeled, stoned and diced

6 ice cubes

edible rose petals (optional)

1 Process the yogurt and milk in a food processor gently until combined.

2 Add the rose water and honey, process until thoroughly blended, add the mango with the ice cubes and process until smooth.

3 Pour into glasses, decorate with edible rose petals and serve.

(979) Mini Colada

Children love the flavor of coconut and milk, so this junior cocktail should be very popular.

Serves : 2

6 measures cold milk

4 measures pineapple nectar

3 measures coconut cream

1/2 scoop crushed ice

cubes of pineapple and a cherry

1 Shake all the ingredients except the fruit together over ice until well chilled.

2 Pour into long glasses with more ice cubes, finish with pieces of pineapple and a cherry on a stick, and drink through straws.

(980) Kiwi Dream

This is a thick and luscious ice cream-based smoothie with the refreshing tang of kiwi and lime. Enjoy it as soon as it's ready.

Serves : 2

2/3 cups cup milk

juice of 2 limes

2 kiwi fruit, peeled and chopped

1 tbsp sugar

14oz vanilla ice cream

slices of fresh kiwi fruit

strips of fresh lime peel

1 Process the milk and lime juice in a food processor gently until combined.

2 Add the kiwi fruit, sugar and ice cream and process until smooth.

3 Pour into iced glasses and dress with slices of fresh kiwi fruit and strips of fresh lime peel.

(981)

Fuzzypeg

A child's delight both in taste and its incredibly strange color! It could be made with other drinks too.

Serves : 1

2 scoops vanilla ice cream
1 measure lime juice cordial
cola
ice

1 Blend the ice cream and lime cordial together for 5-10 seconds with a little cola.
2 Pour into a tall glass filled with ice and top up with cola.
3 Drink through straws.

(982)

Peppermint Ice

This luxury smoothie can vary in color – you may prefer mint chocolate chip ice cream and find it is almost white. You could add a few drops of coloring to make it brighter.

Serves : 4

²/₃ cups cup milk
2 tbsp peppermint syrup
14oz peppermint ice cream
sprigs of fresh mint

1 Pour the milk and peppermint syrup into a food processor and process gently until combined.
2 Add the peppermint ice cream and process until smooth.
3 Pour the mixture into iced glasses and decorate with sprigs of fresh mint.
4 Add straws and serve.

(983) Spiced Hot Chocolate

This is a seriously good version of hot chocolate, not for everyday but perhaps as a treat after building a snowman or singing carols on Christmas Eve.

Serves : 4

3½ cups milk

7oz good dark chocolate (at least 70% cocoa solids) broken into small pieces

2 tsp sugar

1 tsp mixed spice

4 sticks cinnamon

2 tbsp whipped cream

1 Put the milk, chocolate, sugar and mixed spice into a saucepan over a medium heat.

2 Whisk, stirring constantly, until the chocolate has melted and the mixture is simmering but not boiling.

3 Remove from the heat and pour into heatproof glasses or mugs with cinnamon sticks and top with a little whipped cream.

(984) Mexican Chocolate

Mexican chocolate is well worth using – the flavor and texture is quite different.

Serves : 6

3 cups water

1½oz tortilla flour

2in piece of cinnamon stick

3 cups milk

3oz dark chocolate, grated

sugar to taste

extra grated chocolate

1 Pour the water into a large pan, stir in the tortilla flour and add cinnamon.

2 Stir over a low heat for 5-10 minutes until thickened and smooth.

3 Gradually stir in the milk and beat in the grated chocolate, a little at a time, until melted and fully incorporated.

4 Remove from heat, discard the cinnamon and sweeten to taste with sugar.

5 Ladle into heatproof glasses and sprinkle with extra chocolate.

(985) Banana Cocktail

Here's how to pack all your day's nutrition into one delicious glass but serve it cool or chilled for the nicest result.

Serves : 1

1 small banana

2oz thick Greek-style natural yogurt

1 egg

1-2 tbsp light brown sugar or clear honey

ice

sprig of mint

1 Whizz the banana, yogurt, egg, and sugar in a blender with one or two cubes of ice for about 2 minutes.

2 Pour into a tall glass and finish with a sprig of mint.

3 Add a small measure of rum or brandy too, if you wish!

Melon Cocktail

(986)

If you cannot find all three melons at any one time don't be put off, two types will do well, as long as you have watermelon and one of the other two.

Serves : 4

1 cup natural yogurt

3 1/2 oz galia melon, cut into chunks

3 1/2 oz cantaloupe melon, cut into chunks

3 1/2 oz watermelon, cut into chunks

6 ice cubes

cherry

1 Put the yogurt and the galia melon chunks into a food processor and process until smooth.

2 Add the cantaloupe and watermelon chunks along with the ice cubes and process until smooth.

3 Pour the mixture into glasses and dress with a cherry.

Pinomint Splash

(987)

This is virtually non-alcoholic. You could replace the crème de menthe with green coloring if you want the effect without the alcohol.

Serves : 1

4 measures milk, cold

1/4 measure peppermint cordial

1 measure coconut cream

2 measures pineapple juice

ice

dash of crème de menthe, iced

1 Shake all the ingredients, except the crème de menthe, together over ice until well frosted.

2 Dribble or paint the tiniest drops of crème de menthe down the inside of a chilled tall thin glass.

3 Slowly pour in the cocktail and add some more crème de menthe.

4 Drink through a straw.

Tropical Delight

(988)

A velvety-smooth, delicately scented drink without alcohol. This can be served at any time of day – and it's delicious for breakfast.

Serves : 4

2 large ripe mangoes

1 tbsp confectioner's sugar

scant 1/2 cups coconut milk

5 ice cubes

flaked toasted coconut

1 Peel the mangoes, coarsely chop the flesh and discard the stones.

2 Place the flesh in a blender with the sugar and blend until completely smooth.

3 Add the coconut milk and ice to the blender and process until frothy.

4 Pour into 4 tall glasses and sprinkle with flaked toasted coconut to serve.

Lime and Lemon Cooler

If you're looking for something stronger, add a shot of gin or vodka to each glass.

Serves : 3

egg white
3-4 tbsp powdered sugar
2 limes, each cut into 8
1 small lemongrass stalk, chopped
4 ice cubes
$1/2$ cup water
4 lime slices
soda water

1 Rim the glasses first with egg white and a little sugar.

2 Place the lime pieces and lemongrass in a blender with the rest of the sugar and ice cubes. Add the water and process for a few seconds.

3 Strain the mixture into the frosted glasses, add a lime slice to each glass and top with soda to taste.

Pineapple Smoothie

This is a popular combination for a smoothie, one smooth sweet fruit and one tangy and textured fruit. You might like to try your own variation.

Serves : 2

$1/2$ cup pineapple juice
juice of 1 lemon
$1/3$ cup water
3 tbsp brown sugar
$3/4$ cup natural yogurt
1 peach, cut into chunks and frozen
$3^{1}/2$oz frozen pineapple chunks
wedges of fresh pineapple

1 Blend all the ingredients, except the pineapple wedges, in a food processor until smooth.

2 Pour into glasses and dress the rims with wedges of fresh pineapple.

The Big Apple

This is a fun cocktail to make with the children. Prepare several together for convenience and add cognac or Calvados for the adults.

Serves : 1

1 crisp eating apple
juice of $1/2$ lemon
juice of 1 orange
$1/2$ measure grenadine
crushed ice

1 Scoop out the centre of the apple to form a cup, leaving the base intact. Rub the inside with lemon juice.

2 Discard the core and place the flesh in a blender with the juices, grenadine, and crushed ice. Blend to an icy pulp and spoon back into the shell.

3 Drink with straws and then eat the apple!

Spicy Banana Shake

Banana blends well even when partly frozen and it tends to give create a luxuriously thick finished drink.

Serves : 2
1¼ cups milk
½ tsp mixed spice
5oz banana ice cream
2 bananas, sliced and frozen

1 Blend the milk in a food processor with the mixed spice, the banana ice cream and half the frozen banana.
2 Add the remaining bananas gradually and process until well blended.
3 Pour into tall iced glasses and drink with straws.

Fruit Cooler

A great breakfast energizer and healthy start to the day, once you have done your work-out!

Serves : 2
1 cup orange juice
½ cup natural yogurt
2 eggs
2 bananas, sliced and frozen to decorate
slices of fresh banana

1 Pour the orange juice and yogurt into a food processor and process gently until combined.
2 Add the eggs and frozen bananas and process until smooth.
3 Pour the mixture into glasses and decorate the rims with slices of fresh banana.
4 Add straws and serve.

Red Pepper Reactor

The warm sweet pungent flavor of peppers comes through so much more when it is thoroughly processed, so you will be pleasantly surprised by the result.

Serves : 2
1 cup carrot juice
1 cup tomato juice
2 large red peppers, deseeded and roughly chopped
1 tbsp lemon juice
freshly ground black pepper

1 Pour the carrot and tomato juice into a food processor and process gently until combined.
2 Add the red peppers and lemon juice.
3 Season with plenty of freshly ground black pepper and process until smooth.
4 Pour the mixture into tall glasses, add straws and serve.

995 Fig 'n' Hazelnut Smoothie

An unusual combination making a luxury smoothie for very special occasions when you find figs in season.

Serves : 2

1½ cups hazelnut yogurt
2 tbsp freshly squeezed orange juice
4 tbsp maple syrup
8 large fresh ripe figs, chopped
6 ice cubes
toasted chopped hazelnuts

1 Pour the yogurt, orange juice and maple syrup into a food processor and blend gently until thoroughly combined.
2 Add the figs and ice cubes and process again until smooth.
3 Pour into glasses and scatter some toasted chopped hazelnuts on the top.

996 Ginger Crush

A fiery carrot and tomato mix for ginger lovers, so be prepared for it to liven you up.

Serves : 2

1 cup carrot juice
4 tomatoes, skinned, deseeded and roughly chopped
1 tbsp lemon juice
1 oz fresh parsley
1 tbsp grated fresh root ginger
6 ice cubes
½ cup water
chopped fresh parsley

1 Put the carrot juice, tomatoes, and lemon juice into a food processor and process gently until combined.
2 Add the parsley to the food processor along with the ginger and ice cubes.
3 Process until well combined, pour in the water and process until smooth.
4 Pour the mixture into tall glasses and garnish with chopped fresh parsley. Serve at once.

997 Carrot Chill

Carrot is really very sweet, especially when raw and very young carrots are used. Makes a great combination with the peppery watercress.

Serves : 2

2 cups carrot juice
1 oz watercress
1 tbsp lemon juice
sprigs of fresh watercress

1 Pour the carrot juice into a blender.
2 Add the watercress and lemon juice and process until smooth.
3 Transfer to a jug, cover with film, and chill in the refrigerator for at least 1 hour,
4 When thoroughly chilled, pour into glasses and dress with sprigs of fresh watercress. Serve at once.

998

Banana and Blueberry Smoothie

Freeze the bananas and the blueberries in advance to give a thicker, more refreshing result.

Serves : 4
3/4 cup apple juice
1/2 cup natural yogurt
1 banana, sliced and frozen
5 1/2 oz frozen blueberries
whole fresh blueberries

1 Pour the apple juice and the yogurt into a blender, add the banana and half of the frozen blueberries and process well until smooth.
2 Then add the remaining blueberries and process until smooth.
3 Pour the mixture into tall glasses and decorate with whole fresh blueberries.

999

Carrot Cocktail

Pineapple and carrot are a delicious combination, producing a thick and refreshing drink packed with vitamins.

Serves : 1
3oz raw carrots, peeled and roughly chopped
1 slice pineapple, roughly chopped
1 tsp lemon juice
1 tbsp clear honey
ice
sprig of parsley or mint

1 Place the carrot, pineapple, lemon juice, and honey in a blender and whizz for 1-2 minutes until smooth.
2 Serve over ice with a sprig of parsley or mint.

Sunset Smoothie

Orange and carrot are a classic combination. Because carrot is already quite sweet, the orange simply brings out the full flavor.

Serves : 2

3/4 cup carrot juice
3/4 cup orange juice
5oz vanilla ice cream
6 ice cubes
slices of orange and strips of orange peel

1 Pour the carrot juice and orange juice into a food processor and process gently until well combined.
2 Add the ice cream and process until thoroughly blended, then add the ice cubes and process until smooth.
3 Pour into chilled glasses and dress with orange slices and peel.

Prairie Oyster

For times when you really can't lift your head off the pillow, it's the only thing to try.

Serves : 1

Worcestershire sauce
vinegar
tomato ketchup
1 egg yolk
cayenne pepper

1 Mix equal quantities of Worcestershire sauce, vinegar and ketchup and pour into a chilled glass.
2 Add the yolk carefully without breaking.
3 Do not stir, sprinkle with cayenne pepper and down it all in one!

Glossary of Drinks

Amaretto: Almond-flavored liqueur from Italy

Amer Picon: French aperitif bitters, flavored with orange and gentian

Angostura bitters: rum-based bitters from Trinidad

Anisette: French liqueur, flavored with anise, coriander, and other herbs

Aperitif: A drink before the meal to encourage the appetite, which could be a commercial product or a mixed cocktail

Applejack: North American name for apple brandy (see Fruit Brandies)

Aquavit: Scandinavian grain spirit, usually flavored with caraway

Armagnac: French brandy produced in Gascony – it is rarely used for cocktails

Bacardi: Leading brand of white rum, originally from Cuba and now produced in Bermuda – also the name of a cocktail

Baileys Irish Cream: Irish, whiskey-based, chocolate-flavored liqueur

Benedictine: French monastic liqueur flavored with herbs, spices, and honey

Bitters: Spirits of varying strengths flavored with roots and herbs, used in cocktails to add a kick or depth of flavor, or for medicinal purposes. Most common are Amer Picon, Angostura, Campari, Fernet Branca, Orange and Peach Bitters

Bourbon: American whiskey made from a mash that must contain at least 51 percent corn

Brandy: Spirit distilled from fermented grapes, although many fruit brandies are based on other fruits (see Fruit brandy)

Calvados: French apple brandy from Normandy

Campari: Italian bitters flavored with quinine

Cassis: Blackcurrant-flavored liqueur, mainly from France

Champagne: French sparkling wine made only in the Champagne-producing regions, under strictly controlled conditions

Chartreuse: French monastic liqueur flavored with a secret recipe of herbs. Green Chartreuse is stronger than yellow

Cobbler: Originated in America, ideally a drink for hot climates. Usually in a highball glass filled with crushed ice, sugar, spirit, and decorated with fruit

Coconut liqueur: Coconut-flavored, spirit-based liqueur. Malibu is the best-known brand

Coffee liqueur: Coffee-flavored, spirit-based liqueur. Tia Maria, based on Jamaican rum, and Kahlua from Mexico are the best-known brands

Cointreau: Best-selling brand of orange liqueur, flavored with sweet Mediterranean oranges and Caribbean bitter orange peel (see also Triple Sec)

Collins: A spirit-based cocktail topped up with a soda, such as ginger ale

Cooler: A long mix of spirit, sugar or syrup, and soda or ginger ale, over crushed ice decorated with fresh fruit

Crème de banane: Banana-flavored liqueur

Crème de cacao: French, chocolate-flavored liqueur, produced in various strengths and colors

Crème de menthe: Mint-flavored liqueur – may be white or green

Crème de noyeau: Liqueur made from apricot and peach kernels

Crème violette: Violet-flavored liqueur

Crème Yvette: American Parma violet-flavored liqueur

Cup: a long refreshing drink made from wine, cider, or fortified wines, lengthened with mixers, with various added fruits or juices, served before food

Curaçao: Orange-flavored liqueur, produced mainly in France and the Netherlands, but originating from the

Caribbean – available in a range of colors including white, orange, and blue

Daisies: There are many variations on the original – spirit, raspberry syrup, lemon juice, crushed ice, and fruit
Drambuie: Scotch whiskey-based liqueur, flavored with honey and heather
Dry gin: See Gin
Dubonnet: Wine-based aperitif, flavored with quinine – available red and blonde

Eau-de-vie: Spirit distilled from fruit – tends to be used (mistakenly) as interchangeable with fruit brandy
Egg nogg (Noggin or Grog): Variations on a mix of brandy, rum, milk, egg, and sugar sprinkled with nutmeg. Can use other spirits and is usually iced

Falernum: Caribbean syrup flavored with fruit and spices
Fernet Branca: Italian liqueur with a bitter flavor
Fix: A mix of spirit, lemon, sugar, water, and fruit on crushed ice in a highball glass
Fizzes: Mix five parts chilled sparking wine with one part grenadine or other fruit syrup
Flip: A favorite sailor's drink as it was originally made with rum, brandy, or port, with egg and sugar, shaken and then sprinkled with nutmeg or ginger
Fraise: Strawberry spirit liqueur
Framboise: Raspberry-flavored liqueur
Frappé: Well-iced drinks, usually liqueurs or spirits, served over finely crushed ice and drunk with a straw
Fruit brandy: Strictly speaking, brandy is distilled from fermented grapes, but many fruit brandies are distilled from whatever the fruit type is, such as apple and apricot – plum brandy, also known as slivovitz, is usually made from Mirabelle and Switzen plums

Galliano: Italian liqueur, flavored with honey and vanilla
Gin: A colorless, grain-based spirit, strongly flavored with juniper and other herbs. London, Plymouth and dry gin are most commonly used for cocktails
Grand Marnier: French orange-flavored, cognac-based liqueur
Grappa: Fiery Italian spirit distilled from wine must
Grenadine: Non-alcoholic, pomegranate-flavored syrup – used for sweetening and coloring cocktails

Highball: A spirit, liqueur, or wine served in a long tumbler with ice and topped up with soda or ginger ale. The glass also takes its name from the drink. The name is said to have originated in St. Louis in the late nineteenth century – on many railroads, if a ball was hoisted up on a pole at a depot, it signalled to an approaching train driver that he should speed up. Subsequently it has come to mean a speedily made drink

Irish whiskey: Unblended spirit made from malted or unmalted barley and some other grains – suitable for many cocktails

Julep: A long drink of spirit or liqueur, sugar, and mint served in a frosted glass with crushed ice

Kahlua: Popular Mexican brand of coffee liqueur
Kirsch: Colorless cherry-flavored eau-de-vie, mainly from France and Switzerland
Kümmel: Colorless Dutch liqueur, flavored with caraway

Lillet: French herb-flavored liqueur, based on wine and armagnac
Liqueur: Distilled spirit flavored with such things as fruit, herbs, coffee, nuts, mint, and chocolate
London gin: The driest gin (see Gin)

Madeira: Fortified wine from the island of the same name

Malibu: Leading brand of coconut liqueur – based on rum
Mandarine Napoleon: Belgian, brandy-based liqueur flavored with tangerines
Maraschino: Italian, cherry-flavored liqueur – usually colorless, but may be red
Martini: Popular Italian brand of vermouth produced by Martini and Rossi and also the name of a classic cocktail
Melon liqueur: Spirit-based melon-flavored liqueur – Midori is the leading brand
Midori: Japanese liqueur (see Melon liqueur)

Noilly Prat: Leading French brand of very dry vermouth

Orgeat: Almond-flavored syrup

Pastis: Aniseed-flavored liqueur from France. Brand names include Pernod and Ricard
Pernod: See Pastis
Plymouth gin: A less dry type of gin than London gin (see Gin)
Port: Portuguese fortified wine that may be white, ruby, or tawny – white and inexpensive ruby are most appropriate for cocktails
Pousse-café: A drink poured in layers to float on top of one another, which also gives its name to a narrow straight-sided stemmed glass
Punch: Originated in India in the eighteenth century based on rum and incorporating five different drinks. It has become a mix of many drinks, alcoholic and non, carefully blended so no single flavor dominates all the others

Quinquina: French wine-based aperitif, flavored with quinine

Ricard: See Pastis
Rickey: A spirit served in a long glass over ice, topped up with soda and flavored with lime or lemon to give a sharp dry tang. A twist of peel should be added

Rum: Spirit distilled from fermented sugar cane juice or molasses – light, golden, and dark each have distinctive flavors and all are widely used, together and individually, in cocktails and punches

Rye whiskey: Mainly American and Canadian whiskey which must be made from a mash containing at least 51 percent rye

Sake: Japanese rice wine

Sambuca: Italian liquorice-flavored liqueur

Schnapps: Grain-based spirit – available in a range of flavors, including peach and peppermint

Scotch whiskey: Blends are a mixture of about 40 percent malt and 60 percent grain whiskey and are most suitable for cocktails – single malts should be drunk neat or simply diluted with water

Shrub: A slow maturing drink. Fruit such as currants or citrus fruits and sugar are boiled or left to marinade until ready to sieve through a jelly bag, then mixed with brandy or rum, bottled and left 6-8 weeks to mature

Slammer: A cocktail mixed by slamming it in a glass on the bar

Sling: A long drink of spirit, fruit juice, or cordial topped up with soda water

Slivovitz: Plum brandy (see Fruit brandy)

Sloe gin: Liqueur made by steeping sloes in gin – previously homemade but now available commercially

Smash: A crush of mint leaves, a little water, and cubed sugar which is flavored with rum, brandy, gin, or whiskey and served in an old-fashioned glass on the rocks with a slice of orange and twist of lemon rind

Sour: Spirit, lemon juice, sugar, Angostura bitters, and egg white shaken

Southern Comfort: American whiskey-based peach-flavored liqueur

Strega: Italian herb-flavored liqueur

Sugar syrup: A sweetener for cocktails, made by dissolving sugar in boiling water (see syrup de gomme)

Swedish Punsch: Aromatic rum-based drink, flavored with wines and syrups

Syrup de gomme: Sweet sugar syrup, sometimes available bottled

Tequila: Mexican spirit distilled from the pulp of fermented maguey cacti. To be called tequila it must be produced in Government defined regions of Mexico otherwise it is known as mescal

Tia Maria: Popular Jamaican rum-based coffee liqueur

Toddy: Also known as Grog – a drink of spirit, lemon, sugar, cinnamon, and either hot or cold water

Tom Collins: Lemon or lime juice, sugar, dry gin, shaken over ice, strained into a highball glass and topped up with soda

Triple Sec: Colorless, orange-flavored liqueur. A relative of curaçao, but stronger and drier

Vermouth: Wine-based aperitif flavored with extracts of wormwood – both sweet and dry vermouths are widely used in cocktails

Vodka: Colorless, grain-based spirit, originally from Russia and Poland. Flavored vodkas, such as lemon, raspberry and chilli, are becoming increasingly popular and widely available

Whiskey: Spirit distilled from grain or malted barley – the main types are bourbon, rye, Irish and Scotch.

Cocktail Index

Favorite cocktails